ANGELS
&
MORTALS

Cover art by Anne Kilgore

ANGELS & MORTALS

Their Co-Creative Power

Compiled by Maria Parisen

This publication is made possible with the assistance of the Kern Foundation

Quest Books
The Theosophical Publishing House
Wheaton, Ill. U.S.A.
Madras, India/London, England

The Theosophical Publishing House
306 West Geneva Road
Wheaton, IL 60187

A publication of the Theosophical Publishing House, a
department of the Theosophical Society in America.

"This publication is made possible with the assistance of the Kern
Foundation."

Library of Congress Cataloging-in-Publication Data

Angels & mortals : their co-creative power / compiled by Maria
    Parisen. -- 1st ed.
        p.   c.m.
    "A Quest original" -- T.p. verso.
    Includes bibliographical references and index.
    ISBN 0-8356-0665-1 : $14.95
    1. Angels.   2. Theosophy.   I. Parisen, Maria.   II. Title : Angels
    and mortals.
BP573.A5A64   1990
291.2′ 15 -- dc20   90-50205
                                                                        CIP

Printed in the United States of America
by Versa Press

This edition is printed on acid-free paper that meets the
American National Standards Institute Z39.48 Standard

Contents

Contributing Authors

John Algeo, Ph.D., is Professor of English at the University of
Georgia, Athens, where he has served as director of the
linguistics curriculum and head of the department of English.
He has authored a number of scholarly books, and, as a student
of the ancient wisdom, wrote *Reincarnation Explored*. Dr. Algeo
serves as a consultant for a variety of organizations including
the National Endowment for the Humanities, and is currently
a Vice-President of the Theosophical Society in America.

Nathaniel Altman, a graduate of the University of Wisconsin, is
a writer and counselor living in Brooklyn, New York. He is
the author of over a dozen books on subjects such as vege-
tarianism, holistic health, palmistry and nonviolence. He
coauthored (with Jose A. Rosa, M.D.) *Finding Your Personal
Power Spots*, on which this article is based.

Laurence J. Bendit, M.D., 1898-1974, psychiatrist, lecturer, and
author, was awarded three degrees from Cambridge University
(M.A., M.D., and B. Chir.). Dr. Bendit also studied under Dr.
Carl Jung. He made a substantial contribution to the literature
of psychology and theosophy, including the books *Self
Knowledge: A Yoga for the West,* and *The Mirror of Life and Death.*

Geoffrey Farthing has authored *Exploring the Great Beyond, When
We Die* and *Theosophy, What's it all About?* He became interested
in esoteric studies in 1932 and has been a deep student since
that time. Mr. Farthing is the Founder and Trustee of the
Blavatsky Trust which has the object of promoting a knowledge
of the writings of H. P. Blavatsky and the teachings of her
Masters. He is currently on the executive committee of the
Theosophical Society in England and lectures internationally
for this organization.

Matthew Fox, a Dominican Scholar, is Director of the Institute in Culture and Creation Spirituality at Holy Names College, Oakland, California. In addition to lecturing widely, he has authored many books on spirituality and personal transformation, including *Original Blessing, The Coming of the Cosmic Christ*, and *Meditations with Meister Eckhart*.

G. Don Gilmore ministers to the members of the Plymouth Congregational Church in Spokane, Washington. He is the author of several books, including *Angels, Angels, Everywhere; Letters from a Previously Unpublished Angel; Extra Spiritual Power* and others. In addition, Gilmore has a daily radio program heard in the northwest called "Perspective on Living."

Michael Grosso, Ph.D., received his doctorate in philosophy from Columbia University. He currently teaches philosophy and humanities at Jersey City State College, and researches the evolutionary implications of extended human abilities. Dr. Grosso is the author of *The Final Choice* and a number of articles.

Hildegard of Bingen, 1098-1179, is becoming well known today as a prolific, energetic, and original feminist. In addition to being abbess of a large Benedictine abbey in the Rhineland valley, she was a prominent artist, scientist, doctor, poet, composer and spiritual teacher, with nine books and seventy poems to her credit. Spiritual visions began to appear to her at the age of forty-two, which she documented as thirty-six illuminations and text, entitled *Scivias (Know the Ways)*.

Jim H. Hindes, a graduate of the University of California at Berkeley in Philosophy, first became interested in the work of Rudolf Steiner in 1966. He attended a theological Seminary in Germany (Die Freie Hochschule der Christengemeinschaft), and was ordained as a priest in "The Christian Community, Movement for Religious Renewal," an independent church able to incorporate many of Rudolf Steiner's insights into the framework of traditional Christian theology. Since then he has worked as a pastor of congregations in Germany, England, and the United States. His writings include numerous articles on religious and theological themes, and translations of books.

Geoffrey Hodson, 1886-1983, was born and educated in England. He served with distinction in the British Army during World War I, after which he became interested in and devoted to Theosophy. A gifted and noted clairvoyant, he cooperated with physicists, archeologists, physicians, and other scientists to demonstrate the research potential of superphysical faculties of perception. Hodson authored over forty books, including *The Christ Life from Nativity to Ascension, Hidden Wisdom in the Holy Bible, Volumes I-IV,* and *Kingdom of the Gods,* from which this article is taken.

Stephan Hoeller, Ph.D., is Associate Professor of Comparative Religions at the graduate school of the College of Oriental Studies in Los Angeles. He is also a member of the lecturing faculty of the Philosophical Research Society and director of the Gnostic Society in Los Angeles, an organization interested in Jungian psychology, the Kabbalah, Tarot, classical Gnosticism, myth, and literature. In addition, Dr. Hoeller is author of *The Gnostic Jung, The Royal Road,* and *Jung and the Lost Gospels.*

Dorothy MacLean has been involved in human and planetary transformation all of her life—from wartime employment with the British government to cofounding the Findhorn community in Scotland, and in her work with the Lorian Association in Canada. Her gift of clairvoyant perception of the angelic kingdoms allows her to help others learn the benefits that can be gained from mutual contact and cooperation with these realms.

David L. Miller, Ph.D., holds the Chair of Watson-Ledden Professor of Religion at Syracuse University, with teaching and research interests that include theology, mythology and depth psychology. Dr. Miller is well known in Jungian circles and is currently a member of several professional organizations, including the American Academy of Religion and the International Society for Neoplatonic Studies. Besides serving on the editorial boards of several journals, his authorship includes the books *The New Polytheism: Rebirth of the Gods and Goddesses* and *Christs: Meditations on Archetypal Images in Christian Theology.*

Jeanine Miller, M.A., has a cosmopolitan background that gives her ties to Australia, England, China, France and other countries. With a Masters Degree in Vedic studies, she served as research assistant in the British Museum library for twenty years, and has lectured extensively for the Theosophical Society. Miller has published several articles and books, including *A Reappraisal of Yoga* which she coauthored with George Feuerstein.

Sallie Nichols, author of *Jung and Tarot: An Archetypal Journey*, was a student of Jungian psychology for many years, and studied at the C. G. Jung Institute in Zurich while Jung was still alive and active. She lectured frequently on the topics of symbolism, the Tarot, and Jungian archetypes, and presented a seminar series entitled "A Tarot Trip into Jung's Psychology."

Maria Parisen of Troy, Michigan, is a long-time student of angelology and has led workshops in Tai Chi, meditation, and other esoteric subjects. Her career as a nurse has inspired her to become a practitioner of the art of Therapeutic Touch.

Israel Regardie, 1907-1985, as personal secretary to Aleister Crowley, became well versed in the principles of magic and the system of the Golden Dawn. He was born in England, but eventually moved to the United States where he became a chiropractor and taught psychiatrists. Regardie authored many books, including *The Tree of Life: A Study in Magic, A Garden of Pomegranates,* and *The Art of True Healing.*

M. C. (Mary Caroline) Richards, Ph.D., currently lives in a community with mentally handicapped adults which is based upon biodynamic agriculture and gardening, following the suggestions of Rudolf Steiner for healing the soil and the soul. She is a poet, craftsperson, and author, with books in print including *Centering: In Pottery, Poetry, and the Person; The Crossing Point; Towards Wholeness: Rudolf Steiner Education in America,* and a collection of poems, *Imagine Inventing Yellow.*

C. R. F. (Charles) Seymour was a confidant of Dion Fortune and a member of her Society of the Inner Light. He functioned as High Priest and teacher of esoteric studies, and garnered a wide knowledge of the pagan traditions during his lifetime. Many of his articles were collected in the book *Forgotten Mage: The Magical Letters of Colonel C. R. F.*, by Dolores Ashcroft-Nowicki.

Michael Stanley, M.Sc., Ph.D., teaches comparative religion, philosophy, psychology and symbolism of sacred scriptures at the New Church College in England, where he is Principal. His career began in physics at Columbia University in New York. Ministerial work eventually called to him, however, and Dr. Stanley was ordained in 1971 at the Church of New Jerusalem in England. He has developed a system of psycho-spiritual counseling based on Swedenborgian thought, and lectures throughout England, the United States and Australia.

Emanuel Swedenborg, 1688-1772, was born in Stockholm, Sweden. His father was an eminent bishop in the Swedish Lutheran Church, and the family was ennobled in 1719. Emanuel was educated at Upsala University in science, cosmology, and philosophy. At the age of fifty-five he began to have spiritual experiences that resulted in the opening of his clairvoyant faculties. Two years later he abandoned his scientific labors to devote himself to an intensive study of the Christian scriptures. This study resulted in a unique and voluminous body of interpretive Christian teachings from his clairvoyant perceptions and insights.

Marie-Louise von Franz, Ph.D., worked directly for Dr. Carl Jung for thirty-one years. A world-renowned Jungian analyst and prolific writer, she is expanding Jung's theories into new and important avenues. Her provocative thinking has produced such books as: *On Dreams and Death: A Jungian Interpretation, Individuation in Fairytales, Shadow and Evil in Fairytales, The Grail Legend* (co-authored with Emma Jung) and many others.

Jay G. Williams, Ph.D., is currently Chair of the Department of Religion at Hamilton College in Clinton, New York. He has authored many books and articles on a variety of theological and mythological topics, including the Bible, Buddhism, Judaism, and *The Secret Doctrine.* His latest book is *The Riddle of the Sphinx.* In addition, he has participated as Assistant Field Supervisor in two archeological excavations in Israel.

Peter Lamborn Wilson became well versed in Sufism, Islam and other Eastern religions after spending fifteen years of nomadism in Asia and India and working in Tehran at the Iranian Academy of Philosophy. Wilson has contributed to many journals including *Gnosis* and *Parabola,* and currently works for *Semiotext(e)* magazine. His books include *SCANDAL: Essays in Islamic Heresy,* and *The Drunken Universe: An Anthology of Persian Sufi Poetry,* which he coauthored with Nasrollah Pourjavady.

Acknowledgements

Many thanks to all who helped bring a little of the angels to earth with me these past few years, especially theosophical friends who endured my early slide talks and tactfully set me on a clearer course; Michael Martin and Robert Thibodeau at Mayflower, who buried me in possibilities then mercifully left me alone in the "stacks"; all the publishing, library, and museum folks and artists who came through beautifully, even on short notice; Pamela Kent for her creative help with the manuscript; Shirley Nicholson, senior Editor at TPH, for encouragement and a firm hand; summer conventioneers who launched ANGELS AND MORTALS in high style; John Crocker for new beginnings; Bing Escudero for his well-worn chair and little notes at a very strenuous time; my mother, Alice Prusnick, for my introduction to her Angel, a delightful, unpredictable, rascally friend; and to Jon, Jonathan and Dan who have managed to survive late dinners, no dinners, and no mom for longer than I care to admit.

I wish to thank the following publishers for permission to reprint their material:

"The Nature of Angel Forms" is reprinted by permission of the publisher, from *Angels, Angels Everywhere*, by G. Don Gilmore. Copyright 1981, The Pilgrim Press, New York, NY.

"The Incarnation of the Angels" is from *The Mysteries Today and Other Essays*, by Laurence J. Bendit, London: Theosophical Publishing House, 1973. Used by permission.

"The Old Gods" by C. R. F. Seymour is excerpted from Chapter 5 of *The Forgotten Mage*, edited by Dolores Ashcroft-Nowicki, published by the Aquarian Press, 1986. Reprinted with permission of the Thorsons Publishing Group Limited, Denington Estate, Wellingborough, Northamptonshire NN8 2RQ, England.

"The Magician and the Holy Guardian" by Israel Regardie, is from *The Tree of Life: A Study in Magic*, (York Beach, ME: Samuel Weiser, Inc., 1972), pp. 82 to 84 and parts of 179 to 182. Used by permission of the publisher.

"Theologia Imaginalis" is an essay by David L. Miller which originally appeared in *The Archaeology of the Imagination*, edited by Charles E. Winquist, copyright 1981 by the American Academy of Religion, used by permission of Scholars Press, Atlanta, GA.

"Daimons and the Inner Companion" is reprinted, in abridged form, from *Projection and Re-collection in Jungian Psychology: Reflections of the Soul* by Marie-Louise von Franz, translated by William H. Kennedy. Reality of the Psyche Series (La Salle and London: Open Court Publishing Company, 1980), chapters 5 and 7, by permission of the publisher.

"Temperance: Heavenly Alchemist" is Chapter 12 from *Jung and Tarot: An Archetypal Journey,* by Sallie Nichols, © 1980 Sallie Nichols (York Beach, ME: Samuel Weiser, Inc., 1980), pp. 165-177. Used by permission.

"Journeys: Black Elk," "The Miraculous Night Journey," and "Dionysius and the Paradiso" are reprinted from *Angels* by Peter Lamborn Wilson. Copyright © 1980 by Thames and Hudson Ltd., London. Reprinted by permission of Pantheon Books, a division of Random House, Inc.

"All Beings Celebrate Creation: Illuminations of Hildegard" is a chapter from *Illuminations of Hildegard of Bingen,* commentary by Matthew Fox, O.P., copyright 1985 by Bear & Company, Inc. Used by permission of the publisher, Bear & Company, Inc., PO Drawer 2860, Sante Fe, NM 87504.

"Angelic Nature: From the Works of Emanuel Swedenborg" is reprinted from *Emanual Swedenborg: Essential Readings,* edited by Dr. Michael Stanley, published by The Aquarian Press, part of the Thorsons Publishing Group Limited, Denington Estate, Wellingborough, Northamptonshire NN8 2RQ, England, 1988. Permission to use these extracts from the original *Arcana Caelestia,* and *Heaven and Hell* has also been granted by The Swedenborg Society, Swedenborg House, 20-21 Bloomsbury Way, London, WC1A 2TH.

"The Greater Gods and Ritual" quotes two chapters ("The Greater Gods" and "Ceremonial") from a book by Geoffrey Hodson titled *Kingdom of the Gods,* used by permission of The Theosophical Publishing House, Adyar, Madras 600 020, India, (1952) 1987.

"Humans and Angels Now" is a chapter from *To Hear the Angels Sing* by Dorothy MacLean, Issaquah, WA: Lorian Press, 1984. Used by permission of the author.

"Introit" and "Benediction" by Mary Caroline Richards are her "Angel Poems I and II," included in this anthology by permission of the author.

Picture Credits

The compiler wishes to express appreciation to the following for their gracious permission to use these illustrations:

P. 8. The Bible, Rev. xii 10, woodcut by Gustav Doré. From *The Doré Bible Illustrations*. New York: Dover Publications, 1974.

P. 19. "Les Cosmogones," oil on canvas by Wolfgang Paalen, 1941-4. In the collection of Robert Anthoine.

P. 32. "A Healing Angel" from *Kingdom of the Gods* by Geoffrey Hodson, 1952, plate 23, p. 235. Used by permission of The Theosophical Publishing House, Adyar, Madras, India.

P. 52. "Angel of the High Self Initiation: Holy of Holies—Karnak," by Arthur Douët. Courtesy of Inner Light Ministries.

P. 90. "The Alchemist and Angel Guide," woodcut from Musaeum Hermeticum Reformatum et Amplificatum, 1678. Courtesy University of Illinois, Interlibrary Loan, Illinois Reference/Research Office.

P. 98. "Angel with the Key of the Abyss," woodcut by Albrecht Dürer. From Willi Kurth, *The Complete Woodcuts of Albrecht Dürer*. New York: Dover Publications, 1963.

P. 106. "Abraham's Sacrifice" by Rembrandt, 1655. Reproduced by Courtesy of the Trustees of the British Museum.

P. 126. "Dante's Paradise," woodcut by Gustave Doré. From *The Doré Illustrations for Dante's Divine Comedy*. New York: Dover Publications, 1976.

P. 152. "God and Demon," drawing adapted by Dave Gunning.

P. 158. "Genesis" by William Blake, 1825. Reproduced by Courtesy of the Trustees of the British Museum.

P. 188. "Temperance" is card fourteen from the Marseilles Tarot Deck.

P. 206. "Miraj Muhammad," probably by Sultan Muhammad, painting from a reproduction of Nizami's Khamsa made for Shah Tahmasp in Tabriz, 1539-1543. Used by permission of the British Library.

P. 212. "Die Chöre der Engel," (Tafel 9), is an illumination by Hildegard of Bingen. From: *Wisse Die Wege. Scivias*, Otto Müller Verlag Salzburg, 8. Aufl., 1987.

P. 218. "The Angel Appearing to the Shepherds," Rembrandt, 1634. Reproduced by Courtesy of the Trustees of the British Museum.

P. 230. "The Angel of Java," from *Kingdom of the Gods* by Geoffrey Hodson, 1952, plate 26, p. 236. Used by permission of The Theosophical Publishing House, Adyar, Madras, India.

P. 240. "A Guardian, a Formal Presence," 1979, Lee Mullican, collection of the artist. Courtesy of the Herbert Palmer Gallery, Los Angeles.

P. 254. "Angel of Unity," by Arthur Douët. Courtesy of Inner Light Ministries.

Introit - Opening Song

In this valley of mountains,
this ocean of deserts,
we gather. We put our ears to the ground
and listen for steps. We put our eyes to the glass
and look for visions. We put our hands to the
clay and touch a swelling breast.
Far out to sea someone sails.
We gather into an ear, a glance, an embrace
to receive our angels. Around us they hover,
plaiting their feathers, gazing into the crystal
of the inner eye, holding the neck of a wild swan.
Ha! Hear their rustle, they are ready to speak.
They tell us to press on with our questions—to
rethread our needles, wedge our clay and prepare our canvas.
They tell us their crystal is ground in our devotion.
The swan carries them through our clay spheres,
their braids are the layers of our colors.
Our worlds are one, they say. Look! They are all about us! . . .
weaving and dancing, afire with high heat, pale and
pearl-like, silvery, and carved like hard wood. What
are they singing? "In art is a communion of worlds!"

M. C. Richards

Introduction

Angels, in a rich kaleidoscope of life and form, are an intriguing part of human experience. The current fascination with mythical, magical, and metaphysical beings includes a lively curiosity about angels, especially in their cross-cultural forms. For angels are shapeshifters, appearing in whatever guise is familiar and appropriate to their human hosts. Their appearances, names and activities not only express a mysterious, many-dimensioned nature but presently also reflect our beliefs, expectations, and way of life.

Most of us, if we think of angels at all, conceive of them as winged messengers from somewhere "above" who descend occasionally for making momentous announcements or rescuing humans. We have vague notions of their superhuman intelligence, love, and power. But angels seem more a part of poetic or scriptural drama than an everyday reality. They exist as idea rather than fact. And our ideas lack the vitality born of meaningful encounter.

It is time now to consider seriously what angels represent and how they manifest in the world today. Entertaining angels thoughtfully is not only a delightful pastime; it is essential for psychological as well as spiritual growth. For angels reveal a hidden, formative life working within and through all things, a life not separate from our own.

People of various cultures and inclinations experience angels differently, but central impressions are similar: angels exist independently of human thought; they represent or embody an invisible realm about which we must learn; their life is mysteriously linked with ours; and human-angel cooperation is inevitable. As expressions of divine powers and principles, angels are not unearthly humans. They are of another order of reality, invisible, intangible, yet omnipresent.

Outwardly an angelic encounter may be exhilarating, calming, inspiring, or bewildering. Inwardly it is always transforming. Communion with angels enables us to be more fully human, enhancing our ability to relate freely and naturally with others. Much depends on how we respond. An encounter merely personalized, filed neatly according to one cultural or religious view, loses some of its power. We must continue to explore our collective experience of angels, bringing to the study reverence for all forms and attention to universal ideas.

Recent works on angels are wonderfully varied. In comparative studies in scripture, folklore, and literature, angels seem as intermediaries between human and divine worlds—guides and protectors, messengers, guardians, teachers, judges. They always have an authoritative, evocative presence. Esoteric studies reveal Cosmos as a vast hierarchy of lives evolving through Law. Angels and humans are part of a unitary scheme, inextricably linked at every point and at every moment.

Visionary accounts confirm the universal human experience of unseen forces, personified in the gods, devas, orishas, and angels of all times. The higher order of such beings are said to help humans move beyond mortal consciousness. Clairvoyant studies describe angels as radiating centers of divine influence, whose self-luminous forms reflect a ceaseless movement of transcendent force. In this view, angels are energy transformers who mediate the manifestation of subtle energies. Communications from angels tell us that humans must move beyond mere manipulation of matter to a clearer understanding of its inherent meaning. We must not only bring the earth's life into balance again but bring the human family together.

The works of depth psychologists complement traditional angel studies. Here angels are seen as autonomous, archetypal powers manifesting through all things. Humans are polytheistic beings who serve as a focus for the outworking of patterns of meaning as well as content. Sacred psychology calls for renewing our commitment to a science of the soul, in which imagining is primary.

Though science does not recognize angels in their traditional forms, we need the scientific perspective here. There is no room for sentimentality or wishful thinking about angels. We must be as clear in our observations as possible, even when subject and object necessarily co-mingle. Even now science helps us appreciate the dynamics of an unseen world, where things defy our usual notions of space-time. We must consider also that angels, by nature, may not be accessible or amenable to classification. They may be essentially on the fringe of reason's grasp. We confine them temporarily, imperfectly, while we focus attention in unfamiliar terrain and prepare ourselves to cooperate with their hidden purposes.

Angels challenge us to inquire directly into the mystery that is at once Angel, Human, and Nature. They encourage us to wake from self-preoccupation and to break through to a new way of being. It seems that humans cannot ignore the gods, as they confront us anew in ever more compelling forms. Perhaps it is only by welcoming them, with an eager intellect and open heart, that we become capable of probing the mystery of our origins and destiny. In communion with angels we assume the responsibility and rigor of an inspired creative life.

The present work is meant to complement the many fine studies of angels available to students of comparative religion. The articles demonstrate some ideas common to different traditions and bring in provocative ideas from psychology. Commentaries before each section help highlight a few key ideas and sometimes add a theosophical perspective. We hope the study will help illumine the student's experiences and inspire to further open, energetic enquiry.

I
Experiencing
the Ephemeral

We mortals have forgotten our eternal nature. Earthbound in a tangle of habits and prejudices which bring suffering, we escape only by flight. Wings symbolize psychological and spiritual transformation. Unfolding of "winged" awareness is a gradual movement into purer realms of knowing. Flight is not to a place above or beyond earth, but a soaring through the particulars to their unitary, ephemeral soul. Winged awareness ascends to its angelic nature, and returns to gift the earth with the heavenly vision.

Spiritual flight means release of fixed ideas and selfish patterns of living that keep us from truly experiencing life. We must move beyond preoccupation with the dazzle of phenomena to an appreciation of their deeper meaning. Physicists now affirm the mystic view that the material world is a fleeting crystallization of a more fundamental, numinous realm. The interior order is essentially motion, patterning akin to light. Earthly images, whether in material or thought form, are carriers of this intangible reality.

Esoteric philosophy suggests that angels not only "inhabit" realms which interpenetrate the earthly sphere, but that they ARE numinous substance in its ceaseless ebb and flow. Indirectly, they too are evolving through physical form. Matter and spirit are an inseparable unity. Even forms humans create, including thought images, are ensouled by invisible intelligences. The quality of our thoughts determines which angels respond, and we are quite unconsciously living with and through angels all the time. So long as we are ignorant of the powerful, formative forces moving through us, humans will be the unwitting "playground" of the gods.

Though it is essential that we become more sensitive to subtle energies, deliberate development of psychic powers is not necessary. What is important is the development of intuition, a refined sensitivity to the hidden meaning of things. Only a calm, focused awareness penetrates form to reveal its hidden significance. Patient, selfless attention carefully separates fancy from fact. Nature yields her innermost secrets only to those who prepare well. She requires only that they, in turn, create something beautiful for others.

1

The Nature of
Angel Forms

G. DON GILMORE

A high percentage of the mail received in response to my request for stories of experiences with angels contained the emphatic proclamation that angels are messengers. It was ironic to read claims of total ignorance on the subject of angels alongside this traditional, almost arbitrary, definition.

The word angel is derived from the Greek term *angelos*, which comes from the Hebrew expression *mal'akh*, usually translated as the concrete noun "messenger." But the traditional definition weakens under the weight of a scholarly examination of angel history. From the earliest times, angels were not considered single-purpose beings. The idea of an angel as a messenger suggests but one form, like the advertising image of the retail florist association: The Greek god Mercury, the messenger of the heavens, resplendent with wings on his hat and ankles, is dispatched to deliver a bouquet of flowers to someone as swiftly as possible. On the other end of the spectrum of angel definitions is that of the author of Hebrews: "The truth is they [angels] are all spirits . . . [Heb. 1:14, JB]."

Originally there were no stereotypes of angels. Angels were seen as performing a number of functions. They may have taken the form of messengers, but not all did the same thing. At this point let me define angels as those *forms, images, or expressions through which the essences and energy forces of God can be transmitted.* More succinctly, an angel is a form through which a specific essence or energy force can be transmitted for a specific purpose. The image or form of an angel is a creation of inspired imagination that is built up in group consciousness over the years by those who have visualized angels in a particular way. For example, from the earliest times Jewish, Christian, and Muslim angels (excluding archangels) were not relegated to a single category,

THE BIBLE, Rev. xxi. 10, Gustave Doré
  "And I saw a new heaven and a new earth . . ."
Through the companionship of angels, our vision of earthly life is
illumined and transformed, bringing about a Celestial City of harmony
and goodwill.

like messengers; rather, they were described, among other things, as *choirs of singers, a military presence, members of a heavenly court, guardians, helpers, sustainers, protectors, and judges.* Today about the only angel category available is that of a winged cherub people refer to as a messenger.

As vivid as some of these angel images may have been centuries ago, the process of building up angel forms today has all but disappeared. It's not that the essence or energy force of what we call angels has ceased to exist, it's just that the multiple expressions through which the angels previously worked have diminished, due to a shortfall of energy supplies from those who no longer believe in, have faith in, or even think about them. But the angel essences or energy forces do exist, and desire to supply people with extra resources in their daily activities; what is lacking is people's willingness to re-vision their role in contemporary life. In other words, angel images need to be updated and multiplied.

Perhaps no one has done more research on the subject of angels than Gustav Davidson. In his *A Dictionary of Angels* he describes a memorable moment during his angel research.

At this stage of the quest I was literally bedeviled by angels. They stalked and leagured me by night and day. . . . I remember one occasion—it was winter and getting dark—returning from a neighbor's farm. I had cut across an unfamiliar field. Suddenly a nightmarish shape loomed up in front of me, barring my progress. After a paralyzing moment I managed to fight my way past the phantom. The next morning I could not be sure (no more than Jacob was, when he wrestled with his dark antagonist at Penniel) whether I had encountered a ghost, an angel, a demon, or God.

Without committing myself religiously, I could conceive of the possibility of there being, in dimensions and worlds other than our own, powers and intelligences outside our present apprehension, and in this sense angels are not to be ruled out as a part of reality—always remember that we create what we believe. Indeed, I am prepared to say if enough of us believe in angels, the angels exist.[1]

Such is the testimony of one who has probably given more attention to this field of inquiry than anyone in recent times. Davidson's book is a solid collection of personal enthusiasm focused on the reconstruction of damaged forms. It is in every way a labor of love. Unfortunately, he was alone in most of his labors. His colleagues were few. To the contemporary mind, his work was mostly a curiosity, and certainly not a reality.

Those in previous generations who were the builders of the angel forms may well be today the enthusiasts for Unidentified

Flying Objects. UFOs and attendant phenomena have unquestionably galvanized the imaging energies of people all over the world, much as angels did several hundred years ago. Biologist-writer and UFO expert Ivan Sanderson suggested that UFOs come not from another planet but from another set of dimensions— another whole universe! That, Sanderson concluded, is why we have not been able to catch one.[2] So when the UFO forms travel into our space operating according to another set of laws, people see them differently, but the imaging power of the beholder always determines what is seen.

The building up of angel image forms takes time and patience and extra effort. Concentration is the labor of perception. Elizabeth Barrett Browning put it well:

> Earth's crammed with heaven
> And every common bush afire with God
> But only he who sees takes off his shoes . . .
> The rest sit around and pluck blackberries.

It goes without saying that blackberry-pickers outnumber those who would be observers of the angels.

Angel forms have not become extinct. Each Christmas they are superficial appendages to all the activities of the season. There is nothing more pathetic than the flippant way angels are treated during Yuletide. It appears to be a commercial conspiracy to denigrate angels to the form of silvery pasteboard effigies crammed into the background of a window display in a downtown department store. Little wonder that trolls and fairies have superseded the angels in the public mind. I'm afraid that if there were no Christmas carols the nativity angels and their mission would be forgotten.

Even the last bastion of angel cultivation, the Roman Catholic Church, which for centuries advocated all-out devotion to the angels, seems to have lost enthusiasm for angels. A Roman Catholic friend told me that as a child she felt surrounded by the presence of the angels, because of the influence of the church, but that "It is not so today—certainly not with my kids. Perhaps when the statues were removed from our church and the curtain of mystery was drawn aside, the angels went too."

Angel forms dramatize the fact that we are not alone, that we are surrounded by a loving concern. The book of Hebrews describes it as "so great a cloud of witnesses [Heb. 12:1]." The author may not have been referring to angels, but the analogy seems appropriate.

From creative consciousness, the All-in-All, God the Creator, has come pouring out a vibratory force of love and concern that can be personified in angel forms without taking anything away from the direct relationship people enjoy with God.

Let me share a recent angel experience. One cloudy Saturday afternoon I stretched out on our sun deck and drifted into that twilight zone between sleep and being awake. Gradually I felt a warmth on my face and down across my body. It was as though something was gently holding me, soothing me. With eyes still closed, I saw an angel form hovering nearby, projecting renewing energy into my tired body. My angel was a joyous presence whose touch was like the balm of Gilead. I would never have demeaned my celestial guest by envisioning it clothed in the customary angel apparel. The angel in my theater was a unique presence, not a traditional image; my visitor was warm like the summer wind blowing in from the heights of a love that knows me better than I know myself. When I opened my eyes at last, I saw the logical explanation for my angel phenomenon. The sun had come out from behind the clouds. One may rightly argue that angel experience is more than being warmed on a sun deck, and I would agree. But people no longer need to depend on angel forms that have no relevance in their lives. We can be what the French call "the realizers," who pick and choose from the traditional or create new angel forms to channel the essences and energy forces of God.

This was certainly the way of Jesus. At the time of his arrest on the Mount of Olives, he turned to one companion who had just drawn a sword, chopped off a servant's ear, and was ready to take on anyone who would harm Jesus. "Do you think," said Jesus, "that I cannot appeal to my Father, and he will at once send me more than twelve legions of angels [Matt. 26:53]?" Thus Jesus deliberately created a unique form with which to identify the unseen resources. It may indeed have been an individual expression, but he called it like he saw it.

No matter how objective or legalistic people try to be on the subject of angels, in the last analysis angel forms exist in the eyes of the beholder. This does not mean that the components of God's love—those essences and energy forces—are simply products of the imagination. In fact, people have nothing to do with their creation or their activity. But the forms, those images through which the Spirit flows, must be constructed by people in their minds. It is a matter of what they see (or visualize) is what they get (in expression).

There is enormous subjectivity when it comes to angel experiences. A friend warned me, "Be careful about those crazy poets with their extravagant words. Beware of people like John Milton and his angel ecstasy—carrying on about 'that glorious force, that light ineffable, that fair beaming blaze of majesty.' The man is beside himself." Those words came from a man who likes everything precooked, preplanned and nailed down. He leaves no room for the spontaneous, the unrehearsed, or serendipity. He is like one of those people who attended a conference where the popular Indian medicine man Rolling Thunder was to speak. They came early with notebooks, tape recorders, and cameras and got good seats up front. When Rolling Thunder arrived, he asked that the chairs be pushed back and that the would-be audience make a circle. Then, instead of giving the customary lecture, he announced, "I'm going to teach you to dance." The teaching was the dance in which all participated and made their own unique discoveries. He closed with the words "All things are manifestations of your belief system. If you let go of your fixed realities, your limitations, your fears, your doubts, magic can enter your life."

That day Rolling Thunder was helping create a myth. The dance was a story that involved everyone present. It was a metaphor addressed to times in which we live. It was a symbol of what the growing life should be. When Rolling Thunder chose the dance over the lecture, his myth-making was no less appropriate to the situation. The genius of the myth-makers of history has been that they choose the forms of expression consistent with their own inner leading. Those who say that myths are illusionary or irrational do not understand what myth really is. Myths are the products of creative imagination, which the dictionary defines as "the power to represent the real more fully and truly than it appears to the senses and in its ideal and universal character."[3]

Angel forms are the result of myth-building; they provide a story, metaphor, or symbol through which the essences and energy forces of God may be expressed. According to William Irwin Thompson, myth in this sense is "an imaginative description of reality in which the known is related to the unknown through a system of correspondences."[4]

Primitive peoples mythologized what they observed in the processes of nature. That is how the legends of angelic activities associated with the moon, sun, stars, and weather came about.

The stories may have been fanciful, but in order for people to live with the inexorable processes, personalizing of the phenomenon was necessary. And this ancient method of humanizing the elements (e.g., angel of the sun, angel of the moon, angel of the winds) helped them become aware that there was something out there like the beneficial care of God in nature.

Author A. Clutton-Brock told of being in the Maritime Alps one June and discovering a spring in the shade of a sweet chestnut tree on the southern slope of a mountain.

Then I knew suddenly how southern people had come by their myth of the water-nymph. Standing myself in the blazing sunlight, I almost saw a water-nymph among the waters of that shade. Water nymphs had always seemed to me frigid, unreal fancies; but now the spring, in its shadowed beauty and contrast with the parched heat of the mountain side, became alive, became almost a person. It was not the legend of the water-nymph that brought her to my mind, it was the life and beauty of the stream that almost brought her to my eyes. The stream seemed so clearly to be occupied with a lovely, friendly business of its own that I almost saw a lovely friendly creature doing it.[5]

Although Clutton-Brock denies it, the legend of the water nymph probably influenced him, at least subconsciously. That legend added to the beauty of the scene activated by certain energy forces flowing through his water-nymph image, produced an exciting moment that might later have been saluted as no more than a pleasant sensual experience, a picturesque setting or just a nice trout stream to recall.

In the stories of people's encounters with angels, the experience is always colored by the personality of the beholder, and that is as it should be. The personal dimension has everything to do with the angel shapes. In fact, one's own myth-making and development of a variety of personal angel forms will make possible a connection with a wide range of spiritual energies needed in life. So the more angel imagings one can create and experience, the better.

One noon hour I sat with a surgeon friend at the Seattle-Tacoma airport, watching an incredible display of auric light and color blending into a focused configuration over Mount Rainier. My friend is very scientifically oriented, so he was attempting at first to place what we were seeing into some generic classification or category. But nothing fit. There we sat, watching the bewildering, intoxicating happening, not knowing what it was but exhilarated by what was going on out there. It did indeed draw us out of our routine selves and make that day, as he put it, "glittering and glistening with possibility." Much later, I began to realize that what we had been watching was what some experts on the subject call the aura of a mountain angel. Whatever name you give it, for our part it lifted us quite angel-like while we waited for our flight.

It is unfortunate that today angel-less religion is more often the rule than the exception. People caught up in a world of mechanical processes and boring routine feel empty and lonely. They are at the mercy of impersonal forces that by their very nature separate human beings from a recognition of who and what they are and, even more important, all that they have going for them. Religion ought to be a vehicle for freeing people today from their emptiness and loneliness, but the erosion of interest in angels, which is a by-product of denying the higher dimensions of imagination, delivers people into a state of incompleteness. Loren Eiseley described this condition as the losing struggle between "Yam, the old sea dragon of the original Biblical darkness, and, arrayed against him, some wisp of dancing light."[6]

Not many people would prefer the darkness to an angel-like "wisp of dancing light," but there is little question that the wisps have been dismissed and people have elected to muddle through on their own. Yet we are haunted by an urge as deep as life itself, an urge that has driven our species from prehistoric times. We are at heart searchers for the transcendent who actually refuse to believe in or employ the agents of the transcendent, those angel-like "wisps of dancing light."

Christians might want to inform me in no uncertain terms that Jesus has filled all their emptiness, loneliness, and incompleteness in life. But note that even Jesus was not without spiritual allies: a personal company of angels. Following his experience with the tempter, the Greek text reads: "Then the devil left him, and, look! angels came and began to minister to him [Matt. 4:11]." This particular angel form appears to come from the Greek *diakoneo*, which has to do with "minister." This special sort of angelic ministry combines comfort, refreshment, sympathetic sharing, and just being there. And in the Garden of Gethsemane, Jesus was again supplied with another form of angel activity. Following his agonizing prayer that he be delivered from death, "there appeared to him an angel from heaven, strengthening him [Luke 22:43]." Here we have the image of an angel steadying Jesus' nerves and helping restore his depleted energy reserves.

Other angel images in Jesus' life include his "twelve legions of angels," which were apparently constantly vigilant with swords drawn ready for battle. At Jesus' birth a heavenly host was heard singing over shepherds' fields: "Glory to God in the highest, and on earth peace among men with whom he is pleased [Luke 2:14]!" Angels also played a significant role in Jesus' resurrection drama. They appeared to the women who had come to visit the tomb on that first Easter, saying, "Do not be amazed; you seek Jesus of Nazareth, who was crucified. He has risen, he is not here; see the place where they laid him [Mark 16:6]."

What rings out from all these angel experiences is the incredible affirmation that angels await us in even the most unlikely places. There is a diversity of angel forms to be celebrated, and there is an element of surprise to be realized, but unless people revive their childlike wonder and imagination, they may never experience such things. The educational system tends to put the lid on the creativity and imaginativeness that we as children possess naturally. But the great educator John Dewey said, "Every great advance in science has issued from a new audacity of imagination."

Most creative people understand that because the universe extends far beyond the power of their senses, it is through the use of their imaginations that they can perceive the realities of the unseen and draw them into expression. Thomas Edison complained that once he had been able to work peacefully and productively in his laboratory in Menlo Park, New Jersey, but that after he became famous he found it difficult to make new discoveries. Professors from nearby Princeton University kept dropping by and warning him that he couldn't do this or he couldn't do that, that what he was doing was against this law or that. All this nagging negativism inhibited the great inventor to the point that he stopped trying to come up with something new. He turned off the channels of his creative imagination, which was the source of his inspiration and productivity.

J. B. Priestley worried about the way Christianity has attempted from early times to become legitimate in the eyes of the secular world by clinging to the premise of "stubborn fact." He lamented the effort of some church people who, lacking creative imagination, had attempted to make the miracles and marvels of the faith conform to a historical precedent rather than allow them to remain mysterious truths set in mythful forms. Alluding to a point made by Carl Jung, he wrote, "A culture first shaped and colored by Christianity has reached us perilously lacking in the fructifying mythic element which thousands of generations . . . found necessary for their imaginative lives. We are still myth-making, but in a negative inferior way."[7] It may not be that bad, but it is at least a legitimate concern of those who wish to see a revival of angel interest and a resurgence of creating contemporary angel forms. Angel images should be given the same sort of marvelously innovative expression that artists have given the image of Jesus in recent times. Jesus' face has been painted to reveal dozens of expressions with which people can identify and use to connect with his spirit. Why can't the same thing be done with the angels?

In some quarters, angel myth-making in art is catching on. A most creative piece of angel art appeared in an advertisement in an unlikely place. Not in a theological journal or a church newsletter or a devotional guide, but in the magazine *Runner's World!*[8] The advertisement read: "The Isaiah 40:31 Poster—Catch the Vision." The year was 712 B.C., when the prophet Isaiah caught the vision inspired by God. It revealed the promise for the ultimate restoration of humankind. Now, centuries, later, the vision takes on new life as it is reported in the award-winning painting by artist Daniel Moore. The painting shows a man running along a tree-lined road at early dawn. The blue sky overhead is filled with fleecy clouds that give him the appearance of being borne off the ground by angel wings.

Notes

1. Gustav Davidson, *A Dictionary of Angels* (New York: Free Press, 1971), pp. ix, xii. Reprinted with permission of Macmillan Publishing Co., Inc. Copyright © 1967 by Gustav Davison.

   This is a first-rate study of angels and a sourcebook for developing one's own angel forms.
2. Bryce Bond, "Ivan Sanderson on U.F.O.'s and the Unexplained," *Argosy,* UFO Special Annual Edition, 1977, p. 63.

   This extraordinary interview covers a wide range of material relating to UFOs. The late Sanderson was one of the most informed people on this subject.
3. Webster's *New Collegiate Dictionary* (Springfield, Mass.: G. & C. Merriam Co., 1958).
4. From p. 137 in *At the Edge of History* by William Irwin Thompson. Copyright © 1971 by William Irwin Thompson. Reprinted by permission of Harper & Row, Publishers, Inc.

   Thompson does not claim to be a prophet, but he does know what is going on and he communicates masterfully.

5. A. Clutton-Brock, *The Spirit: God and His Relationship to Man* (London: Macmillan, 1935), p. 282.

Few writers can communicate their sense of the "personal" in the beauty of nature as this writer. He keeps raising the question of why we misunderstand myths and talk so much nonsense about them.

6. Loren Eiseley, *The Unexpected Universe* (New York: Harcourt Brace Jovanovich, 1969), p. 76. Used by permission.

Eiseley was a naturalist, but also one of the most perceptive writers ever. Anyone would be deeply touched in spirit as well as enlightened in mind by Eiseley's work.

7. J. B. Priestley, *Man and Time* (New York: Dell, 1968), p. 144.

Priestley's section on the problems of Christianity's acceptance of and dependence on history and the rejection of myth is stimulating reading.

8. *Runner's World*, May 1979, p. 7.

2

On Reimagining Angels

JAY G. WILLIAMS

Old Images

Neither secular skeptics nor liberal Christians, believing that angels are at best metaphors and at worst superstition from an earlier age, have taken their existence very seriously. Angels may be mentioned in hymns and in Scripture; they may be depicted by cardboard cutouts in the annual Christmas creche, but they have, it is generally concluded, no substantial reality. Lumped together with fairies, hobgoblins, and other fantastic creatures, they are thought to be no more than creations of the human imagination. And, quite frankly, it *is* difficult to imagine angels inhabiting a world that knows of Voyager II fly-bys, nuclear spills, and the mysteries of DNA.

At the same time, it must be admitted that angels, though modelled on ancient Near Eastern prototypes, are a unique contribution of specifically Biblical religion. It is difficult to escape the fact that Jews and Christians have long believed in them as especially important denizens of the universe. Some scholars believe angels a late "foreign import," tracing angelology back to the Persian prophet Zarathustra, but there is strong evidence that Biblical angelology is not only earlier but of a different nature. While the *Amesha Spenta* of Zoroastrianism are more-or-less personified abstractions of various virtues, angels in the Bible are not abstractions at all. They are concrete, living realities. That is to say, there is nothing allegorical about Biblical angels. They appear in this world.

Not all of the Biblical creatures grouped together by tradition as angels are, strictly speaking, such. The Genesis account of Adam in the Garden ends with the man and woman being driven out of Eden. They are forbidden reentrance to their original

THE COSMOGONS, *Wolfgang Paalen*
*"The personal dimension has everything to do with the angel shapes.
In fact, one's own myth-making and development of a variety of personal
angel forms will make possible a connection with a wide range of
spiritual energies needed in life."*

G. Don Gilmore

home and are no longer allowed to eat of the tree of life. Barring their return are cherubs and a flaming sword. (Gen. 3:24) Cherubs today are envisioned as sweet baby angels, but the original cherubs had an entirely different, even ferocious nature. Composite creatures thought to be part lion, part eagle, part bull, and part human, in Assyria they were placed as guardians of the royal palaces. In Israel they not only were said to guard Eden but were depicted as surrounding the ark of the covenant, the earthly image of Yahweh's throne. In effect, they were, for ancients, the outward manifestations of potent and forbidding divine holiness.

Seraphs were also of a strange, even eerie nature. The book of Numbers (21:4-9) describes them as fiery serpents sent to punish Israel for her sins. Moses, in response, makes a bronze serpent and raises it on a pole to avert further disaster. Doubtless, this bronze serpent, placed eventually in the Temple in Jerusalem, became an inspiration for Isaiah's vision. In Isaiah 6:1-5 the prophet sees seraphs with wings flying around the throne of God in the temple, chanting the famous song,

> Holy, holy, holy is the Lord of hosts;
> The whole earth is full of his glory.

Malak, the word usually translated as "angel," means in Hebrew "messenger." In a broad sense, virtually anything could serve that function. The burning bush of Moses was, or at least contained, a *malak* (Ex. 3:2). It would appear that the angel with whom Jacob wrestled was a human messenger sent by his brother Esau (Gen. 32:4-32). The prophets were also thought of as *malakim*; the last of the minor prophets is named *Malachi* (my messenger).

The Bible, however, usually depicts angels as super-human. They speak, eat, and wrestle, but they also can suddenly appear and disappear and exhibit other powers not known to mortals (see Judges 6:11-24). In the early books of the Bible angels are anonymous, but in later literature they are given definite names such as Michael, Gabriel, Raphael, and Satan. Most angels, however, remain nameless. Yahweh is conceived as the Lord of the Sabaoth (hosts), vast angelic armies which stand ready to fight God's battles in the world (Cf. I Kings 22:19). Humans have only become acquainted with a few angelic leaders, not with the rank and file of the heavenly hosts.

The New Testament does nothing to minimize angelic reality. Indeed, the whole gospel story occurs within an angelic parenthesis: angels announce both the birth of Jesus and his resurrection.

Jesus, himself, seems to have been a firm believer in angels (see, for instance, Matt. 13:41, 49, 16:27, 24:31, 36, etc.). In Acts 12:6-11, Peter is freed from prison by an angel, while in the book of Revelation the number and variety of angels is almost staggering. In a word, it takes considerable hermeneutical sleight-of-hand to avoid recognizing how important angels really are in the Bible.

It is not surprising, therefore, that angels continued to play an important role in the life of both Judaism and Christianity. In the former, in fact, angelology was greatly developed by the Kabbalists. More angelic names were discovered and rites for the invocation of angels were common. It was believed by some that if an angel were summoned in the correct way, it could not fail to appear.

Christianity also preserved the angelic tradition, although eventually, to avoid abuses, the use of angelic names was limited to the three mentioned in Scripture (Gabriel, Raphael, and Michael). Theologians invariably found a place for angels within their worldviews and debated endlessly about issues to do with angels. Thomas Aquinas, the great Medieval rationalist, wrote extensively on angels; his *Summa Theologica* (Ia, Q. 50-64) even contains a confident, thoroughly developed account of how angels think (Q. 58).

Moreover, there have always been some Christians who have claimed to experience angels, either in visions or in the flesh. One thinks of Joan of Arc whose voices included that of the Archangel Michael, and St. Teresa who is memorable for her description of her confrontation with specific, well-defined angels. These women, however, are but two among a vast throng who have not only believed in angels but have claimed to experience them *in corpore*.

It should also be noted that angels have sometimes appeared to some who for the orthodox Christian are doctrinally beyond the pale. The whole of Islam, for instance, depends upon Gabriel's memorable revelation to the prophet Muhammad, a revelation which was to produce not doctrinal change, but a whole new orthodoxy. The *hadith* describes the prophet's experience very graphically:

Then solitude became dear to him and he used to seclude himself in the cave of Hira, and therein he devoted himself to Divine worship for several nights before he came back to his family and took provisions for this [retirement]; then he would return to *Khadijah* and take [more] provisions for a similar [period], until the Truth came to him while he was in the cave of Hira; so the angel [Gabriel] came to him and said, Read. He [the

Prophet] said, "I said I am not one who can read." And he continued: "Then he [the angel] took hold of me and he pressed me so hard that I could not bear it any more, and then he let me go and said, Read. I said, "I am not one who can read." Then he took hold of me and pressed me a second time so hard that I could not bear it any more, then he let me go again and said, Read. I said, "I am not one who can read." [The Prophet] continued: "Then he took hold of me and pressed me hard for a third time, then he let me go and said, 'Read in the name of thy Lord Who created—He created man from a clot—Read and thy Lord is most Honourable.' "[1]

What Muhammad eventually read, of course, became the Koran, the memorable message from Allah to the world.

Also, most striking was the experience of Joseph Smith, the nineteenth-century American who founded the Church of Jesus Christ of the Latter Day Saints, largely because of his confrontation with the angel Moroni.

Joseph Smith, through whom, by the gift and power of God, the ancient Scripture, known as *The Book of Mormon*, has been brought forth and translated into the English tongue, made personal and circumstantial record of the matter. He affirmed that during the night of September 21, 1823, he sought the Lord in fervent prayer, having previously received a Divine manifestation of transcendent import. His account follows:

". . . Not only was his robe exceedingly white, but his whole person was glorious beyond description, and his countenance truly like lightning. The room was exceedingly light, but not so very bright as immediately around his person. When I first looked upon him, I was afraid; but the fear soon left me.

"He called me by name, and said unto me that he was a messenger sent from the presence of God to me, and that his name was Moroni; that God had a work for me to do; and that my name should be had for good and evil among all nations, kindreds, and tongues, or that it should be both good and evil spoken of among all people.

"He said there was a book deposited, written upon gold plates, giving an account of the former inhabitants of this continent, and the source from whence they sprang. He also said that the fulness of the everlasting Gospel was contained in it, as delivered by the Savior to the ancient inhabitants;

"Also, that there were two stones in silver bows—and these stones, fastened to a breastplate, constituted what is called the Urim and Thummim—deposited with the plates; and the possession and use of these stones were what constituted *Seers* in ancient or former times; and that God had prepared them for the purpose of translating the book."[2]

Angels, then, have not always confirmed orthodox Christian opinion but have occasionally been the agents through which the Church has been challenged, criticized and/or chastised. In every era, however, there have been some who have attested to the reality of angels and have therefore helped to perpetuate the tradition.

On Imagining

All of this leads us to some basic questions, questions which I would like to raise, not "in the faith," but from a more universal and transcendent standpoint. Although it is an interesting question, I will leave to other theologians inside the Church to determine whether or not a belief in angels is essential for the Christian faith. Instead, I would like to ask whether the Biblical conception of angels points to a reality which lies beyond mere ethnic or religious worldview, to a reality which is at least potentially experienceable wherever you live and whatever you believe.

This is a difficult question because it is impossible to know reality untouched by human imagination. What we have by way of evidence are the testimonies of human beings, and these human beings came to their experiences with minds which hardly resembled *tabulae rasae*. Joseph Smith, for instance, not only knew the Bible but conceived of angels in a way that strongly exhibits the influence of classical and Medieval art. Nevertheless, the experiences have been reported, and that ought to raise questions in the inquiring, modern mind.

The history of human thought has taught us that when something does not "fit" into a worldview, it does not do to pronounce, out-of-hand, that something as "superstitious." One must at least inquire into the possibility that the worldview itself is at fault. When we look back over the history of human intellectual development, we see that when something in human experience has not "fit" it has often been a sign that a new paradigm was developing. Kepler's data just didn't cohere with the accepted astronomy of Ptolemy, and it was astonomy that had to be radically revised. Einstein's mathematical investigations did not support the regnant Newtonianism. Eventually, the latter had to give way to a new, largely counterintuitive conception of the universe. As history proceeds, it becomes ever clearer that no worldview or human formulation is eternal.

But, one might argue, angels are not a new discovery; they are rather a discarded conception from the ancient past. True enough, but if they represent genuine human experience, they either must cohere with the worldview, or the worldview must be modified to accommodate them. Worldviews can be considered acceptable only so long as they adequately account for all legitimate human experiences.

Determining which human experiences are legitimate, however, is a problem, for the regnant worldview largely controls not only what experiences we regard as legitimate, but what experiences we actually have. As human beings, we are bombarded at every moment by a great welter of external and internal stimuli. If we were to experience everything that we potentially could experience, we would very quickly go mad. Therefore, we simply do not see, hear, and feel everything that goes on around us. Our sensations are unconsciously screened, so that we perceive only what it appears useful to perceive. The irrelevant is left largely unnoticed. The same is true internally. We do not remember all our dreams; neither are we conscious of all our thoughts and feelings. Although each person is unique to a certain extent, this screening process usually conforms to the worldview society holds in common.

In a word, if we do not really believe in angels—if they do not cohere with our worldview—our minds will unconsciously and/or consciously screen out those experiences which, for others, might indicate angelic presences. Most of us have had odd feelings of uncanny eeriness, of tremendous exaltation, of disturbing edginess. Could these have been angelic encounters which our screening process has emasculated?

For most of us there is a sharp distinction between what is fact and what is imaginary. We frequently ask: Is it real or am I imagining things? In truth, however, this line of distinction is never very sharp. Much of what we call the world of reality is the product of our corporate imagination. Consider, for instance, what sort of reality a ten-dollar bill, a national boundary, or an atom would have apart from our corporate imagination of them. We imagine that a ten-dollar bill is worth ten times as much as a one-dollar bill, though both are of the same size and shape, and as a result, it is. But remove the imagination, and the whole basis for our economic system collapses. Economics is, literally, a fantastic affair. It is imagination which fuels our demand for products, dominates the vagaries of the stock market, and values one type of labor more than another.

The same may be said for political boundaries and, parenthetically, for political life in general. National boundaries are divisions, not of nature, but of human imagination. The St. Lawrence River is "there," but it is imagination that says it separates one people from another. There would be no border if people did not so imagine it. Nevertheless, despite its source in imagination, the border, once established, becomes a geopolitical fact which may be the source of great conflict. Millions have died defending such imaginary lines.

The atom, however, appears different. That, many would say, is really there; it is a matter of fact. However, no one has ever seen an atom. All atomic theory is precisely that: theory designed to explain certain known phenomena through the postulation of an unseen object. Diagrams of the atoms, any physicist will admit, are not really accurate pictures of how things are; they are imaginative constructions designed to conceive the largely inconceivable. Science, with its non-empirical mathematics created through human quantitative imagination and its models of the unseen universe, is as much a product of human fancy as any other aspect of culture.

Distinctions between reality and imagination, then, are at best arbitrary. Just as we, together, create atoms to answer certain questions and then, on the basis of that imagining heat our homes and blow up the cities of our enemies, so it may well be that corporate imagination created the angels who, through the power of common consent, became fact. Traces of angels were found everywhere. People envisioned angels both in dreams and while awake. Although medieval philosophers admitted that angels are essentially incorporeal and thus in themselves unimaginable, the imaginative pointings to that unimaginable reality became, by common consent, factual.

Today the atom is "fact." But given the history of science, it seems probable that one day this feature of our scientific imagination will dissolve, and atoms will become as irrelevant to science and as unbelievable to scientists as angels are for the average physicist today. That will not mean that the phenomena which led to the imaging of the atom will have gone away. Either they will be overlooked or will be accounted for in a new fashion. Given the scrupulosity of science, the latter option is more likely, but it is not necessary. In the history of science there have been many examples of science simply forgetting about the phenomena for which old concepts had been designed to account.

Human imagining takes place on at least three different levels or planes. On the lowest and most universal level, the body is "tingled" by various sensory stimuli of both external and internal variety, and it transforms these tingles into conscious images. Even here culture and personal experience intrude to shape the imaging in particular ways. One should not think that there is something called "raw experience" which, in itself, is purely objective and is then interpreted in subjective ways. Right from its inception, human imaging is affected by language and mind set. Believing, one might say, is seeing. As Edward Hall says,

> It has long been believed that experience is what all men [sic] share, that it is always possible somehow to bypass language and culture and to refer back to experience in order to reach another human being. This implicit (and often explicit) belief concerning man's relation to experience was based on the assumption that, when two human beings are subject to the same "experience," virtually the same data are being fed to the central nervous systems and the two brains record similarly.
>
> Proxemic research casts serious doubt on the validity of this assumption, particularly when the cultures are different. . . . People from different cultures not only speak different languages but, what is possibly more important, inhabit different sensory worlds. Selective screening of sensory data admits some things while filtering out others, so that experience as it is perceived through one set of culturally patterned sensory screens is quite different from experience perceived through another.[3]

Secondly, there are those imaginings clearly created by human culture. We have already reviewed some examples of such imagining—money, national boundaries—and there is no need to give more examples. Perhaps it should be added only that while some features of the social imagination are virtually universal, others are quite culturally bound.

Third, there are imaginings that are individual and hence not shared by society as a whole. These are the images normally called "imagination." The common distinction between "reality" and "imagination" usually points to the difference between imagination more-or-less assented to by society as a whole and imagination of a more personal and individualistic sort. When the latter becomes accepted by society, imagination is transformed into fact. When it is not, the person so imagining is likely to be branded psychotic or at least highly idiosyncratic.

Since our modern worldview seems to preclude angels, any

experience of them appears today peculiar, perhaps even abnormal. Angels have been banished to the fringe. As inhabitants of the old three-story universe, they no longer can live in post-Newtonian space. Nevertheless, certain primordial experiences do not go away. There is, for instance, a common feeling, once expressed in terms of guardian angels, that there is a power which guides, sustains, and protects the individual. Even very secular people sometimes attest to this experience in moments of danger and/or stress. There is also the perhaps less common experience of being suddenly "called" or directed or filled with purpose. The light breaks, the penny drops, and life is transformed. And there is that eerie sense of holiness, of overwhelming power, which attracts and yet repels. These "ground experiences" just will not disappear. Although already shaped by our "psychic grid" and hence "impure," they seem to point to a reality behind anything our minds can invent.

Clearly, however, if one is to take seriously the reality of angels in the modern world, one must reimagine what or who they are, for many aspects of the old traditional angelology are no longer acceptable to us. We have our own blinders on.

For instance, we know now that the universe as a universe is not divided into three tangible levels. Heaven is not literally above us nor is hell beneath our feet. Angels, therefore, cannot be more-or-less tangible messengers between heaven and earth. This observation, however damaging to traditional conceptions, hardly destroys angelic reality. Although Medieval people often spoke of heaven as "up there," sophisticated theologians have always known better. God is not, for Thomas Aquinas, a great big being in the heavens but the source of all Being. Angels for him might take corporeal form in order to communicate with humans, but such a form was regarded as visionary. Angels were seen as spiritual beings without material substance.

The discovery by moderns that God is not "out there" has led some thinkers to assert with Carl Jung that God is "in here." Deity can be found, not by going up but by introspection within the human mind. Angels, then, become inhabitants of the unconscious who make themselves known in dreams, reveries, and visions.

I would like to argue, however, that God is neither "out there" nor "in here," for both are the product of human imagining. If God exists, the divine reality is in another dimension entirely, a dimension which impinges upon our own but for which we have no univocal words at all. And if angels have any reality, they too are in a dimension which is neither up nor down, neither out nor in.

On Reimagining

In order to reimagine angels for our time, we must first assess at least briefly the essentials of modern cosmology. There was an era, scarcely more than one hundred years ago, when both scientists and lay people thought of the world as a self-contained, more-or-less mechanical reality composed of indivisible building blocks called atoms and operating according to immutable natural laws. The Law-giver had long since been banished from true science, leaving only a self-explanatory cosmological machine. The task of science was simply to discover exactly how each part of the mechanism works.

Today some may think this is what science is about, but most scientists, following the lead of theoretical physics, have come to doubt this vision of reality. Newton's world, like Aristotle's before it, has turned out to be a complicated but fallible product of the human imagination.

Atoms, the building blocks inherited by modern science from the ancient Epicureans, have been found to be neither indivisible nor solid. In a word, they are not atoms at all. The stuff of atoms (those curious subatomic particles) seems to operate in a strange world characterized by neither space nor time nor causality. The continuity of matter, so apparent on a visible level, is entirely subverted inside the atom. Laws become probabilities; once certain attributes become obvious illusions. The world of post-Einsteinian physics is neither a mechanism nor even a knowable reality. It is as though we see only the white caps of matter on an ocean of emptiness whose depths are both unexplored and apparently unexplorable. Heinz Pagels, a well-known interpreter of modern physics, reminds us that while classical physicists like Aristotle once thought of nature as abhoring a vacuum and of matter as existing everywhere, the modern conception of the universe is the reverse. Whether one looks at the universe or the atom, space is empty; matter is the exception, not the rule.

At the same time, the notion of a vacuum, which was once considered purely empty space, has also been transformed. The vacuum, he says, is not really empty; it is a plenum. What was thought to be a void yields particles and antiparticles coming into being and passing away with apparent spontaneity. Matter, as we know it, is not permanent but arises from and returns to the vacuum. What does this mean? Pagel writes "Space looks empty . . . nothingness of space."[4]

Let us use this image of the ocean of emptiness to reimagine the cosmos and its source. We shall begin by thinking of this world of space and time as like the surface of the ocean, an ocean which constitutes another, fifth dimension. Matter which is constantly coming into being and passing away, is the manifestation of vibrations from the Depth, vibrations which make a Mahler symphony look like one note without overtones, played on a monochord. The world we sense, according to this image, is ordered as it is by the great vibratory source whose ground bass is the essential pitch of the universe. Matter is the vacuum vibrating. The cosmos is a symphony.

Everything operates in harmony with that Source—everything, that is, except human consciousness. Peculiarly, consciousness has somehow been cut loose and appears deaf to the harmonies essential to human life. We could hear the music of our being—the inner ear is there—but we do not. Thus, while we *are* ourselves vibrations from the one Source of harmony, our consciousnesses invariably produce cacophany, what Buddhists call *dukkha* or suffering and Christians denominate as "sin."

The whole problem of humanity, then, is to recover that lost hearing in order to sense those primordial rhythms and harmonies of our nature and to dance out life accordingly. Meditation is to listen again to the heartbeat of the universe and its overtones; it is to reproduce in life that essential ground note and its harmonies.

The whole world, of course, is a manifestation of the music of No-thingness. Vibrations can be apprehended everywhere—in the subatomic world of quarks, in the macrocosmic world of interstellar space. Our deafness, however, bars any easy access to these shaping, cosmic vibrations. It is only occasionally that certain moments in nature and history, and in dream and vision, make audible for us the vibrations from the source. We might call these moments "angels," that is, messengers of the creative harmony.

Such angels have no independence or power of their own. They are like motifs in a cosmic symphony. Angels have no substance; they are not things. Indeed, there *are* no things in the ordinary substantial sense. All reality is composed of vibrations which would immediately cease if the Source were to observe silence. As Rumi, the great Sufi poet, writes:

Jay G. Williams

> All day and night, music,
> a quiet bright
> reed song. If it
> fades, we fade.[5]

It is this bright reed song that sustains each one of us. One might say that each person has a special song, or, as it were, a guardian angel.

The key to living is listening quietly and carefully for those inner harmonies which are creative and sustaining, while shutting out the cacophany which disrupts and makes inharmonious the song of the self. At its worst, human music itself can be part of that disruption and can produce in our consciousnesses death-dealing noise. There is such a thing as demonic music. In fact, noise *is* the demonic. On the other hand, great music itself can open the consciousness to those deeper harmonies of the cosmos and can, at least, hint of the angel's song.

There is a long-standing but largely neglected Western tradition arising from the Pythagorean and Platonic traditions that speaks of the harmony of the spheres. Human music, according to this tradition, is but a pale reflection of that deeper, inaudible music that is the cosmos. This essay is written to assert agreement with that general notion. But it is not the planets which create the harmony. It is rather that the harmony from that other oceanic dimension creates the planets and, as it were, sings through them. And when we hear a piece of cosmic music, what rings in our ears, whether we know it or not, is the angel's song:

> Glory to God in the highest
> And peace among humans of good will.

Good will is the harmony of the cosmos made audible in human consciousness. It is that good will which is the true end and meaning of every human life.

Everything I have said, of course, is metaphorical. I am imagining, not presenting facts. My aim is not a literal picture, for the world is not a symphony nor is emptiness an ocean. Moreover, I am well aware that I have explained neither why humans are deaf nor where cacophony comes from. And yet I would beg you to listen, for beyond the metaphors of human imagination, in the heart of reality, the angels do sing.

References

1. Maulana Mohammed Ali, *A Manual of Hadith*, 2nd ed. (Atlantic Highlands, N.J.: Humanities Press, 1978), pp. 2-3.
2. Joseph Smith, trans., *The Book of Mormon* (Salt Lake City: The Church of Jesus Christ of the Latter-Day Saints, 1961), r.p.
3. Edward T. Hall, *The Hidden Dimension* (Garden City, NY: Doubleday & Co., 1969), p. 2.
4. Heinz R. Pagels, *The Comic Code: Quantum Physics as the Language of Nature* (New York: Bantam Books, 1984), pp. 243-244.
5. John Moyne and Coleman Barks, *Unseen Rain: Quatrains of Rumi* (Threshold Books, 1986), p. 2.

A HEALING ANGEL, from Geoffrey Hodson, The Kingdom of the Gods
"to make contact with the angelic kingdom . . . to appreciate its nature
we need to have something of the quality of the real artist. This is the
higher octave of feeling which is not in any way emotional . . . it goes
with the sense of mystery, of wonder which leads on to that of the
livingness of all things."

Laurence Bendit

3
The Incarnation of
the Angels

LAURENCE J. BENDIT

The word 'science' means 'knowledge.' Hence, anything which adds knowledge to our minds is, literally and exactly, 'scientific,' 'knowledge-making.' It is only by degradation that the word 'science' has come to be applied only to certain methods of learning. In much the same way, we see 'catholicism' or 'universality,' used only in the restricted sense of the encircling and limited theology emanating from the Vatican.

With the new, emerging mentality, it seems reasonable to propose that the field of science be enlarged so that it will include much which is nowadays considered as 'unscientific' because it does not fall within a framework dictated by the intellect and excluding the parallel function, feeling. Feeling, at a certain level, is the opposite of intellect in that while the latter separates the knower from what he wants to know, emotion (*ex*, 'out' and *moveo* 'I move') means a reaching out from oneself towards the object. So, while intellect 'objectivizes' (*ob*, 'away' or 'apart' and *jaceo*, 'I throw'), the result of emotion is to 'con-fuse'—to 'melt together.' Hence, emotion and science as at present understood are incompatible, and, so far, the upstart, modern science has strenuously pursued objectivity and tried—with limited success—to avoid the confusion which feeling brings.

We are, however, moving into a new mental age and if we are really concerned with science in the larger sense, we must gradually find that we cannot ignore the feeling aspect of our minds in order to concentrate only on the aspect which thinks, is logical, and has all the virtues which the emotional person lacks. In Vedantic philosophy *Vairagya* or emotional objectivity is the first quality of the would-be yogi, and leads on to discriminative understanding or *Viveka*. Scientists, or those who have the scientific attitude without necessarily being trained in any particular branch

33

of technical science, should by now have developed this power of mental objectivity sufficiently to be able to carry it with them out of the womb of intellect into the wider field which includes feeling. The feeling needs to be similar to that we have as emotion, but without the 'movement-out' of emotion which identifies us with the object to which our feelings are directed.

This higher octave of feeling is doubtless that sometimes known as Buddhi. But Buddhi can also be seen in another aspect where it is the climax of the thinking function when it reaches beyond logical, step-by-step building. It then becomes what L. L. Whyte has termed 'pattern-thinking' as distinct from 'atom-thinking,' Teilhard de Chardin the quality of the 'noosphere,' the psychologist 'intuition,' and others 'true perceptivity' as distinct from ordinary perception. It is also the difference between intelligence and mere intellect.

This introduction was written with a particular subject in mind which cannot fall directly into study from the viewpoint of intellect-science. For the latter requires to be able to measure, weigh and in other ways to compare object with object, effect with effect and so on. And this subject of study cannot be fitted into this framework. I refer to the whole question of what in India is called the kingdom of the *devas,* in the West, of the *angels.* I will even suggest that, just as we study animals under the heading of zoology, the physical earth as geology, we should now use the term *angelology.* And since we are dealing with entities which (so it seems at first) are non-physical and hence non-mensurable, it becomes futile to try and discuss—as it is said was once done— how many angels could sit in comfort on the point of a (physical) needle: there is no connection between such a physical object as a needle and the angel who has no physical organism to sit with. On the other hand, as I shall try and explain, feeling-science could have much to say about this kingdom, both in the positive sense of trying to understand it and in the negative of 'debunking' the often sickening sentimentality, as well as the anthropomorphism of what is said about them.

First, however, we must try to find some premises from which to begin our study. Of prime importance is *whether angels or devas actually exist.* And here we find a diversity of views. Intellect-scientists of the old school would categorically say that they do not. More modern ones, less dogmatic, might be a little more open; though the tendency is today to think in more general and impersonal terms, of a 'life-stream' behind biological forms rather than of intelligent and more personalized entities.

Depth psychology offers us a viewpoint which in some ways is two-edged. For analysts of the non-materialistic schools know that, at a certain point in individual self-discovery, they will dream and see visions of angelic and other mythological figures which are of great importance to them. These convey 'messages' from somewhere beyond the ordinary personal mind. They tell us about ourselves and the state we are in, and in that sense they are 'divine messengers.' But is is usually assumed that these images are created by the mind of the dreamer, emanate from within, not that they represent self-existent entities of any kind. But the more intelligent psychologist allows for the point of view of clairvoyants who tell us of angels or devas in terms of independent beings which they see or which, sometimes, seem to 'visit' them and teach them. Indeed, I myself once asked Professor Jung the question whether he thought that humankind would have the use of images of angels, 'elementals,' centaurs, unicorns and the like if they did not, somewhere, somehow, exist in the universe in their own right. I may, of course, have misunderstood him, but the impression he left in my mind is that he replied that if they did not so exist we should not have model images to use for our own purposes: we should not be able to use them as symbols, characters in the drama created by our minds to teach us about ourselves and our spiritual needs.

The 'opposite number' to the psychologist is the clairvoyant, often deplorably ignorant of the powers of dramatization of the mind, and more concerned with attempts to observe the psychic world outside than with what one's own mind is doing. They often profess to despise psychology, believing that visions give them a position superior to the mere mortal who has not got psychic powers of direct observation, however flawed these may actually be. Books appear, supposedly relating teachings given to such a chosen individual by an angel—though whether the latter is supposed to speak English or to use words is usually not made clear. Occasionally these 'teachings' have the quality of true inspiration, repeating the profound truths of the Perennial Philosophy, though sometimes they degenerate into pure fantasy.

Both the psychologist who insists on pure subjectivism where angels are concerned, and the clairvoyant who takes the opposite view, miss half the theoretical possibilities: the first in not accepting at least the idea of the actual existence of angels, the latter in repudiating the creative and inventive powers of the internal mind. So both may be wrong, while both may also be half right: which leaves us with the question of how to make use of any dream or vision we may have of a denizen of the angelic kingdom.

This question is of considerable importance to the true student and can be resolved only in a pragmatic manner. For whether or not we see an angel objectively or 'invent' it with our mind is, from this angle, unimportant except in theory. What matters is that, at this moment of time, we have seen something with the value of myth. Myth has been said by Annie Besant, as well as by depth psychologists, to be in effect truer than so-called fact: i.e., fact at the physical level. For it goes deeper and has more true meaning to the individual who experiences it. So students need to consider *what their vision means to them, in terms of their state of mind when it occurred.* That is, what 'message' it brings from the spiritual or divine Self within.

This, of course, applies principally to the kind of angelic visitation which makes serious impact on the individual. But it also applies to all other kinds of observations, at all levels, physical, psychic or psycho-spiritual. For, if there is any validity in clairvoyant reports, there is a population of entities in the psychic worlds which are not particularly exalted, however large they seem to be in terms of physical space, however fascinatingly beautiful—or ugly—, however interesting. Their impact is comparable to that of watching bird or plant or animal life in the physical realm, and the effect they have on us depends on what they show us or make us feel: the level of our being on which they impinge; a matter to which we shall return a little later.

We have not yet answered the question we started with, as to the actual and real existence of the angelic kingdom. What seems like a digression, above, was, however, a necessary first step: to observe, one has to determine the viewpoint from which one is observing, as well as the mechanism for doing so—i.e., on minds and how we use them. Now, we come to two important points with regard to evidence in favour of angelic reality. One is that humanity in every part of the globe and at all times in history—save perhaps for a small minority of modern, sceptical sophisticates in the so-called civilized world—has believed and still believes in angels, devas, fairies, gnomes, leprechauns, sylphs, centaurs, fauns, satyrs, local gods of trees and rocks and streams. Intellect-science tends to denounce such ideas as superstition. Perhaps later—as in the case of E.S.P.—it may discover that when the superstition is discarded there remains a solid basis of reality at the core of a popular belief.

Then we have the evidence—which can only really be assessed

in terms of feeling: 'Does it ring true?'—of endless people, both educated and illiterate, who claim to have seen and experienced for themselves the reality of 'the little people' or of greater and more important beings such as we call angels. Some of these observers, of course, are hysterics, unbalanced people; others, may be glamored by moonlight in woods and on hills, perhaps assisted by having taken alcohol or other drugs which loosen the solidity of brain-consciousness. But some are sober, perceptive individuals who are not likely to be merely self-deceived.

If we take the latter only into account, we find a certain consistency in what they have to tell us; from which we can go further in trying to understand what it is all about.

Let us assume, at least for the present, that there actually exists a kingdom of nature which is that of the angels or devas. They are not incarnate as humans and animals are incarnate and, for the most part, are invisible to the eye, inaudible to the ears—existing outside the range of our senses. It is not difficult to make this assumption if we can rid ourselves of the idea that life and consciousness can only function through bodies like our own, largely made up of molecules of carbon, hydrogen, nitrogen, oxygen; and also of the idea that Mind can only operate in the same terms as our ordinary, workaday mentalities. God, the Creator, is surely not limited to such a pattern, and must be capable of other kinds of organic structures. He may be able too to originate minds in which the world-picture (the *maya* by which we live and learn and evolve) would be quite other than our own. I have elsewhere suggested that if our perception of space-time were different, so that time was the element fixed, as to us space is fixed, and space flowed through time, we should be so different from what we are that two humanities might meet and mingle without either being aware of the very existence of the other—except when consciousness rose to the level where space and time as we know them ceased to exist. (I shall come back to this detailed point: it is significant.)

On this basis it is reasonable to postulate that the devic kingdom, which is said to live on earth alongside humanity, really exists, not so much parallel with us in having a similar mind and consciousness, but, as it were, at right-angles. The devic mentality would 'cross' the mental track of the human being, each one working in its own particular direction as ships on different courses cross one another's wakes.

This alone would account for angel and human remaining

unaware of one another as we are today. But there seems to be a further side of the matter: that the devic realm covers a wide range between the highest and most transcendental and the densest and most material aspects of what we call Nature. It runs from Supernature which we scarcely know, through Nature as we know it, into Subnature which, again, we do not know, and is concerned with everything which is manifest in the whole universe. Its function is to build—and destroy—everything which is formed or formulated, at every level from the highest spiritual down or out to the most material. And it does this because it exists as a hierarchy in which different grades or steps may be indicated. Yet it needs to be seen as a whole. In much the same way, the advanced intellect-scientist of today views things less as separate packages of life than as an integral process running, to use Teilhard's phrase, 'from Alpha to Omega,' with the whole alphabet between: a single vast evolutionary process which needs to be understood as a mathematician understands an integral equation which includes an infinite number of differentials.

So we can speak in one breath of archangels, angels and the whole traditional nine orders of the angelic hosts (of which the Christian Churches speak but about which they have no knowledge or eschatology) down to the tiny, evanescent creatures among the flowers and plants in our garden; and doubtless further, into the level of atoms and subatomic particles; and perhaps beyond into realms of which we human beings have no cognizance whatever, if for no better reason that they lie outside the range of ourselves as earth-humanity.

In common parlance the word 'angel' has come to mean not merely a messenger but a messenger from God. This specialization in the sense of the word is not without significance. We may take it to point to the 'crossing point' of the human with the angelic kingdoms at a level beyond that of the personal mind, in the realm of Being as against that of workaday existence. In other words, when we perceive an angel, we do so at the level of the peak experience, hence the vision brings with it something of a numinous quality, a sense of the divine presence. But if both tradition and what clairvoyants tell us is correct, the angelic kingdom extends well 'below' that of the divine or numinous; and here the Vedantic division of the multiple worlds into *rupa* and *arupa* levels is of great help. 'Rupa' means 'form,' 'Arupa' means 'formless': or, extended in space-time versus unextended. This division corresponds in our own world-image and our image of ourselves, respectively to the spiritual and the psycho-physical levels. In the same way we may think of *rupa devas* and of *arupa devas*—the word 'deva' being of course, Sanskrit for our Greek-based word 'angel.'

The 'divine messenger' perceived at peak moments seems to be an image projected from the *arupa*, spiritual, or unextended levels, and stands for the 'higher' ranks of the whole devic kingdom, as humanity stands for the higher rank in the biological. From this we can postulate that this kingdom devolves into the rupa or form worlds, first as the devas clairvoyants and other sensitives know about as covering a valley or a range of mountains, to more localized foci of natural energy such as give rise to the idea of local gods; and then on into the still less developed forms of the various traditional kinds of 'fairy' life, naiads, kelpies, undines, sylphs, gnomes, leprechauns and even smaller creatures. Maybe some day these may be classified into species and varieties and so on, much as we classify animals and plants today: but that would require a perceptivity far beyond that of almost any human being as yet in existence.

Even then problems might arise because, if what some sensitives tell us is true, one would have to account for the disappearance of the 'fairy' life which appears when snow falls and try and determine what happens to it when the snow melts. A hypothesis on this matter may be that in reality many of these lowest denizens of the great kingdom of invisible nature which includes great angels as well as tiny 'fairies' do not have permanent form at all, but, *at all levels* represent vortices of energy, not in any human form; and that the shape in which we human beings see them are projected by our mind, clothing these vortices in forms with which we are familiar. So, when these vortices take on a particular character as in snow, ice, water, fire, air, when the physical state which they represent changes, they fade back into the pool of more or less undifferentiated energies which lie behind all natural phenomena. When circumstances allow, this sea of energy becomes active in the manner appropriate to these circumstances; whirlpools, as it were, become manifest, and we have a show of a particular order of 'nature spirits' which lasts as long as they are needed. It is we, or at any rate, those with less differentiated vision, and with preformed pictures, in our minds, who then dress these vortices up, give them more or less human-like bodies, faces and clothes. The human shape is not intrinsic to the devas although, it seems, certain levels of kingdom have the power of mimicry of the things they perceive, and so produce strange figures in imitation of actual people or things. All this, of course, is quite unscientific, even from the angle of feeling-science: but it makes interesting speculative material none the less.

Two matters arise out of this discussion: First, what is the role of the devic kingdom, on this planet at least? And how can we human beings come closer to them in consciousness?

These two questions seem to be interrelated. For the angelologist even at this beginning stage suggests that the role of the devic kingdom comprises the carrying into effect of natural law—a term which some prefer, with justification, to that of 'the will of God.' Their minds are such that they are simply agents of those laws, just as our mind is such that our function is less simply to carry out the laws than to develop variations in what automatic Nature would do. In this sense the devas can be considered as representing, incarnating, Nature and its laws at all levels, physical and mental, perhaps spiritual too. Continuing this line of thought, it would then appear that the rupa level of the devic kingdom is as I have said represented in everything having form, or every idea or feeling formulated, within our scope—and perhaps beyond it. In other words, every physical object, every feeling, every idea or 'thought-form' is *the incarnation of the devic life at some level of its hierarchy.*

The human beings hammering a piece of iron, digging in the ground or writing a poem are, whether they have any sense of it or not, acting or reacting in conjunction with the angelic kingdom. They may try to 'conquer' Nature, opposing what the angels are trying to do; they may co-operate with them; they may misuse them; but in all cases they are in contact with the angels! In the same way the scientist weighing and measuring some physical object is weighing and measuring a devic 'body' but does not realize it in those terms. And when we non-scientists look at the world around us even in the most casual manner, we are in the presence of the devic kingdom itself, embodied in the things we see. When we think, the form taken by our thoughts, the form of feelings we have, are equally devic 'bodies.' So that we need not be clairvoyant or have any other kind of developed E.S.P. to make contact with the angelic kingdom. On the other hand, to appreciate its nature we need to have something else, something of the quality of the real artist. This is the higher octave of feeling which is not in any way emotional, let alone sentimental. It is difficult to define this quality save that it goes with the sense of mystery, of wonder which leads on to that of the livingness of all things. Even 'dead' bodies are alive, for by that we merely mean that a lower form of devic life has taken over an organism in order to dissolve that body. Truly perceptive people are aware of the living quality of a common pebble, a piece of metal and what have you, let alone of growing things like plants, animals and human beings. The sky, a rainbow, a shower of rain shows them *life* just as much as does a person, though in a different form. This is why 'peak experience' can occur at any time and in any place when the busy-ness of the mind is stilled for an instant and the individual *perceives*, in quietness and silence.

Is this difficult? Yes, because it is too simple, and our lives are usually lived in action and complexity. What we need is not to do but *to stop doing*, and find the wonders of the quiet mind. Then, as H. P. Blavatsky tells us, we shall hear the 'Voice of the Silence,' which is that of the gods or angels among whom we dwell. Maybe this essay merely reflects the fantasy in my own mind: but I suggest that the basic idea is one worth pondering in quietness. It may bring much richness to our lives.

More About the Angels

> The angels keep their ancient places;
> Turn but a stone and start a wing.
> 'Tis ye, 'tis your estranged faces
> That miss the many-splendoured thing.

So wrote Francis Thompson about the devic kingdom and our blindness to it despite—as I suggested earlier—the fact that we live in and by and through it in its manifest form in both the physical and psychic worlds. The poet goes on to tell us that if our eyes were opened, there

> Shall shine the traffic of Jacob's ladder
> Pitched between heaven and Charing Cross

—bringing the vision of angels into London's crowded city.

These lines support my thesis that, if we learn to see in the right way, we shall realize the universal presence of the order of life we call angelic or devic. But this raises the question, Why bother? Of what use is it if we do realize it? And you, the writer, tell us that all manifestation, hence all that we perceive physically or psychically is, whether we know it or not, perception of the angelic work. Why go further?

It is a good question and if I have suggested not a fantasy but a certain truth about the world we live in, it can be answered by inquiring why we human beings want to inquire into anything except the most utilitarian problems. The fact remains that we are inquisitive, that what we discover through inquisitiveness not only enlarges the mind, but can also perhaps reflect into the utilitarian sphere itself.

This applies particularly to the sense of the livingness of things; which is another way of saying, to the sense of the devic life behind all phenomena, at whatever level. To seek to become aware of this is not to seek for sensation and excitement, but to try to reach into the nature, the quiddity of things, to see what *is*, with an added order of perceptivity which has nothing to do with clairvoyance or other forms of mere E.S.P. A new field of exploration opens up to us to which there is no bound, provided we do not fall into the trap of trying to enclose this field within the framework of space-time and anthropomorphism in which our minds ordinarily work. If we circumvent this snare, we shall find our consciousness moving out from the realm of phenomena into that of the Numinous—the arupa, to use that word again— from the realm of images to that of archetypes and, to quote a rather misleading phrase, 'from the unreal to the Real.' The words are misleading not in their basic idea, but in that the 'unreal' is in fact the *relatively* Real, and so is comprised within the Real Itself.

If, on the other hand, we fall into the error of trying to reduce the boundless into the limited, which happens basically through a lack of self-knowledge, hence through the bias of our minds, we then tend to try and reduce the more-than-personal to the level of human personalities. And in this way we may come to believe that a human-like angel has chosen us as a recipient for teaching which, in effect, derives from within our own selves and may be merely repetition of things already said, or may be of no real value whatever. And yet, we have to begin at the beginning in such a study, and so, to start with the commonplace things around us or in our own minds if we want to go beyond them.

There is a reason for starting this article with a poet's words. For those real artists—not such who dare to call themselves and who probably are not—are invariably in touch with the deeper levels of life. If not, they are not artists. But, in addition to this, they must also be in close touch with Nature, since, if not, they have nothing to express the Numinous with. This fact may not be so obvious in some forms of art as in others. Yet poet, painter, musician, all have to use natural forms, sounds, colors, shapes, textures and the rest, as the vehicle for their work: otherwise it remains unexpressed, unobjectivized. I have capitalized the word 'Nature'—that which is *natus*, or born—because it is the Numen in manifestation, the expression of God's Law and will; and if my thesis is correct, this means that it is the field of the devic or angelic life. Hence, artists may be said to have, if only unconsciously, entered the field of awareness of this kingdom. Their art, moreover, consists in using Nature—the devas—to embody their vision of the Numinous in a new and 'non-natural' way: they bring the human mind to work on Nature and mold it to their purpose; yet they do so, so that the vision is implied, contained within the form, and so becomes an indirect expression of the deeper vision itself. What Edward Arlington Robinson says about poetry applies to all art forms. They say that poetry 'is a language that tells us something which cannot be said.' And Joyce Beavis, in a lecture, put it that poetry is the ability 'to say something by saying something else.' It is the 'something else,' which 'cannot be said' which makes the work of art, and which makes, for instance, a painting one, whether it be 'primitive,' representational, impressionistic or abstract: it conveys the sense of the divine, the Numinous, the *arupa* or spiritual behind whatever subject is depicted, be it 'beautiful' or not, provided therefore that artists have inner vision; which, in turn, means certain personal qualities, which may be active in them, whatever else they lack.

This may seem to have taken us a long way away from the angelic kingdom. Yet it has direct reference to some of the qualifications needed if we want to study it directly as such: to become in our own way and degree angelologists. For, as I have suggested, the angelic life is to be seen everywhere and at every level of manifestation. It exists in the process of death and decay as well as in that of construction and creation. It is in our thoughts, our feelings. And it goes beyond what we know as the realm of existential forms into that of Essential formlessness, far beyond what we as human beings can reach. Artists are the most obvious examples of ones who sense the gamut—or at least the first octave—of the span of devic life. But it is perhaps only if they become, not only persons of deep feeling, but also feeling-*scientists*, that they may find themselves able to see something of the mechanics of the co-operation of the human mind with the devic.

To be such scientists, certain qualities of feeling must be theirs, notably that of awe and wonder whereby the observer feels, as it were, apart from the thing being observed; but one needs also the quality of love, the Martha to the Mary of wonder, which reaches out and touches the object observed. Many people have this, but if we are to act as scientists in this field—as in any other—there has to be also a great deal of mental objectivity such as can only be acquired through deep self-knowledge. This is all the more important because it is so easy in dealing with the non-physical to deceive oneself and to confuse the subjective contents of one's mind with objective material or with objective, self-existent entities. I refer once again to the powers of dramatization which the mind possesses, its ability to project from itself 'thought-forms' which take on the character of independent beings. If would-be observers do not understand this power, they will give shapes to things which do not really exist in those shapes, even if existing in their own right and not by virtue of being projected from the observer's mind. To give human form and especially faces to devas is one example: the more intelligent observers describe them as more in the nature of patterns of energy, beautiful and fascinating, but certainly not human; whereas 'fairies' take on the form in which the mind is apt to think of them. It is important also to become sufficiently self-aware to realize how much more dramatic it is to believe oneself to be the pupil of a deva than to acknowledge even to oneself that this 'deva' is in reality oneself, if it be a deeper level of oneself, and that one is not in reality singled out as a special channel for whatever information is received.

At the same time, one has to see that it is in no way necessary to be 'psychic' in the ordinary sense of that word to be able to understand at least something of this angelic world. One can be highly perceptive and positively sensitive without being in any way clairvoyant; and indeed, for most of us it is better so, since perceptivity and self-knowledge go hand in hand in correcting the distortions which the personal mind introduces into clairvoyance of the usual kind.

Let us now consider as far as we can the communication which can be established apart from the arts between the devic and human kingdoms. Perhaps the most obvious example is that of the gardener with a 'green thumb.' To be so endowed does not require great technical skill, however useful this may be. It is something which belongs to the plant-lover, not to the commercial exploiter who uses the vegetable kingdom for simply utilitarian purposes. The power of the mind in agriculture is not merely a matter of belief. Indeed, it was realized in the laboratories of the late George de la Warr near Oxford, when he found that mental attention to a row of wheat seeds brought about a much better growth than in a row not specially 'treated.' When similar prepared soil and grains were put in the hands of a gardener uninterested in any special ideas, both rows grew equally. Other experiments were performed with similar results, thereby confirming that a special attitude of mind affected the growth of plants.

True, in this case, the mental aspect lay probably less directly in the direction of wonder-love for the plants than in the scientific interest in a field which came to include them—one might perhaps suggest that there was 'wonder-love' for the whole subject of so-called radionics, etc. But the results were there to see.

We know also of the 'genius with machines': not only can such a person see what is wrong with one and repair it, often more through 'hunch' than an intellectual analysis of its symptoms. Moreover, there are some people for whom an assembly of pieces of metal seems to function better and more smoothly than for the one who considers it merely as a soul-less object. The successful engineer has a kind of sympathy for the engine which, in the common phrase, 'pays off,' though not necessarily in cash.

This leads us to the ability to postulate various aspects of human-deva co-operation or contact.

1. A human being may simply observe: look at a view, a tree, an animal, without attempting to affect it. If one 'feels' it, penetrates behind the phenomenal aspects, he or she may come to realize the quality of life—devic—behind what is observed.

2. One may learn to work with this life, improving plant species, cultivating the ground and the plants and animals on it. If one is nothing more than a materialistic exploiter, he or she is likely to destroy at least as much as is being created—as is happening today. (The destruction itself can be an aspect of devic life acting in a negative manner as far as humanity is concerned.)

3. One can take the manifestations of this life in, for instance, metallic ores, bring another aspect of the same life—fire or electricity—to bear on it, and so produce things which it is reasonably safe to say the devas—Nature—alone would never produce.

It is clear how far we are from intellect-science in all this, and how easily it can become a kind of primitive animism: but animism need not be primitive if it is an intelligent appreciation of the 'spiritual' or 'soul' principle in every created object. For animism is primitive if it does not reach up beyond the *rupa* and personal levels into that of the *arupa* or formless which we call those of spirit.

Evidently, in speaking of the life-background of objects we have so far concerned ourselves only with the 'lower' ranks of the devic hierarchy. It is only when writing of the artists' inspiration that we have touched on the source from which these lower, executive, ranks derive.

Now, however, we need to consider the 'higher' or formless devas which exist beyond the personal, existential level in that of Being or Essence: of the Numinous. As human beings, we reach these levels directly only in moments when we cease from being 'estranged.' These moments of peak experience bring us into direct contact with the crossing point where, I have suggested, the devic and the human minds meet; though 'meet' is perhaps too weak a word. Rather should we say, merge and become identical: human is at this level deva, deva is human.

Intuitively, we have long felt this. In every religion there is the principle of the guardian angel, the daimon, and so on, the idea that somewhere in the depths of our beings there is this direct and individual touch with the angel which is also ourselves, and which we can call upon in various ways, not only to guard us against danger. Those with more extended feeling-knowledge know that such a call does not go unheeded, that, in a certain sense, the guardian angel is only too anxious to respond and to help. It may be that we want assistance in dealing with somebody in distress, or sick; and if we think in terms of invoking angelic help, it will be there almost before we have invoked it. There is an influx of power which is not that of our own little personalities. We may or we may not be aware of what is happening. And if we are trying to help somebody in distress, it is wise to ask for that help, not in terms of what we think is needed, but to hold the thought of what is in reality best for the person we are working for: in other words, as it were to leave it to the higher powers to do what is proper. It may be, for instance, that the truest form of healing for a particular individual is not to be restored to physical vigor but to die: the truest 'making whole' or 'holy' of that person at that moment of time.

In other words, we should offer ourselves as channels between our higher or inner selves and the individual we are coping with, get our little personal egos out of the way as much as we are able: which brings us back again to the need for emotional detachment, which can only be reached through self-knowledge.

We thus can discover two main divisions in the study of the devic life. Just as we can distinguish between ourselves as personalities and ourselves as inner, spiritual beings, so can we see the angelic hierarchy in terms of *rupa*, or formed beings, however evanescent these forms may be especially at the lowest levels, and *arupa* or space-time-less Beings, apparently of the same nature as our own Essential Selves.

I have touched only on the fringes of this subject. It may be that what this article says may appeal to certain people and help give shape to their unformulated and hence rather confusing experience. I am far from suggesting that what I have called angelology should be taken up by all: there are, as the Hindus say, 'as many ways to God—i.e., understanding—as there are individual men.' But, especially for those with the feeling-artistic temperament, it may be of use if one thinks in terms of the existence of this kingdom of intelligent beings we call devas or angels, linking our own intelligence with theirs, learning to work with them—i.e. with, not against Nature—and avoiding sentimentality and emotionalism, let alone any sense of self-importance. If we do this, we shall surely find that life, even in its most commonplace forms, acquires a new dimension of richness and interest from which we, as human beings, are 'increased,' as was the poetess, by the most simple events.

II
Gods, Guardians, and the Religious Spirit

The religious spirit celebrates unity in diversity and the infinite as inseparable from finite things. It mandates integrity of relationship from deep within the human psyche, ordering an unfoldment of powers which makes possible communion and cooperation. Religions embody wide-ranging ideas about God, angels, and saviors. But what is vital is the underlying vision of wholeness . . . a celebration of diversity, commitment to connectedness, and furthering of altruism. It is the religious spirit, as it enriches individual lives, that entitles and empowers humans to rapport with angels.

Angels, it seems, appear especially in times of fundamental change. When we are in crisis, when life lacks substance and the way forward is clouded, angels are said to help us refocus. Their purpose is not to entice us from the earth, but to help us regain earthly balance. Herein lies a subtle danger. For as angels draw our attention to greater realities, their radiance invites fascination, a numbing preoccupation with their forms. Perhaps this is why intuitively we may recoil from reverencing angels to the exclusion of the wider vision.

People everywhere worship the same spiritual reality. Paths to the Infinite vary, however, as do ideas about how near we may approach the ultimate Source of being. Intermediate realms or states of consciousness, very different from our familiar space-time world, are part of our nature. Esotericists agree that superphysical intelligences in these causal realms are involved in the emanation and evolution of all worlds. Esoteric philosophy affirms that all phenomena, even spiritual realities, arise from natural, knowable causes and that humans can cooperate with Nature's innermost life.

Angels manifest the psychospiritual fabric of Nature. Depth psychologist Roberts Avens says, "The world is a subtle reality, a celestial Earth which is unimaginable without the constant presence of Gods. All things and events in the world are established and maintained in Being by divine influx."[1] In our consideration of things "heavenly," we cannot exclude the operation of forces of disintegration. Both creation and destruction, involution and evolution, are within the province of angels. It is said that the celestial gods magnify, while the earthly gods diminish. Their might is equal and their movement measureless.[2]

Ancient systems of spiritual training, based on known laws of the subtle spheres, have established a sound base of support for enhanced awareness. Expansion of consciousness inevitably involves suffering as it challenges, sometimes drastically, our thoughts and feelings about life. As vision widens, a hidden side of ourselves surfaces into everyday awareness. There is an unsettling identification with the subtle, powerful collective life of humanity and Nature. That hidden side, brought forward vividly by angelic encounters, reveals forces of darkness as well as of light.

Religious practice supports and helps transform the mortal personality in preparation for spiritual flight. A universal discipline is the practice of virtue, reflection on spiritual ideals, intense study, and selfless service. The formula, though apparently simple, is transformative. It substantially refines human nature and lifts the earnest aspirant into communion with angels. It also helps the neophyte to focus spiritual aspiration and energy in every arena of earthly life. Thus, as we enter the realm of the gods, we naturally intensify our commitment to the earth. The blending of angelic and human natures renews our sense of purpose and releases an immense, abiding joy.

Some say angels of the higher orders have passed through the human stage of evolution. As regents of the soul realm, they understand the spiritual plan for humans. The esoteric tradition suggests that Lords of Compassion, who have gone beyond humans in understanding, love, and power, help us through an abyss that seems to separate us from the Divine. Perhaps without the aid of such angels, humans would never move beyond the idea of God as wholly other. These beings can help initiate us into the mysteries of our own being if we are willing to open ourselves to them.

The Guardian is an especially important figure, explored variously in religion, psychology, and the arts. This angel appears to the soul to lead it on an inner journey to God, to the heart of manifested things. Marie-Louise Von Franz states that the inner companion is, in psychological terms, the inner teacher or Self. It is at once "the most individual core of the individual person and simultaneously the human self . . . the self of all humanity." Once the soul is conscious of the guardian angel, and becomes a "clear mirror of this image," it proceeds "in its company as with an escort."[3]

1. Roberts Avens, *The New Gnosis: Heidegger, Hillman and Angels.* Dallas: Spring Publications, 1984, 123.
2. C. G. Jung. "Sermons to the Dead." *Parabola.* Vol. VI, No. 4. "Demons" October, 1981, 80.
3. Marie-Louise Von Franz, this anthology, p. 186.

4

The
Old Gods

C. R. F. SEYMOUR

Part 1

Who or what were the Old Gods? Pause for a moment and reflect on this, then note what pictures float up from memory's storehouse as the conscious mind focuses attention on the question. The answer will show, to some extent, what religion you hold. An atheist might well dismiss the whole question as meaningless, holding that there is no God and no gods. He is probably right and certainly not altogether wrong.

To understand the Old Gods we must enter into the spirit of paganism. Let us see what the pagans themselves had to say. Seneca wrote:

The wisest among men understand him whom we call Jove to be the Guardian and ruler, spirit and soul of the universe, the Lord and Maker of this mundane sphere, to whom every name is applicable. Dost wish to call him Fate? Thou wilt not err. He it is on whom all things are dependent. . . . Dost wish to call him Providence, rightly wilt thou do so; for by his counsel . . . provision is made for this world so that it may proceed in an orderly fashion, and unfold his deeds to our view. Dost thou wish to call him Nature? Thou wilt commit no sin; for he it is from whom all things are sprung and by whose spirit we breathe life. Dost wish to call him the World? Thou wilt not be mistaken, for he . . . is all infused in its parts.

Over a temple at Sais in northern Egypt was the inscription, 'I am all that was, and is, and is to come.' An Orphic teaching runs, 'One is the Self Begotten, and all things were derived from this same one.' The Egyptians called God *Ua Neter*, the One God, they were as much monotheists as the Jews, the Arabs and the Christians who officially believe in saints, archangels and jinnee.

Proclus in his *Elements of Theology* gives the same teachings, as the following will show, related to the Qabalistic Tree of Life.

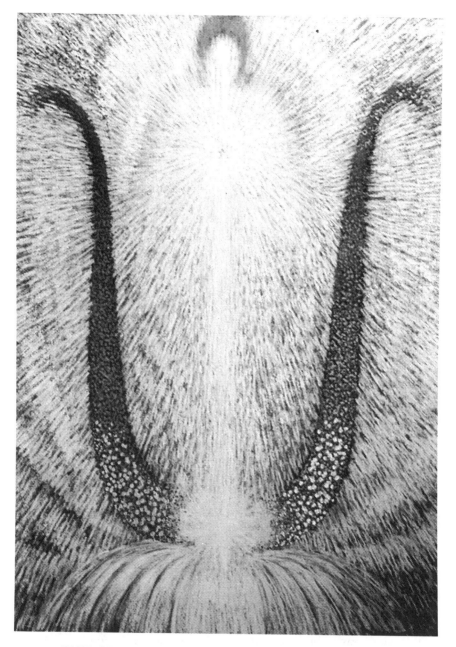

ANGEL OF THE HIGH SELF INITIATION
HOLY OF HOLIES—KARNAK, *Arthur Douët*
*"For an initiated pagan, the gods, as distinguished from God, represented
divine intelligences and hierarchies of intelligences who were, and
are, living out a form of experience which is other than man's experience."*

C. R. F. Seymour

(A) The One Originative	The Qabalistic Unmanifest, called
Principle of the	by Proclus The One and the Good.
Universe	The First Principle. It is
	'Unparticipated,' and is
	'Unparticipable.'
(B) The Many or High	The Qabalistic Manifest. The ten
Gods	Sephiroth in Atziluth

The high gods are the 'Participated' and the 'Participable' as well as the source of all that participates. They are above being, life and intelligence. These gods are divine henads or unities, the outshinings of the One and the Good. They are the Ten Holy Sephiroth, and are derivative terms proceeding from the first principle. Their attributes pre-subsist them in a unitary and supra-existential mode.

In connection with the above and with the aid of the Tree of Life consider the implications which are contained in the following propositions of Proclus.

Prop. 126. A God is more universal as he is nearer to the One, more specific in proportion to His remoteness from it.

Prop. 128. Every God, when participated by beings of an order relatively near to Him, is participated directly; when participated by those more remote, indirectly, through a varying number of intermediate principles.

These propositions when studied in the light of the descent of life force through the Four Worlds of the Qabalists give a clue to the use of god-forms, and to the varying functions of certain gods, like Osiris, Thoth and Isis.

To the uninitiated the pagan systems look chaotic, but there is a clue. It goes by function and not by name. So to answer the question posed at the opening of this chapter we may say that for an initiated pagan, the gods, as distinguished from God, represented divine intelligences and hierarchies of intelligences who were, and are, living out a form of experience which is other than man's experience. They were, and are, undergoing this experience of living on the various planes of consciousness in this universe in much the same way that man undergoes the experience of living on this earth.

We can divide these intelligences and hierarchies into three main classes, which in turn have many subdivisions. There are the high gods which correspond largely with the Qabalistic names of God, the archangels and lesser gods corresponding to the great devas, jinnee and angels, and the humanized gods such as Osiris, Orpheus, Im-hotep, etc., which are somewhat similar in conception to the Christian saints.

Behind these high gods are unmanifested divine aspects which are not usually personalized, and are named as the Unmanifest, Chaos, Old Night, etc. They could be said to correspond to the Unmanifest and the Three Veils of Negative Existence as used in the Mystery schools of the Western Tradition.

Within the above classification there is another and smaller one: that of the sun-gods, the underworld- and moon-gods, the earth-gods and the mind-gods. This last is important for it contains the 'principles' which were and are used by the pagans for the practical working of their rites and for meditation work.

The first classification gives us the broad background of paganism. The second gives us the foreground of the stage on which the action takes place in the pagan Mystery dramas. Therefore, for the pagan both past and present the gods as a class represent the type of experience of which it has been said, 'I do not believe that our experience is the highest form extant in the universe.'

The gods were personalized and named by the initiates in the same way, and for the same reason, that modern science names certain types of experience as electromagnetic, radioactive, etc. The Old God names are labels for certain types of divine experience which the initiates of old met up with in the course of their researches into the nature of the unseen. To sum up we may say, by using methods similar to those used centuries ago we can get similar experiences of the divine, for the old classifications still hold good. This again means the message which the Egyptian Thamus gave to the islanders of Palodes is false.

Part 2

The Mystery schools based their training methods on the maxim, 'As above, so below.' They taught that man is a replica of the Great Cosmos, he is the little cosmos. The ancient teaching of Hermes is the method to be followed in this exposition of paganism, and it takes 'mind' in its various forms as the working basis of its training methods.

It postulates that mind is everywhere and directs everything. For example: the earth is the outward symbol of an indwelling intelligence in a manner analogous to a man's body, which should also be the outer symbol of an indwelling intelligence. This intelligence incarnates to gain experience as does man.

All upon the earth lives, moves and has its being and is dependent upon this intelligence, called the Earth Soul or Earth Mother. These indwelling cosmic intelligences are graded. The grade above that which controls the earth, is that of the sun. This intelligence controls the whole solar system, which in its outer spatial form is its body. The planets and all they contain live, move and have their being within the all-inclusive being of this solar intelligence, considered to be the Great Father and giver of life to the Earth Mother.

The same idea holds good with regard to these vast transcendental intelligences which control the systems of solar intelligences and even the cosmos itself. Each god lives, moves and has its being within the vaster intelligence of the grade above it, the grade above fertilizing the grade below it. If you wish to study this more deeply you will find the ideas developed more fully in Proclus, *The Elements of Theology*, Propositions 113-17.

These ideas are worth bringing into the sphere of everyday life. For example think of the multitude of little lives that have their being within the vaster life, being and intelligence of a man. Study the living contents of your next boil with a microscope, then meditate by analogy on man and the gods, and the cosmos, keeping in mind the axiom, 'As above, so below.'

Compared with man these cosmic gods are superior and perfect, while man is inferior and imperfect. The object of the initiated pagan was to gain conscious touch with these superior beings in whom he had his own beingness. He based his methods on the psychological maxim, 'As a man thinks, so he becomes.'

The second great hypothesis on which they based their training was, 'The mind gains conscious touch with that upon which it broods.' The method of Loyola depends upon this, and his system is one of the most successful that Christianity has produced and is essentially magical in its methods and results.

It now becomes necessary to define the word 'pagan.' According to the *Oxford Dictionary*, it means 'heathen, unenlightened person,' yet Socrates, Plato and all the great intellects of the ancient world were pagans. Jesus ben Joseph was the flower of a pagan civilization. The word comes from the Latin, *paganus*, meaning in, or of, the country. When Christianity came to power it was used to denote those who worshipped the old gods at their shrines on the hills and in the vales, in contradistinction to the Christians, who were mainly town-dwellers.

The modern pagan, too, is a lover of open air, one who worships

God made manifest in nature. In Qabalistic terminology he worships Adonai Ha Atretz, the Lord of the Earth. He sees God most clearly in the countryside and finds Him in the open spaces. He knows that God is just as present in the stuffy chapel, and the slum dwellings, and in the public houses as He is in the wooded vale and the dim forest glade.

For him the approach is not via a priesthood for every pagan is his own priest or priestess, he is the master of his own soul, and his own saviour, he has no belief in a supreme personal God. He denies all that the Church holds dear, including bishops, priests and even deacons. However, he remembers gratefully the great pagan mystic who walked and taught in Galilee, a man who, when he was tired of working in the towns and slums, went out into the hills to commune with his Father, Adonai, to obtain by meditation refreshment for body and soul from the open spaces and night skies. He learned to draw near to the Great Mother and to be at One with Her.

As with Jesus, so with the modern pagan; communion with nature is his means of worship and of rest, of refreshment for body and soul and spirit. Religion is for him a conscious linking of phenomenon with noumenon. Once this has been mastered the pagan is his own high priest, and he is independent of the priesthood as Jesus was independent of the Temple and the priests in Jerusalem. The third great hypothesis upon which modern initiation bases its system of training is, every man can become his own priest by right of *function*.

Part 3: The Background of Paganism

> The mind of Man is this world's true dimension,
> And knowledge is the measure of the mind:
> And as the mind, in her vast comprehension,
> Contains more worlds than all the world can find,
> So knowledge doth itself far more extend
> Than all the minds of man can comprehend.
>
> Rupert Brooke

The cosmic background to pagan religious thought is formed by the idea of the 'oversoul' or 'world soul,' which Plotinus calls the Divine Creative World Soul, and which he describes thus:

First let every soul consider that it is the World Soul which created all things, breathing into them the breath of life—into all living things which are on Earth, in the air, and in the sea, and the stars in heaven, the Sun, and the great heaven itself. The Creative World Soul sets them in their order and directs their motions, keeping *itself* apart from the things which it orders and moves and causes to *live*.

It will be seen from this quotation (*Enneads*) that the Divine Creative World Soul is the ultimate form of creative energy to which the mind of man can reach. The other great and divine souls, such as that of the solar logos, our sun, of the great Earth Mother, of the various stellar logoi, are born and persist as this Oversoul grants them life . . . but this oversoul lives for ever and ever and never ceases to be *itself*. This is not the Earth Soul, which is of a lesser grade.

To use the terminology of the Qabalah, in its first manifestation this creative oversoul is the Supernal Triad of Kether, Chokmah and Binah, and *as such*, it is the primal manifestation of that Unmanifest which the Qabalists call the Ain, the One, the Absolute; that which has its own mode of being behind that purely human convention which is called the Three Veils of the Unmanifest. The Ain thus corresponds to the *itself* of the passage quoted above.

Emerson, as the prophet of modern paganism, in his work *Oversoul*, writes with regard to man, the microcosm: 'The Soul of man is not an organ, but animates, and exercises all the organs: it is not a function like the power of memory, of calculation . . . it is not a faculty . . . it is the background of our being in which all faculties lie.'

'As above so below.' The ancient initiates, recognizing the limitations of human thinking and of human methods for expressing their thinking, postulated as a working hypothesis the theory of the Divine Oversoul, analogous to the Soul of man. And this theory of a Divine Creative Oversoul which is analogous in its working to the Soul of man, and with which the human soul can get conscious communion, is the background of both ancient and modern Mystery school training.

We can divide up the Mystery systems of the Western Esoteric Tradition of today into six groups—Qabalistic, Chaldean, Egyptian, Greek, Celtic and Norse. It is not easy to decide which of these is the oldest. When educated people thought of human history as beginning in about 5,000 BC, it was generally considered that the Egyptian system was the oldest and that Egypt was the Mother of civilized religions. Today this assumption is considered a doubtful one. There are schools which think that the Druidic branch of the Celtic religion and the Egyptian Mystery systems are both offshoots from a common and still more primitive religion which they call Iberian, a system which was in vogue between 10,000 and 5,000 BC. If this theory is true it will explain the likeness as well as the curious differences between the British Druidic systems and the Mystery religions of ancient Egypt. The Celts themselves are not Iberians, but in their wanderings conquered or displaced the more ancient Iberian tribes and added their predecessors' religious practices to their own.

It must here be remembered that these ancient religious systems were not collections of dogmatic teachings which are supposed to be capable of demonstration by, and to, reasoning minds. They were practical systems for obtaining 'religious experience,' in its widest sense; and as most of them were based upon a technique for using the subconscious mind, they could not be rationalized or made reasonable in the modern sense of that term.

The ancient initiates found these systems reasonable because their sole religious criterion was that of utility. A system was valid if it produced religious experiences. If it did, all well and good—if not, the priest died! Invaders coming into a new country found that the old power centres were easier to work, and the old and local methods often gave more satisfactory results than their own. This is why so many of the old centres have remained in use for religious purposes down to the present day. Many Christian churches are sited upon old pagan centres that have been in use from time immemorial.

From a practical point of view it is far easier to open up, and gradually modify an ancient centre of religious power, than to start a new centre and a new system that is alien to the country, to the oversoul of the place and to the race. Looked at from the pagan initiate's point of view the key idea is this: that man can get into intimate touch—almost at will—with the world soul once he has realized that the mind touches that which it constantly and sympathetically thinks about.

Part 4: General Classification of the Gods

The object of this section is to classify the gods of the pagan initiates from the practical point of view. This classification may not recommend itself to the historian or to the scholar. In the first place it is limited. In the second place it deals with deities which are unlike those of the classical religions and philosophies. And, finally, it is according neither to popular historical importance nor to the conventions of esoteric religion, but to the efficiency of gods when they are used in accordance with a certain technique.

The reader may say here: 'What does this mean? Can I for example see, hear and touch the Great God Pan?' Certainly. You can make Pan your constant companion and you can bring the 'Pan within' to life in exactly the same way that the orthodox Christian saint by a certain technique brings to birth the 'Christ within.' But you are not recommended to do this without safe-guards, for the pagan who has called into over-activity the 'Pan within' can be as unbalanced a person as the Christian saint who has roused into undue activity those forces which are sometimes called the Christ Within.

If you are a monotheist, and not that much-abused person, the dualist, you must, logically, recognize that Pan and Christ are but two aspects of the same thing, which temporarily, for the sake of convenience, will be called God. Both aspects are good—in the right place and in the right proportions. Both are harmful when misplaced in time, or space, or both. Spiritual adultery is just as common as physical and in the long run it is even more undesirable.

In *The Mystical Qabalah* by Dion Fortune there is given the system for the classification of the pagan gods which is used by the initiates of a number of modern schools. Briefly, it divides all the gods of the pantheons into ten classes, called the Sephiroth, and presupposes that they emanate from an unmanifested state of being which is the source of all that has been, is, or will be. The Neo-Platonists call it the One, as opposed to the Many. These ten classes are:

1.	The space—time gods	—Kether
2.	The all-fathers	—Chokmah
3.	The great mothers	—Binah
4.	The builders	—Chesed
5.	The destroyers	—Geburah
6.	The sun-gods	—Tipareth
7.	The virgin nature-gods	—Netzach
8.	The wisdom-gods	—Hod
9.	The underworld- and the moon-gods	—Yesod
10.	The earth-gods	—Malkuth

From the practical point of view the student need, for the present, concentrate only upon numbers 1, 6, 9, 10 and 8, which reduces his classification to the space- or time-gods, sun-gods, moon- and underworld-gods, earth-gods and the gods of wisdom.

The more common types of symbols for these cosmic intelligences are:

1. The space-gods. The point within the circle. 'The Serpent that devoured his tail.' ⊙ , and occasionally ♆ . The signs ♐ and ♄ are also used for Chokmah and Binah respectively as the positive and negative functions of the Kether space—time gods. The zodiac is also a symbol for Chokmah.

2. The sun-gods: ⊙ .

3. The moon-gods: ☽ .

4. The signs of the Four Elements are used for various elemental deities:

△ fire; ◬ air; ▽ water; ⍷ earth.

5. The sign ☿ for the gods of wisdom.

A short comparative list of the more common forms is:

1. Space-gods:

Qabalah	— Eheieh.
Greek	— Chaos, Nox and Eros. Zeus, Jupiter as sky-gods.
Egyptian	— The Eight Gods of Hermopolis with Thoth at their head; Amen and Ptah; Nu and Nun.
Chaldean	— Apsu, Mommu and Tiamath. Anu as the All-Father.
Celtic	— Lir and Beli.
Nordic	— Odin or Tiwaz or Tyr.

2. Sun-gods:

Qabalah	— Aloah va Daath.
Greek	— Apollo and Helios.
Egyptian	— Ra, Horus and Osiris.
Chaldean	— Shamash. Asshur, Enlil, Merodach or Bel.
Celtic	— Lugh or Angus Og, Dagda, Bile and Hu.
Norse	— Balder.

3. Moon-gods and the underworld-gods.

Qabalah	— Shaddai El Hai.
Greek	— Semele, Pluto, Persephone.
Egyptian	— Isis of the Moon and Thoth as Tehuti, Khensu and Osiris.
Chaldean	— Nin-gal and Sin. Ishtar. Allatu and Nergal.
Celtic	— Celi as the husband of Keredwen. Midir and Etain of the Fairies. Bile, Manannan Manawyddan Mab Llyr the Welsh Lord of Hades. Brigid and Gwynn ap Nudd.
Nordic	— Mani the moon-god. Ran and Hel the Goddesses of Death.

4. Earth-gods:

Qabalah	— Adonai.
Greek	— Demeter, Gaea as Earth Mother and Ceres.
Egyptian	— Isis.
Chaldean	— Ishtar. Tiamath as Earth Mother.
Celtic	— Keridwen and Dana (Irish), Brigantia. Cernunnos.
Nordic	— Rinda. Thor and Sif, the God and Goddess of Crops.

5. Gods of wisdom:

Qabalah	— Hermes, Thoth.
Greek	— Hermes. Pallas Athene.
Egyptian	— Thoth.
Chaldean	— Nabu or Nebo, and Sin.
Celtic	— Ogmios and Briganda. Ogma (Irish), Myrddin (English). Dagda ('The Lord of Great Knowledge').

Nordic   — Odin, with Loki as the
              God of Evil Wisdom.

This list is a brief one, and it refers only to the cosmic intelligences, i.e., to the type of beings that Iamblichus in his book *The Egyptian Mysteries* calls 'the gods.'

In the Mystery schools of Egypt and the Gnostic schools at Alexandria, the 'many' gods were considered to be the emanations or the 'outshinings' of the 'One' God who was the super-essential deity, or, as we should say, the Unmanifest Cause of All. Iamblichus divides the divine hierarchy into the gods and the superior races, and it is clear that he considered the former as representing or personifying qualities in the Divine Mind rather than as personalities or individuals.

For the ancient initiate, mind was 'the leader and King of the things that actually are.' Thus we can best understand these pagan gods by thinking about them as the great directing minds of this universe.

When studying these deities, the student, in the course of meditations made with some degree of proficiency in the technique of the Mystery school method, is bound to come across certain curious phenomena which have been described as the Memory of the Earth. A. E. in *The Candle of Vision* (p. 56) has dealt with this subject and the student is advised to study this great writer's theories. But for the present we may take the 'Memory of the Earth' as a working hypothesis. The *modus operandi* will be discussed later, and if the student will tentatively accept this theory, he will save himself a good deal of worry about details, and this will result in accelerated progress.

The student is advised to read and re-read these classifications of the gods. He may not agree with them. If he has been educated in what is called the classical tradition he will probably disagree heartily. But it must be called to mind that we are not dealing with the classical pantheons. The criteria of the classical records are not the same as the criteria that are applied to results obtained from the recovery of Earth Memories. The latter are empirical; the former are not. The main object is to get a working process that can be relied upon to give adequate results when recovering the past.

The more these gods are reflected upon in solitary meditations the more such meditations pass inwards into sympathetic contemplation and the easier it becomes to develop, from latent existence in the subconscious mind, the long-hidden memories of the ancient Wisdom religions.

Part 5: The Gods and their Functions

The souls came hither* not by sending, and not of their own will; or at least their will is no deliberate choice, but a prompting of nature. . . . The Intelligence which is before the World contains the destiny of our abiding yonder † no less than of our sending forth; the individual is 'sent' forth as falling under the general ordinance. For the universal is implicit in each, and not by authority from without does the ordinance enforce itself; it is inherent in those who shall obey it and they carry it always within them. And when their season is come, that which it will is brought to pass by those in whom it resides; bearing it within them, they fulfil it of their own accord; the ordinance prevails because the ordinance has its seat in them, as it were pressing upon them weightily, awakening in them an impulse, a yearning, to go to that place whither the indwelling voice seems to bid them go.

(Dodds, *Select Passages Illustrating Neoplatonism*)

When striving to unravel the complexities of the numerous pantheons it is necessary to call to mind the fact that the gods are but symbols for certain manifestations of divine force. Their names are the X, Y and Z which enable the theurgist to work out this system of divine algebra and to function as a priest.

Isis, for example, is a man-made personification of a certain type of divine force. Again X may stand for many things which are not of this physical plane. Isis too stands for many non-material things. There is Isis as the Earth Mother, as the Virgin Lady of Nature, as the Queen of Heaven, as the Moon, as the Cosmic Mother, and so on.

There are many forms in which electricity can be used—as a motor agent, as light, as heat, as a curative agent, or as a means for executing a criminal. What electricity is *per se* we do not know, but we do know how to make use of it in various particular ways. What the gods are *per se* we do not know, but the theurgist does know how to bring into function a god-form, i.e., a divine symbol —in many particularized ways.

From a practical point of view this is all that really matters. The divine within reaches out to the divine that is without, the contact is made, and the divine machinery is set in motion upon

---

*'Hither' is a technical term for the material world. (Seymour)

†'Yonder' is a technical term for the unseen world. (Seymour)

the plane of consciousness that is required. But if there is no Isis within your own soul, you will call in vain to this goddess. You must seek within yourself for the starting-handle.

To understand what the pagan was trying to do one must imagine, as he did, that divine all-embracing power which welling up under pressure from the unmanifest is ever seeking to express itself more and more fully, more and more perfectly. It has been well said that 'God is pressure.'

This pressure is often called Spirit, or Life. In reality it is all these things, and more, for there is the transcendent aspect to this power which the Chaldeans called the Great Silence, as well as the imminent aspect which is the Great Sea. In order to exist—this universal power must differentiate itself into particular units. The One must become the many—the High Gods.

The Qabalists use the system of the Tree of Life to explain the process by which the One becomes the Many. They divide divine manifestation into four worlds or states of consciousness. The most subtle of these worlds is Atziloth, which might be called the world of pure spirit, the Archetypal World, the sphere of the divine archetypal ideas, the plane of the High Gods, or the world of the ten Divine Names. All these things, and many others, it has been called, but it must be remembered that in itself the world of Atziloth is beyond our comprehension. It can be described only by means of analogy and by the use of symbols. Neo-Platonism, as a system, gives a full and very vivid teaching concerning this sphere of the divine activity. But the modern student must not forget that these ancient initiates were carefully trained in the pure dialectical method, a subject little studied today.

The best line of intellectual approach to the comprehension of ideas concerning the world of Atziloth is a study of mystical theology. This art reaches out to the supreme goal by the use of analogy and paradox, by blending the *Via Affirmativa* and the *Via Negativa*, until the super-essential Darkness which is the Ultimate Light of Light is reached in a contemplation that ends in *Agnosia*. One can study these methods even if one cannot use them. A study of Neo-Platonism can take the competently taught student by an ancient, well-trodden road to identification with the 'One and the Many.' But competently taught students are extremely rare for the world has seen few such teachers as Plotinus, Ammonius Saccas or Lao-tzu. These teachers are themselves living embodiments of the divine wisdom-gods. By sympathy they have become 'at one' with the divine wisdom. By their 'at-one-ment' they are able, at least temporarily, to lift the prepared student up to the metaphysical heights of the Light beyond all Lights—the Transcendental One, or to take him down to that abyss beyond all abysses.

The experiences which these teachers produce in the student's soul are evanescent. Yet something remains in memory for the hand of the Initiator has been laid upon the neophyte. When Height has challenged Height, and Deep has called to Deep, one is never quite the same.

The second sphere of the divine outpouring is called the world of Briah, a word derived from the Hebrew verb meaning to create, to produce. The divine ideals have, as it were, become the divine ideas. In Qabalistic terminology this is the world of the archangels, of the creating gods and the all-mothers of the ancient pantheons. It is the world of the great devas of the Eastern systems. In modern language we might call it the sphere of the abstract mind, or the world of abstract thought and ideas.

The third world is called Yetzirah. Now the Hebrew word Yatzar (Yod, Tzaddi, Resh) has several significant (from our point of view) meanings. It means to form in the mind, to plan, to fashion as an artist, and in certain cases to destine for a particular purpose. Now the initiates conceive the physical world to be crystallized astral matter, the astral world to be crystallized mind-stuff, and mind-stuff to be crystallized spirit. The same thing but varying in, shall we say, density.

In this third sphere of being, ideas take form, and the etheric moulds that hold dense matter in its physical form as we know it are fashioned by the divine artists; for Yetzirah is the sphere of the greater localized divinities, and the student will find a good deal given in Chapters 3-6 of *The Egyptian Mysteries* by Iamblichus. In modern terminology Yetzirah may be called the astro-mental world, though one must remember that there is no hard and fast line between the various spheres of being; they shade off imperceptibly one into the other. Dividing them up is like dividing the human mind into the descriptive sections that are used by psychologists. This is convenient for teaching and description, but these hard and fast lines of distinction exist only in textbooks.

The fourth sphere or world is that of Assiah. It corresponds to the physical world in its most subtle form. It is the densest form of the etheric world. In this sphere of the subtle pre-matter of existence are to be found the nature spirits, elementals, and the children of Dana, of the Great Earth Mother, the divinities of mountains, streams and woods.

If we bear in mind the ancient Mystery teaching that 'all the gods are one god, all the goddesses are one goddess, and there is one Initiator,' it will be seen that in the system of the Tree of Life as expounded in *The Mystical Qabalah* there is developed a perfectly logical sequence of cause and effect. From the human point of view the Tree of Life works as a system for enabling a human being to obtain contact with divine things, and again using the analogy of electricity, to put himself in circuit with the power-house of the universe.

Once more the student is warned that he must distinguish between 'the order of that which is' and 'the order of ideas concerning that which is.' One is not now trying to describe a chemical experiment. How these things that have just been described by analogy and by symbol may appear to minds superior to our human minds, we have no idea. To such minds our explanations are certainly childishly inadequate even if they are not entirely inaccurate. But this Qabalistic system of describing and using the mind fulfils the following fundamental conditions for obtaining results. First there is the power. Then there are individuals of various grades in all four worlds of manifestation who understand how to use this (divine) power. And, lastly, there is a method, or rather methods, for using this power insofar as mankind can become aware of it.

The divine life or power—like electricity—is not generated by the individual. The individual uses power which is already existing and the specializing of the divine energy which alone leads to manifestation must take place through individuals, human or otherwise. In theurgy this is a matter of experience as well as of common sense.

The pagans taught that every man is a distributor of this all-embracing, originating divine spirit or power. The initiate, however, was a trained man who, understanding the nature of the divine power, was able to transform it at will. He was a well-trained engineer, and he got his training in the same way that an electrical engineer gets his today—by working practically in an electrical power station. The initiate worked in the power-house of nature after having been taught the theory of his craft in a Mystery school. Then he took his practical training in the sphere of Yesod, which is the unmanifested element of the Four Elements of the physical world, the aether of the wise, the astral light of the ancients.

Thus it will be clear that the pagan initiate looked upon life from a rather different point of view from that of the ordinary man. The ambitious self-reliant man of the world strives to make himself a forceful personality and to get things done by his own driving power. He is his own power-house, and he supplies—or thinks he does—his own energy. The pagan, however, grasped the idea of 'Spirit' as the fountain head of a great 'forming power' which he received into himself. Then he proceeded to manifest it in accordance with the Law of Harmony and by means of a technique that he had been taught.

The various gods and their hierarchies are specialized functional types of this omnipresent divine energy. For example, Venus is the personification of the divine activity that is called attraction; Mars is that of repulsion, the divine destructive force; and Jupiter is a constructive mode of action. Again the religions of the mother and the daughter—Demeter and Persephone for example—are not so much family relationships as psychological stages in the life of the soul. From this point of view, the doctrine of the identity of Kore the Maid and her mother is obvious. The Maid is the psychological parent of the mother, and so the confusion of the persons disappears—the mother is the virgin and vice versa. The One God has become many gods, and each god functions as the head of a divine hierarchy with aspects that are spiritual, mental and astral. Each hierarchy in its turn carries further into manifestation the cosmic principle of the One, which becomes the Many. And each plane of manifestation has its own standard of truth and its own ethic, and these standards are by no means identical.

Cosmically, every man is a unit, but he is also a multiplicity, a hierarchy of divine lives, and in his activities proper to himself he manifests the same principles as the One and the Many. The virgin is the parent of the mother(!) psychologically if not physically. The virgin goddess renews her virginity every winter solstice. This becomes clear if we study the Babylonian Ishtar, who is called 'the Virgin,' 'the Holy Virgin' and 'the Virgin Mother' by her worshippers. Yet this virgin goddess says of herself, 'A harlot compassionate am I.' Among the ancient Jews and Babylonians a veil was the mark of both virgins and prostitutes—Ishtar in certain aspects wears the veil. And Genesis 38:14-15 throws a curious light on this custom. Also, the word *Parthenos*, upon which so much theology has been founded, is worth looking up in a *modern* Greek dictionary, for in ancient days bastards were called *Parthenioi*, virgin-born.

To sum up we may say that in this universe there is an ever-descending stream of divine power and life welling up under pressure from an unmanifested state of being and pouring down into manifestation. The various gods, each on their own plane and functioning according to their own degree, manifest and specialize this life force on planes of being which are more subtle than the plane of physical matter. The pagan by taking conscious thought of the gods can draw through himself the specialized life force of the gods or god with whom he is most in sympathy. Thus by a conscious effort man can forward evolution by increasing his capacity to distribute and to specialize this divine life power.

Again, by the study of the inner aspects of man's existence before conception draws him back into the realms of matter, the identity of Kore becomes manifest, for Kore is the Virgin Mother, the higher self in man; and every man—in terms of his lower self, and excluding the physical body—is one of the *parthenioi*. For the ancients, the moon-mother is a virgin, yet Demeter, curiously enough is the goddess who presides over divorce. (Harding, *Women's Mysteries*, p. 78.) The doctrines of the virgin who has a child, of the perpetual virginity of the mother, of the renewal of the mother's virginity with the death of the child, will yield much spiritual food for thoughtful meditation.

There are many curious paradoxes to be found in the psychological teachings of these ancient myths when once we begin to study the 'Great Silence.' For, as the 'Great Sea' is the root of things that are in matter, so the 'Great Silence' is the root of thoughts that are in mind—divine mind. As the Chaldeans taught, the 'Great Silence' and the 'Great Sea' are cosmic yoke-fellows. They are the duad of the monad which, on each plane of being, forms a divine triad—such as woman, saint, butterfly; Zeus, Apollo, Dionysius; Chaos, Erebus, Nox. Does not the picture of Nox, crowned with poppies or stars, with large dark wings and flying robes, riding in a chariot drawn by two black horses, touch the very depths of your being with a feeling that is subtle and mysterious?

The key to 'understanding' is sympathy, which is strong feeling carefully directed. Once sympathy has been aroused, the soul feels the truth of a 'mythos,' not because it is in any way reasonable, but because something in the depths of one's innermost being has been touched. Pre-natal memories of a divine knowledge that the soul once had long ago—a knowledge temporarily lost while wandering in the realms of mortal generation—begin to stir. By meditation these memories of a lost understanding can be recovered; for in the long dead past, perhaps, one may have known something of the Egyptian, Chaldean, Orphic and Pythagorean systems.

5

The Shining Ones
of the Vedas

JEANINE MILLER

The Vedic pantheon with its variety of "gods" and "goddesses" is a colorful and beautiful one,[1] but one that differs totally from the Greco-Roman pantheons with which most of us are more or less acquainted. The difference lies in the fact that the Vedic "gods" have not yet been completely anthropomorphized and reduced to the measure of human lowliness.

Who are the gods?

In saluting Dawn, the beautiful daughter of Heaven, or Agni, the Fire that rose at daybreak to awaken humankind, or Surya, the Sun that bestirs all creatures to activity and shines on the just and the unjust, or in appealing to the Wind, the Mountain, the Waters, the Rivers, the Lord of the Forest, the poets obviously showed their response to Nature. The whole of Nature was for them alive with a luminous vibrancy, with a quickening power, a refreshing vigor that filled them with dynamic life and *joie de vivre*. But, as we shall see, the "gods" are not just personifications of the powers of Nature, as thought for so long by Western scholars. They are far more.

The word "god," however, is quite a misnomer insofar as the Vedas are concerned, the word *deva* coming from the verbal root *div*, to shine. The devas are the luminous energy principles behind all phenomena, whether of Nature or of the Cosmos, hence can be thought of in terms of the regents of the universe, the custodians of the One Law, the Cosmic Order which they establish throughout manifestation.

To the Christian conception, a multiplicity of gods denies the One Infinite Godhead, source of all. This is again an erroneous surmise which blinded the early Western scholars to a real understanding of the functions of the many "gods" behind which abides the One, *tad ekam*.

70

1. The Origins

Behind the devas, behind the multiplicity of phenomena and noumena, pulsates the Great Unknown Principle, the "That" or "That One" of the great hymns of creation, the One that "breathes breath-less-ly by Itself," nameless, undisturbed (Rigveda X.129.2), "whose shadow is death, whose shadow is immortality" (X.121.2).* That One is the Vedic "God" or Absolute whom no human thought can touch or degrade.

That which originally brought about the onset of manifestation is the Flame-Power of the Divine contemplation:

Darkness there was; at first hidden in darkness this all was undifferentiated Depth. Enwrapped in voidness, that which Flame-power kindled to existence emerged. (X.129.3)

Desire, primordial seed of mind, in the beginning, arose in That. (X.129.4)

The Void, as the vast ocean of space, or the "Waters," contains *in potentia* all the seeds of life that awaken at the first touch of the Flame divine, Agni, first born of Holy Order (X.5.7). The vastness of space becomes embodied in the goddess Aditi, the Mother, the Infinite, the far pervading One who is all embracing, who is Father and Mother and Son, what has been and what shall be (I.89.10). That, furthermore, this universe of ours is not the first one[2] is inferred from one of the hymns of creation:

As of old, the Creator imaged forth the sun and moon, the heavenly, earthly and the intermediate realms, and also the empyrean. (X.190.3)

The gods thus came later in this world's manifestation. This is stressed again and again:

Earlier than the heavens, earlier than this earth,
earlier than the devas and the archangels, That indeed is.
What seed primeval did the billowy-deeps conceive wherein all the gods appeared together? (X.82.5)

In yon billowy-deeps ye devas stood closely-clasped; then from ye, as though from dancers, hot dust was whirled away. (X.72.6)

The devas emerge closely clasped, whirling to incandescent manifestation out of the "Waters of Space." These represent that subtle essence out of which the universe and all therein are fashioned and emerge to separate life. The Greeks called these *aether*, the later Hindus *akasha*.

---

*Unless otherwise noted, all quotations are from the Rigveda.

2. The Role of the Devas in Creation

That which is one has developed into the all (VIII.58.2d).

One whole governs the moving and the stable, that which walks and flies, this variegated creation (III.54.8).

That divine, mysterious Power which resides at the core of Life, that ground of being in which we are all rooted, that One (*tad ekam*) now manifests through a multiplicity of shining, radiating, energizing principles or powers, the intelligent units or devas that represent Life-Light-Intelligence behind all cosmic and natural phenomena.

Furthermore, the blueprint of Universal "Order and Truth" is established with the very first outbreathing of the ONE into manifestation. This is beautifully imaged thus: "Cosmic Order and Truth were born of the all blazing contemplation" of Deity. (X.190.1)

Harmony, order, law, all of these are expressed in the one little word *rita*, the Cosmic Order, the foundation, the blueprint of the universe. Therefore, we can deduce that what encourages cooperation, togetherness, integrity, oneness is of the very essence of the life divine. Of this the devas are the supreme exponents. "Law-abiding, born in law, sublime fosterers of law, haters of falsehood" (VII.66.13ab), they are "herdsmen of the Supreme-Law whose decrees are truth" (V.63.1ab). Theirs is the task of "establishing" and "ordering" the manifest world. Manifestation is a process of demarcating and shaping the inchoate, of fashioning it according to the celestial blueprint, which the devas "vision." For the devas are said to be "rita-visioned"; they mirror in their consciousness the pattern of Cosmic Order, eternal in the heavens, as poetic imagination has described it, and they proceed to establish it in our space-time phenomenal world. They express it through their actions. This is a remarkable admission insofar as it shows the gods receiving the blueprint of the Eternal Harmony and endeavoring to make it "real." The Rigveda here, as elsewhere, vindicates H. P. Blavatsky's statements in *The Secret Doctrine.*

The devas' solidarity, their essential righteousness, their concerted activity are their peculiar characteristics that eminently mark them as the agents of the One Law by which, through which, and in which they live and move and perform their varied tasks. The rishis, ancient sages, conceived an impersonal eternal Law to which all, even the most exalted of beings, are subservient. That Cosmic Order is the "song" of the cosmos. So "the devas revel in the sacred-song of the Cosmic Order" (I.147.1d).

3. Vision, the Means of Human Communication with the Devas

The opening to the world of the devas is effected through the power of vision and the flashing mantra. It is anointed by humanity's ancestor, Manu, thereby giving the seal of sacred approval. It was because of their faculty of visioning—hereditary among the rishis—that they entered into communion with the devas, approached the "thousand branched tree" of life, and were consciously taken into the "gods' council" where they saw celestial entities and apprehended the functions and influences of the powers at work within the cosmos.

The rishis discovered that to sing meant to shine, to illumine. The sounding of the right word which shone forth in the right way signified worship. These radiated from their hearts as they uttered their prayers and thereby attracted the right divinities.[4] "They found the light, receiving visionary insights" (VII.90.4b). So the prayer goes to Agni, "O tireless Knower-of-generations! Bring us the prolific word that it may shine to heaven" (VI.16.36). Such a word opens out the intuition and lets in the light like a flash of lightning. Agni is indeed like Soma, the "Lord of vision," the seer-will that takes humanity to "highest immortality." In another verse he promises "I will place brilliant speech in your mouth" (X.98.1).

The hymn or song of praise is indeed the "flashing song," the bright, fire-hot chant, a "resplendent visionary insight" sent aloft by the seer to be taken up by the god, thereby initiating a rapport and a communion between god and mortals. "Proclaim three light-projecting words [that] milk the honey-yielding udder" (VII.101.1).

Here as elsewhere we find the Word as light, the illuminating power of the Word milks the nectar of heaven. The divine vision-speech is compared to a celestial cow pouring out milk in a thousand streams. The gods generated this celestial "cow" as the divine speech (VIII.100.11).

So the rishi in his contemplation and hymn chanting beholds the god:

Gazing upon the loftier light beyond the darkness, we have reached Surya, divine among divinities, the light supreme. (I.50.10)

I saw the Lord of men [Agni] with his sevenfold progeny. (I.164.1)

I saw the herdsman, the unfaltering one, approaching and departing by the pathways. Arrayed in diverging and converging [forces] he revolves ceaselessly within the worlds. (X.177.3 = I.164.31)

We have beheld the Golden one through our power of vision, as it were through our mind, with our own eyes, with Soma's own eyes. (I.139.2)

"Beholding" is of the essence of the Vedic rishis. This communion culminates in a visitation, an epiphany:

There . . . where the birds vigilantly sing forth their share of immortality, the lordly herdsman of the whole universe, the enlightened One, has entered into me the simple. (I.164.21)

I have known this mighty celestial being,
refulgent as the Sun beyond the darkness;
only by knowing him does one overcome death;
no other way is there to go. (Yajurveda 31.18)

In the culmination of exaltation, the poets entered the divine domains and sang, "We have drunk Soma, we have become immortal, we have gone to the light, we have found the gods" (VIII.48.3).

4. The Devas' Appearance

What do the gods look like? Their appearance varies. Some are said to change form at will. Their main characteristic is of course shining, their bright, luminous quality. Some are evidently a poetic response to natural phenomena: Dawn, the Asvins, the Maruts, or personifications such as Heaven and Earth, the primordial Parents. All are intelligent powers who never infringe upon each others' domain and whose outer manifestation may be a natural element, such as Fire, Wind, the plant Soma, or a visible entity such as the Sun whose various facets are conceived in terms of several gods. They all have an inner being that marks them out as individual.

Dawn, the shining daughter of Heaven, bedecked like a beautiful maid, rises in splendor and unveils her beauty "dispelling gloom of night, ushering in the light," letting loose her herds of light, the harbingers of Surya, the Lord of heaven who pursues her as a lover his beloved. Surya, the Sun, is the "eye" of heaven whose chariot is drawn by one horse, Etasa, or by seven fair-backed tawny horses. He is of course the most concrete because the most visible of the deities. Savitar, that aspect of the Sun that stimulates, impels and invigorates, is the golden deity par excellence. He has golden hands, eyes and tongue; he is bright and lustrous; his chariot is adorned with pearls and golden pins. He blesses all beings with his golden arms. Agni, the Fire, is also a very visible deity, but extremely complex. He has sharp jaws and golden teeth. He is flame-haired and butter-backed, and his flames are roaring waves. Through his mouth the gods partake of the sacrifice.

The Asvins, the heavenly riders and physicians, twin sons of Heaven or of Vivasvat the Sun, strip the covering of darkness as harbingers of the light. They also wear many forms at will (I.117.9) and are "wonder-workers." They are lords of brilliant gold, adorned with lotus garlands, drinkers of honey and bestowers of it as well.

Of all the gods Indra is the most anthropomorphized and perhaps for this reason the closest to the human heart. From our point of view, he is the least perfect of the gods. Because of his great capacity for quaffing the Soma juice, his "belly," which is able to contain whole lakes of the nectar, is often described, as are his jaws and beard. His arms bear his deadly weapon, the thunderbolt, which sunders chaos. It was fashioned for him by the artisan of Nature, Tvastar, sometimes regarded as his father. His bay horses bear him to human rituals where his generosity amply repays human prayer.

Varuna, the awe-inspiring Lord of Cosmic Order, the Universal Monarch, is "thousand-eyed." He has myriads of spies that watch human beings. He tramples on wiles with his "shining foot." He wears a resplendent robe and a golden mantle. By means of his magic or occult power [*maya*]⁵ which is laid down in Heaven (V.63.4), the world order is established, "even like the moon, it bestows its splendour far and wide" (III.61.7cd).

It is by means of this *maya* that the gods change their appearance and counteract the *maya* of their opponents, the forces of darkness. Thus Indra "wears all shapes at his will, effecting magic changes in his appearance" (III.53.8). These magic changes are not elaborated, nor is the hostility between the gods and the demons emphasized as in the later literature. The form of the god waxes in strength and majesty in accordance with the fervor of the invocation or worship of his devotee. This implies that in a state of exaltation the seers were able to perceive the devas more or less clearly.

These descriptions of the devas with their unavoidable anthropomorphic traits fade into insignificance when we enter into the lively relationship of deva and human, into that atmosphere steeped in the fluidity and transparency of flowing water. The luminous gods of the Vedic pantheon bring sunshine, light, joy. They illumine the screen of the cosmos with their special brightness. The poets' own songs, called "fiery-hot hymns," take on the crystal hues of the devas.

5. Human and Deva: The Relationship

The gods are gracious to human beings, "bounteous to every man": "For of one spirit are the gods with mortal men, co-sharers all of gracious gifts" (VIII.27.4ab). Humanity often claims its common origin with the gods and seldom cringes to them. "From time immemorial we here set forth our brotherhood, our kinship in the Mother's womb" (VIII.83.8). Devas and humans are born in the "same Mother's womb," of the same Father.[6] It is because of this kinship that to infringe the statutes of the gods is to "injure as it were a friend" (X.89.8c). The gods differ ethically from humans because they never infringe on the one Law whose statutes they guard, whereas humans do so through weakness or ignorance or evil intent. Humanity, according to the Vedas, was fashioned by the devas. A quaint verse in the Atharvaveda puts it thus: "Having poured together the whole mortal, the gods entered man" (Athv.XI.8.13cd).

In this, one of the most important hymns of the Atharvaveda, we find a description of human beings as the abode of godly powers, as the child of the deities, as the seat of the opposites, of light and darkness, union and separation, love and strife, in short good and evil. This in itself sums up the glory and the predicament of our human race. Humanity stands at that stage where conflict prevails and thereby wreaks havoc in its own domain, the earth, and in its life. But this stage will in due course yield to that further stage that the deva commands, where harmony is established and the tension between the polarities resolved.

The cooperation of humans and devas is called for in order to establish a world of harmony at the phenomenal level, in our space-time dimension, as it is already established at the noumenal level, the realm of the devas. So the poet sings of the ideal world in the Yajurveda:

Where spiritual and ruling powers move together in unison,
that world shall I know as holy, where dwell the shining ones
together with Agni the Flame divine. (Yjv.20:25)

The Rigveda tells us that: "Beyond the statutes of the devas no
one, even if he had a 100 souls, can live" (X.33.9ab). The Atharvaveda
sums it all up thus:

Vast truth, mighty order, consecration, spiritual exertion, prayer, sacrificial
offering, these uphold the earth. (Athv.XII.1.1)

These are expressions of a spiritual venture that translate the
divine order into human terms, the great inspirers of which are
the devas.

6. *Individual Gods*

Indra. In the task of establishing a world, Indra is of paramount
importance and indeed the prototype of human dynamism and
never-ending urge for conquest. He is very far from the storm
god as propounded by the early Western scholars. Indra at the
cosmic level, as demiurge, is the principle of activity and order
that brings an end to the undifferentiated state of chaos wherein
all motion and change are suspended and all seeds of life are
slumbering in the darkness of inertia. This is their "imprisonment."
This bringing to life was presented as the epic fight of Indra with
the power of chaos and inertia, the Dragon Vritra, the personification of obstruction, of that force that keeps back, withholds,
restrains, constricts. At the psychological level, the power of
inertia is that force that prevents people from going forward,
from achieving whatever they are capable of achieving, from
working out their destiny. To sever the life-breath of Vritra is to
render this force harmless; it can no longer have a grip on humans.
This is Indra's achievement, and it results in the experience of
the free flow of the divine life. "The waters are let loose," not
only in the cosmic sense of the creation of a universe with its
laws, directions, cycles and rhythms, but also in the psychological
sense, as those inner impulses emerging from the unconscious
to quench the inner thirst and drive one forward to ever fresher
creativity.

In the struggle to gain the Sun, which represents the achievement of illumination on the part of the seers, Indra is humanity's
best friend. So he is invoked in the battle for the Sun of enlightenment, for the true Sun. Indra, the chosen of the gods, is humanity's

light-bringer, the personification of mind's struggle for freedom. He modifies the primeval state of undifferentiation into a differentiated world with distinctive realms, sequence, time, contrasts, light and darkness. This activity shows mind's function, which is to give shape to the shapeless, to make pathways, distinctions, demarcations where none were (VI.21.3). Indra is the active, indeed dynamic deity who is always on the march. He not only finds the way to human fulfilment but "through might and conflict he made space for the gods" (III.34.7) who in a previous cycle were not immortal. "In the threefold heaven, in the triple splendour, he found the hidden immortality" (VI.44.23).

This immortality is personified in Soma. The prize Indra wins is not only the sun "that men may see," not only the "waters" of life that are released through his action, but also Soma, who is his beverage par excellence. Soma is even equated with his thunderbolt, an interesting hint as to an inner significance: for just as the lightning flash illuminates the darkness of the sky, so the flash of insight lights the darkness of the mind, and in that illumination is experienced the state of exaltation, of wholeness, which the rishis called immortality. Man invokes Indra in the "light-bestowing conflict," for through conflict Indra found for humanity "the way to fulfilment" (X.49.9).

Lead us to wide space, O thou who knowest,
to celestial, fearless light, successfully. (VI.47.8ab)

Varuna. The high gods of the Rigveda are not only called *deva* but also *asura*, which word, in those early days, had a totally different connotation from the later meaning of "demon."[7] The *asura* was not only the possessor of the life-breath (*asu*) but its bestower, hence the creator par excellence. The title of *asura* was applicable to highly spiritual entities for their creative and ruling capacities and especially for what appeared as their "magic" power. A deva that rises to the accomplishment of "creator" is entitled to being called *asura*. Are the asuras the Rigvedic equivalent to the Dhyan Chohans of *The Secret Doctrine*? It may be so.

So Varuna, Indra, Agni, Savitar, Soma, Dyaus (Heaven) are all asuras as well as devas. Varuna is perhaps the greatest asura in awe-inspiring majesty. He is the mighty Lord of the Cosmic Order, the Lord of righteousness, and thereby nearest to our Christian conception of the majesty of God. This is probably why he won such acclaim among the early scholars. His supremacy seems to have extended prior to Indra's domination, in a previous dispensation. But even in the present cycle, he encompasses the world, and his statutes, immovable, are firmly fixed as on a mountain (II.28.8cd) and all the gods obey his ordinances. The "Waters," or Ether, of space are his realms, not the waters we know on earth, though even these, as the counterpart of the etheric realms, fall under his supervision. Ultimately the "waters" refer to the undifferentiated state of primordial matter over which Varuna rules and which he "measures out" in order to shape the universe: "In accordance with the Law, Aditi's Son, observer of the Law, has spread out the world in threefold order." (IV.42.4cd) His cosmic action expresses his occult or magic power (*maya*) and is not an original act of violence, such as Indra's rending asunder of the Dragon of Chaos. Varuna gives the first impulse to demarcating chaos.

Varuna is compared to a mysterious ocean that rules over "the seven," pervading the "three earths and the three realms of heaven" (VIII.41.9). He supports heaven in the seat of Order, watching over all from the center, the Cosmic Tree which he sustains erect, whose "root is high above," whose branches, like rays, descend downwards (I.24.7).

Varuna is the god of sinners whom he fetters for their transgressions and whom the sinners beg for release from their dreaded "noose." The noose represents the effect of disturbing the Cosmic Order. Sinners are chained by their own actions; they have transgressed against the Law whose custodians are the Sons of Aditi—the Boundless, the Infinite, Freedom—at the head of whom towers Varuna. The Adityas are the sons of Freedom because they have chosen to align themselves with the Great Law and are therefore one with it. In this oneness is freedom.

In Varuna, the god of might and of terror, the ancient archetypal image of the awe-ful majesty of certain aspects of Deity, and the experience of the numinous as it strikes the human psyche, are still vibrant. They account for Varuna's often ambivalent role. His might and splendor find expression in some of the most beautiful verses of the Rigveda:

Thy force and might and passion,
Neither these birds in their travelling can attain,
Nor these waters ranging restlessly,
Nor they who hedge in the hugeness of the winds. (I.24.6)

Agni. Some of the devas who have an obvious physical counterpart such as Agni, Surya, and Soma, (fire, sun, plant) may be difficult for us to understand in terms of "god" or "angel," for we, in our rational dismissal of the finer forces of Nature, have taken the "divine life" out of the cosmos. But let us put ourselves in the heart of the Vedic seers, see with them and feel with them.

Agni, the celestial light-finder, seated in secret in the human heart, in the "cave" or ocean, the Flame divine, the "truth bearer" (III.26.1) is the "seven-rayed," the "triple-headed" deity, born of the waters and of the wood and of the stone and of the gods (II.2.1). He dwells in the moving and the fixed (I.146.1).

There lies the fire within the earth, and in plants,
and waters carry it; the fire is in stone.
There is a fire deep within men; a fire in the kine
and a fire in horses. The same fire that burns in the heavens;
the mid-air belongs to this fire divine. Men kindle this fire
that bears the oblation. (Atharvaveda XII.1.19,20)

The dual, indeed many-faceted, role ascribed to the devas is fully apparent in Agni. He is the force that builds the cosmos as well as the destructive power that shatters unwanted forms. He is the great purifying agent hidden in all things. He is the inspiring flame that kindles human aspiration. He is the high priest of the Vedic seers, the envoy of humans to gods, messenger between gods and humans, seated in the altar ready to act on our behalf. For through his ministry he links both heaven and earth. He is the Charioteer of the Transcendent (I.77.3), the redeemer (X.71.10), the perfect vehicle to carry messages from mortals to immortals. He is the "guest" in human tabernacles, the Lord of prayer, "immortal in mortals" who "raises mortal man to highest immortality"—"The one ocean, the foundation of riches, of many births, that shines forth from our heart" (X.5.1), our guardian, our providence, our protector, our spring of life. As a father he calls to us while being kindled on the altar. Rich in light, he is father, mother, brother, friend: "Father and mother of mankind for ever" (VI.1.5d).

Agni, men seek thee as a Father with their prayers,
win thee, bright formed, to brotherhood with holy act. (II.1.9)

To him, lord of the people, prayers ascend for welfare and freedom from all malignities. "In the hidden place" of the heart, the poets, "recipients of visionary insights," . . . "find him when they sing their mantras which they fashion in their heart." (I.67.2).

From thee, O Agni, inspired wisdom, from thee intuitions,
from thee accomplished utterances are generated (IV.11.3).

Agni, "Lord of thought," whom the wise ones kindle by their thought power (VIII.44.19) is also said to be kindled by means of "hymns"; he carries these upwards to the gods as a human "offering," together with the clarified butter and the Soma drops as the oblation. Through his sacrificial ministry he is asked to gain for us "in the heavens the grace" of the various gods.

In the service of Agni, along the paths, they offer up their sweat.
On him their own kin, they mount, as on a ridge on earth. (V.7.5)

The rishis discovered the "inner fire" and its tremendous action in us, and described it in terms of its perfect mirror, the outer fire. They further conceived the sacrifice as a universal process to which all are called, an eternal give and take.

The Sun. Turning to the solar deity, who like Varuna views the deeds and misdeeds of the human race, we find that the sun has many facets and therefore many names and tasks. He is Surya, Savitar, Pushan, but Vishnu and Indra are also solar deities, and Agni's lofty face in heaven is the bright light of Surya (X.7.3).

Surya. Spiritual knowledge is a result of illumination, and the latter finds its full embodiment in Surya. The supreme goal of the rishi is the "finding of the sun," the "true sun" which Indra discovers in the darkness, "encompassed in rock, in never-ending rock" (III.39.3). The sun is the "eye" of the gods, that eye which they themselves have generated and through which they gaze on the finite and the infinite, that is, on the below and the beyond, on humans and all creatures, that eye that symbolizes their omniscience, the very essence of their vision. In the Atharvaveda, Surya is described as "the one eye of what exists that looks beyond the sky, the earth, the waters" (Athv. XIII.1.45). Since that eye, the "sun," is the "atman of what moves and moves not," it betokens a divine presence everywhere. This presence makes the wise ones who foster truth illumined, or in the quaint expression of the Rigveda, "sun-eyed."

This sun of illumination, like Agni its counterpart in so many ways, is kept hidden "secretly concealed in the waters" (III.39.5) or in the darkness, or in the rock. Indra, on his knees finds it and raises it on high for humankind to see.

Savitar. Savitar, the vivifying aspect of the sun, the life-giving principle in whose stimulation all things grow, fills the whole of Heaven and Earth, and fashions the "holy song" of the cosmos. For the universe is the song of the solar deity, that song he cannot help but sing as he performs his varied tasks. Of profound inspiration, as a fine-winged bird, he surveys the regions and the dark, wide spaces of the heavens.

Pushan. In all his outgoings, Savitar becomes Pushan, the unfaltering herdsman, the eternal pilgrim who marches in Savitar's vivifying energy. Savitar who goes through the darkness of space by a downward and an upward path, dustless, well-made paths that have been from everlasting (I.35.11), gives way to the pilgrim shepherd born on those forward paths leading to heaven and to earth. Pushan, the glowing essence of Surya, is herdsman of all beings, the good shepherd who guides his human flock unerringly along the paths and the crossroads, through the darkness where the two-faced evil lurks and obstructs our progress. He guides us right to the heights that lead to luminous riches, to the enlightenment of Soma and Surya. He removes all obstacles that prevent our progress. Hence he is called the "son of liberation" and the "liberator." Friend of all suppliants, he is not only the outer herdsman of creation, guarding the cattle, who "moves onward beholding all creatures," but he is also "inserted in every creature" (VI.58.2). This gives more than a hint as to the inner meaning of Pushan. But even more clearly than this, he is openly stated to be the divine torturer; for it is his "prayer stimulating goad" (VI.53.8) that urges human beings onwards in unrelenting pursuit of their goal, and it is his awl that tears the heart:

Thou glowing Pushan carriest an awl that urges men to prayer. Therewith thou tearest up and rendest to shreds the heart of everyone. (VI.53.8)

Pushan probes the heart, sharpens the mind, tests human beings in all their inner recesses. He is indeed asked to "sharpen us like a razor," for only sharp insight can find the right track that leads to the right road and the right goal. Sharp as a razor's edge is the path of return, say the Upanishads.

Soma. When we turn to Soma, the nectar of immortality, the bestower of inspiration and its matching eloquence, we are faced with the celestial catalyst that takes us to heights of spiritual understanding. Soma is the "thousand eyed," the "Father of thought," the "Lord of intuitions." Far more than a mere plant that gives inebriation, Soma is the "knower," the "inspired and inspirer" (*kavi*) or "poet" in the ancient sense of this word, the enlightener, the "light conqueror, causing illumination," "leader of the poets" (IX.96.18), rishi among the rishis, the king of all celestial seership. He is asked to "unseal the inspired thought" for he "releases the mind-yoked vision even as the thunder releases the rain." His great action is to give the poet "kinship with the gods," and "with the sun unites our eye" (IX.10.8): in awakening inner perception Soma makes human insight equivalent to Surya's divine gaze. Soma thus helps to illuminate us, to render us "sun-eyed."

Like Agni, Soma "produces the gods"; that is, he makes the divine powers manifest, he reveals them in their fullness, whether in Nature or in man. This is an admission that only in a state of exaltation, enthusiasm or ecstasy such as granted by Soma, or in that state of intuitive perception as granted by Agni, can the gods become visible to, or sensed by humans, can the cosmos be illumined by the divine light which is "life."

Soma is lord of heart and mind as well as the "infallible lord of speech." He represents the Word, the evocative power of the Word released from depths unplumbed, the Word as both sound and light, eloquence and illumination; the power of invocation as well as evocation, and the ability to express the resulting insight in eloquent songs or mantras. This Word is that first milk or "primeval milk of heaven which from the very depth of mighty heaven" the seers learn to milk forth from their inspiration.

Soma knows humans in the depth of their consciousness. Like Agni and Pushan, as "light-finder" he "makes all blessings flow," and is the "giver of riches." He calls all the generations to immortality. "He clothes those who are naked and doctors all who are sick"; through him the "blind man sees, the cripple goes about" (VIII.79.2).

His highly esoteric meaning is hinted at in the following verse:

Soma is thought to have been drunk when they press the plant. The Soma whom the Brahmans know, of that no one tastes. No earthly born can taste of thee. (X.85.3.4)

That Soma is evidently the ecstasy experienced in the state of oneness which no ordinary mortal knows, and which Soma, the plant that yields the nectar of bliss, is but the symbol.

Agni is the consumer and kindler to ever greater exertion, Soma the consumed and catalyst to greater and greater expansions of consciousness. Savitar is the impeller and invigorator, Surya the eye of omniscience, and Pushan the guardian of the paths, the remover of obstacles and the divine torturer. All these may appear to us as various glowing aspects of communion with the numinous. But as we have seen, each is an entity in its own right. Not only is each very personal insofar as worshippers are concerned, but each plays a specific role both in the cosmos and in human affairs. The complex of striking affinities among the gods gives a blurred picture of their nascent "personalities," as projected by. human beings. Nevertheless, they all keep their distinctions. Thus, although the poet may salute the "bright and holy light of Surya" as the "face of Agni in heaven," thereby acknowledging their essential kinship, Agni and not Surya is always the messenger of the gods who reveals their presence to humans and Surya and not Agni is always the eye whereby the gods look upon all creation. Both Soma and Agni—both the liquid fire that wounds the heart and the flame-power that burns the whole being—enlighten, purify and grant immortality, but Agni is the high priest who transmutes and transfers the oblation to the gods, while Soma is the kingly response as the exalted vision of godhood, the illumination, the ecstasy.

7. The Devas and the Esoteric Wisdom

The devas of the Vedas can be most fruitfully studied in the light of the esoteric wisdom as it has been revealed to us by H. P. Blavatsky and her successors.[8] The subject is vast, and but a few hints can be given here. Everything in the universe pulsates with deva life, whether this be the intelligence that energizes deva substance (the myriads of tiny involutionary deva lives) or that substance which responds to the impact of divine Intelligence, the call of the high devas and evolutionary Life.

The Vedic seers were aware of various categories of devas, and one or two schemes of classification have come down to us in their barest outlines. The oldest, as it appears in the Rigveda, groups the devas around their threefold habitat: earth, (our terrestrial realm) over which presides Agni with his millions of cohorts; the mid-region (psychomental world) over which rules Indra, or Vayu in previous cycles; and heaven (the spiritual realm, *buddhi-manas*) whose lord is Surya, or Solar Fire. But within these three realms are "many mansions." For heaven is threefold, or as we are told in the Rigveda, there are three heavens. Earth is also threefold, or there are three earths. Similarly for the intermediate region. Our world is said to have a sevenfold foundation— the seven planes of the esoteric tradition. In Varuna himself as the presiding deity, "are placed the 3 heavens and the lower 3 earths disposed in sixfold order" (VII.87.5ab), but there is also a seventh: "Immovable is Varuna's seat; over the 7 he rules" (VIII.41.9).[9]

The four known Elements and their synthesis, Ether, which is not yet manifest, substand all that there is around us. For the Vedic seers, as for all ancient philosophers, "Fire, air, water, earth, were but the visible garb, the symbols of the informing, invisible Souls or Spirits, the Cosmic Gods"[10] as *The Secret Doctrine* says. We live and have our being in the Elements, hence in the very substance of the devas;[11] for without air or water we cannot survive; earth is obviously our habitat.[12]

The devas of Fire and of Manas are the basis of divine alchemy in the cosmos, and they are playing an increasingly important role in our world civilization. Bearing in mind that, according to the esoteric tradition, "the sum total of manas [mind] is pure deva essence," and that we live and move and have our being in Mahat, the Universal Mind, and that the high devas are "flaming fire," "radiant electric" substance, we may understand why Agni the Fire and Soma the fiery drink are lords of thought, inspiration and intuition, as well as of vision, wisdom and ecstasy. The electric fire of Spirit lies back of all phenomena and is the expression of a Lord of light. What manifests on our earth as life and light, and what we feel as warmth or cold, what we see as the many colored crystal in which we mirror ourselves, all these are but the ultimate manifestations of "lives" or "celestial entities," quite beyond our ordinary comprehension and perception, whose task is to weave here in the space-time world the eternal pattern of the heavens.

The close interaction of fire and water is shown in the Rigveda in what could be called "hieroglyphics," specific images of deep esoteric meaning. Thus the lightning bolt is immersed in the ocean of mundane existence, yet remains the "king" to whom all creation pays homage: "Deep in the ocean lies the bolt with waters compassed round about and in continuous onward flow the floods bring their tribute to it." (VIII.100.9) Agni the Fire is also called the "Son of Waters" whom *The Secret Doctrine* identifies with Fohat.[13] He rises upright amidst the flowing waters lying athwart. The spirit flame descends as lightning into the "waters," into the Mother deep that feeds him; the vertical line of dynamic life and the horizontal line of the rippling waves form the cross of manifestation. Deep significance is hidden in this image: "The Son of Waters, upright, clothed in lightning, has occupied the lap of the reclining waters" (II.35.9).

Indra, the god of the mid-region or air (which is "differentiated and compound Ether"),[14] is entering another phase of his dominion insofar as humanity is learning to master the air and travel through space. Varuna encompasses the astral level from where he watches over human emotional responses and morals and our transmutation of the lower desires into higher aspirations.

The task of the devas of the Waters is to nourish all the kingdoms of Nature, to care and tend all life, constantly to pour out their essence and reveal that love principle at work in the Cosmos. Theirs is the task of the "Great Mother" as she "performs her work of body-building under the impulse" of the Divine Desire. Here we find the feminine element in the Vedas.

The Waters in their highest meaning represent the vast depths of space wherein the drama of creation is being enacted, and wherein dwell all beings from the microscopic to the loftiest Lord of Contemplation. They are therefore identified with the womb of Cosmic Order that as blueprint of Harmony was impressed on the Waters or Aether of Space at the very beginning of manifestation. But the Waters also represent the astral plane of desire, which is the somewhat distorted mirror of the buddhic level whence we receive our inspirations, aspirations, intuitions and love. The Mother principle in the Rigveda is stepped down to our level in four goddesses, Aditi, Dawn, Sarasvati and Earth. At the ultimate remove shines Aditi, the boundless, luminous Mother of all, "the mighty Mother of those whose sway is just, Queen of Eternal Order . . . good Protectress, gracious Guide" (Yjv.21.5).

Nearer home, the Waters of space and of earth wherein moves Varuna are the nourishing and purifying Mothers implored for their life-giving balm and auspicious fluid and blessings of all kinds "within the Waters—so Soma has told me—are all healing balms and Agni benign to all" (Rgv.X.9.6). They are "sun-possessing" or solar waters, a deeply esoteric phrase. Dawn herself, the brilliant daughter of Heaven, "the radiant mover of sweet sounds" is the very light or ray of the Waters to whom beautiful hymns are addressed. The great representative of these Waters as Rivers, indeed, the "best" and most motherly of the "seven rivers"[15] is Sarasvati, "mighty among the mighty," the "anointed one," who directs and stimulates the ritual. She too, is the bestower of vision and inspiration, the detector of intuition, to become in the later literature, the goddess of wisdom, of eloquence, of the *Veda*.

Nearest home is Mother Earth to whom is dedicated a magnificent hymn in the Atharvaveda:

"in whom lie the sea, the rivers and other waters,
in whom food and cornfields have come to be
in whom live all that breathes and that moves." (Athv.XII.1.3)

Conclusion

The subtle characteristics of the devas and their reflections in the human psyche were expressed in the Vedas, on the whole, in terms of the powers of Nature, because of humankind's close communion with Nature. Nature is the phenomenal expression of the devas' activity. We cannot dissociate the one from the other. But human beings are also the playground of this same activity. The interblending of the devas' influences reflects an intimate relationship with the human psyche's weaving of its own destiny. From our modern psychological standpoint, the devas appear as variations on the one theme of the pilgrim's perpetual search for light, understanding, achievement and enlightenment, his or her ascent and descent, struggling, questioning and finding. Each deva mirrors and confers on the worshipper something of itself: the flame of desire and aspiration; the ecstasy of life in its deepest essence; the never tiring urge to seek for more experience, more achievement, more meaning; the core of knowledge and wisdom, the completion of fulfillment. All bestow on us that celestial vision resplendent, which is hidden in the Word, the power of evocation, which the rishis find in their hearts.

In later ages, when that communion diminished, these powers dwindled in importance and significance in human eyes and disappeared in the background of the psyche to remain dormant as dim, distant archetypal images. Only the heroic and human aspects of the ancient gods survived, to be grafted on a new but purely anthropomorphic image of God, a vast projection of humanity's own being onto the screen of the cosmos. But the present cycle is fast drawing to an end, and we are told that in the new age the human and angelic evolutions will draw closer. Greater contact and working in unison will be possible in order to establish on earth (that is, outwardly,) that which we have all longed for, the harmony prevalent among the angels in the inner realms of cosmos.

Notes

1. The word *veda* means the eternal *gnosis* or wisdom and comes from the root *vid* to know. The *veda* is thus the fountain source of wisdom. It is contained in four collections of hymns, akin to the Psalms, which we call the Vedas, whence the anglicized adjective, vedic. The four Vedas or collections are: the Rigveda, (or science of the word); the Yajurveda (or science of sacrifice); the Sama Veda (or song Veda) and the Atharvaveda (or Veda of prayer and of the people, as opposed to the priests). As the Rigveda is the oldest, and the other three comprise almost half the verses of the Rigveda, we shall be quoting mostly from that ancient collection which has come down by word of mouth for at least 4000 years. The Upanishads are esoteric treatises composed much later than the Vedas and explaining some of the verses of the Rigveda.
   Rgv. = Ṛgveda (Rigveda); Yjv. = Yajurveda; Athv. = Atharvaveda. ṛ is a semi vowel pronounced almost as the Scottish r.
2. For this eternal recurrence and for the Eternal Principle beyond all speculation, and the idea of Space as the "Eternal Parent" or an Entity, compare the first and second fundamental propositions of *The Secret Doctrine* in vol. I, and pp. 109-111 of vol. I, as well as pp. 176-89 of vol. IV. All references to *The Secret Doctrine* (S.D.) are to the 6 vol. Adyar edition.
3. See S.D. vol. I, p. 322, line 29.
4. See S.D. vol. II, p. 185 for the language of the Gods; and compare vol. II, p. 19.
5. *Maya* in the Rigveda has a different connotation from the later meaning of illusion. It refers to the asuras' creative power, as well as to that power of transformation—later to be used by the demons for deceptive purposes.
6. Compare S.D. vol. I, p. 319: "Man . . . being a compound of the essences of all these celestial Hierarchies. . . ."
7. See "The myth of the 'Fallen Angels' in its various aspects" in S.D. vol. IV.
8. Three outstanding works, among others, wherein is found information concerning the angelic evolution are: *The Secret Doctrine* by H. P. Blavatsky; *The Treatise on Cosmic Fire* by A. A. Bailey; *The Kingdom of the Gods* by G. Hodson.
9. Compare what is said in S.D. IV, p. 187.
10. S.D. vol. II, p. 181, and see following pages.
11. This is well brought out in *The Treatise on Cosmic Fire*. Compare this with Arjuna's vision in the *Bhagavad Gita*.
12. The frequency of the earth is between 7.8 and 8.4 cycles per second. This is the fundamental frequency of the human brain. This shows our close link to earth.
13. See vol. III, p. 399, note 4 of S.D.
14. According to S.D. vol. II, p. 258. Compare also vol. IV, p. 185.

15. The 7 Rivers have many meanings. With Sarasvati as their head they may imply the fountain source of inspiration in a sevenfold division. Compare what the S. D. says on "the seven Rivers of the Sky, the descending Creative Gods, and the seven Rivers of the Earth, the seven primitive mankinds," vol. IV, p. 176-7.

ALCHEMIST AND ANGEL GUIDE
Woodcut from MUSAEUM HERMETICUM
REFORMATUM ET AMPLIFICATUM . . . 1678

"Now the ideal which to the Magician constitutes his greatest treasure, and to which the whole tenor of his life's activities is directed, is the recovery of the knowledge of his Holy Guardian Angel . . . which is real, permanent, and the bountiful, undying source of inspiration and spiritual sustenance."

Israel Regardie

6

The Magician and
the Holy Guardian

ISRAEL REGARDIE

As one of the fundamental pre-requisites to magical training, whether in the Goetic branch or that pertaining to the invocation of the higher Self and the Universal Essences, it has been insisted upon throughout the ages and by all classes of Magicians that purity of life must accompany all Theurgical practice and ceremonial. It seems to be iterated by almost every authority, dogmatically and with certainty by some, somewhat vaguely by others who hand on what they themselves have received half-understood and half-digested from their forbears. All are agreed, nevertheless, that with the pursuit of the magical arts there must be purity and sanctity. I wish to enquire into what is meant by this "purity." Into a discussion of ethics and morals I do not wish to enter, for this would lead me far from the subject of Magic, and I have purposely refrained herein from touching upon this controversial subject which seems to have created more confusion and difference of opinion than almost any other. So far as *purity* in Magic is concerned, however, the student may rest assured with the truth of this one statement, reading into the rest whatever interpretation of morals he so chooses. The whole of one's life should point in one direction, and be concentrated upon and devoted to one set of objectives. When we say, for instance, that milk or butter is pure, what do we mean by this statement? Only this. To the milk we are considering has been added no water or chemicals or any other extraneous substance, and the entirety of its contents is consistent with the main ingredient. Now purity of magical life is to be considered in much the same way. The life of the Magician must above all things be *eka-grata*, one-pointed, and the sum total of his thoughts, emotions and actions, whatever they be, should always be made to interpret and give impetus to the spiritual aspiration. . . .

91

So far as the Magician is concerned this only is important. Whatsoever it is that he is doing, whether eating, drinking or working, that action must be transfigured into a symbol of and dedicated to the service of that Ideal treasured above all wealth and other values in his heart. His whole life should be one continuous concentration. All his training in Dharana and the development of the magical Will otherwise will have been utterly wasted; so much useless energy thrown away as on a dust heap if he does not bring this concentration and this sacramental attitude to bear upon the press of daily life.

Now the ideal which to the Magician constitutes his greatest treasure, and to which the whole tenor of his life's activities is directed, is the recovery of the knowledge of his Holy Guardian Angel, the Augoeides, that nobler part of his consciousness which is real, permanent, and the bountiful, undying source of inspiration and spiritual sustenance. Hence there is, in reality, one perfect ritual in Magic; one goal which takes precedence over all others: the invocation of the Holy Guardian Angel, union with whom should even precede the invocations of the Gods or the Universal Essences, following the procedure laid down by Iamblichus. The soul seeks first and delivers its life into the governance of its Daimon. . . . Union with the Gods and Adonai is sought by means of love, and the commingling of essences is encompassed by surrender of the ego, and the spontaneous renunciation of all that is mean and petty and irrelevant. The supreme invocation implies above all other things the sacrifice of attachment to earthly things. As one who, entering into the interior of the heavenly Adytum, leaves behind him all statues in the outer temple, or as those who enter the inner sanctuary of the Holy of Holies purify themselves, laying aside their garments to enter naked and unashamed, so should the soul approach its goal. . . .

The outcome of the invocation of the Holy Guardian Angel does not result identically with various people. Adonai appears in various manners and guises, according to the individual. "Moreover," Iamblichus also confirms, "the gifts arising from the manifestations are not all of them equal, nor have the same fruit. But the presence of the Gods, indeed, imparts to us health of body, virtue of soul, purity of intellect, and in one word elevates everything in us to its proper principle."[1] Whatsoever the man cherished during his life, and to whatsoever conception of his

---

1. *The Mysteries*. Iamblichus.

Angel he aspired, so will the outcome of the mystical marriage be. According to his love, so will be the offspring. Each student, as he ascends or enters into the mystic Mount Abiegnus of the Rosicrucians, will see before him, stretching forward on the far horizon of the holy land of promise, just that panorama which existed potentially within him before the Vision gave it birth. For the Mount is a symbol for that peak of soul when, gone inward into itself, it draws nigh to its divine root. Then memory and imagination are penetrated and inspired with the superb radiance of another and superior nature. Whatsoever is germinal within the *Ruach* springs into life through the agency and fire of Adonai. Our inspiration will be in like manner to the aspiration, and the type of genius which will be manifested to the world following the mystical union may be poetic, artistic, musical, or any other recognized manifestation. I remember a passage in some one of the Upanishads which deals with this same theme. If one approaches the Self which is Brahma believing that it is Power and Might, that one becomes might and power. Let him, however, approach it seeing in its majesty supernal knowledge and wisdom, and he as a result becomes filled with the Wisdom of the Self. And if he aspires towards it as the creator of Song, he likewise becomes the singer. In other words, just what the Theurgist has conceived in imagination his Angel to be, in just that form does the Angel manifest, welling up from the deepest font of being within the heart as revelation and inspiration. Should there be aspiration towards the Angel solely as the symbol of love and peace and kindliness so does Adonai show to the world that gracious and benign aspect. St. Francis of Assisi is the most outstanding instance of the one, as is the Buddha who aspired to Wisdom that he might find for mankind the solution of their woes and sorrows, the symbol of the other. And this supplies the answer to the question "If Mysticism and Magic endow a man with genius, why is it that so many successful Mystics and Magicians seem to manifest not one scrap of genius?" It is because their aspiration has been a humble one; to become no great figure on earth was their desire, neither did they aspire towards any of the forms of Art. Of their lives they made a sublime work of artistic creation, and applied their inspiration to the walk of everyday life, appearing but humble men and women of gentle mien and aspect. But like the cowled and gowned Hermit of the Tarot they bore the angel light within them, secretly, that all with whom they came into contact day by day might be blessed with Adonai's love, and impressed with the holiness of the spirit and the purity of its effulgence rather than with their own personal attainment. This is the key; for when one inflames oneself in prayer towards the Holy Guardian Angel, as the secret aspiration of the soul will have been, upon that will the Angel seize, in the ecstasy of bliss which ravishes the soul away, to convey his manifestation to the world. . . .

Thus the supreme object of all magical ritual is the communion with the Higher Self. For every man is that the most important step, and no other compares with it in importance and validity until this one union has been accomplished. It brings with it new powers, new extensions of consciousness, and a new vision of life. It throws a brilliant ray of illumination on the hitherto dark phases of life, removing from the mind the clouds which inhibit the glory of the spiritual light. With the attainment of the Vision and the Perfume one sees, as did Jacob Boehme perceive, the entire field of natural existence literally ablaze with a divine incomparable splendour, so that even the trees lift up their heads to the skies, and the grasses in the green meadows chant gently in praise and thanksgiving, offering hymns of glory to the Supernal Light.

In the fullness of the Knowledge and Conversation of the Holy Guardian Angel, the Theurgist is able to foresee with the extension of the light of reason what further steps are to be taken in the great quest which has not ended with the illumination of the Angel, but one, he sees, which has only just begun. The whole universe is a vast range of spiritual hierarchies, and the Holy Guardian Angel stands on but one rung of that great ladder which extends above and below into Infinity. The Theurgist perceives that he is but a spark thrown off from the spiritual essence of a God, and amazingly brilliant though his own Angel be, if, as the principles of his Art teach him, that Angel is but a spark, how much more glorious is the God who gave it birth? Thus his aspiration under the guidance of his Angel is ever directed upwards and onwards, furthering his inner vision to the One Life, to *Ain Soph*, the Unnameable Source of all. Nature does not proceed by jerks or with unbridgeable gaps or leaps. Hers is a graduated march, and this steady forward surge of progress the Theurgist seeks to emulate. Union with *Ain Soph* cannot be effected at once; he must slowly climb the ladder of Life, uniting himself on each rung in love and wisdom with each superior hierarch, until the Boundless Eternal Light is reached. Iamblichus conceives the same procedure in these words: "And when the soul has received Him as its leader, the daemon immediately presides over the soul, giving completion to its lives, and binds it to body when it descends. He likewise governs the common animal of the soul, and directs its peculiar life, and imparts to us the principles of all our thought and reasonings. We also perform such things as he suggests to our intellect, and he continues to govern us till, through sacerdotal Theurgy, we obtain a God for the inspective guardian and leader of the soul. For then the daemon either yields or delivers his government to a more excellent nature, or is subjected to him as contributing to his guardianship, or in some way is ministrant to him as to his lord."

It is not so much that the Holy Guardian Angel yields the government of the human soul to the presence of the God, but that the soul, already united with the Angel and thus forming one complete being, unites likewise with the God. Or it may be that the Angel who has taken unto itself the life of the soul is correspondingly assumed into the large and superior life of the God, who to the Angel is as the Angel was formerly to the soul. Proceeding yet further, Iamblichus adds: "Moreover, after it (that is Theurgy) has conjoined the soul to the several parts of the universe, and to the total divine powers which pass through it; then it leads the soul to, and deposits it in the whole Demiurgos, and causes it to be independent of all matter, and to be co-united with the eternal reason alone. But my meaning is, that it peculiarly connects the soul with the self-begotten and self-moved God, and with the all-sustaining intellectual and all-adorning powers of the God, and likewise with that power of him which elevates to truth, and with his self-perfect, effective, and other demiurgic powers; so that the theurgic soul becomes perfectly established in the energies and demiurgic intellections of these powers. Then also it inserts the soul in the whole demiurgic God. And this is the end with the Egyptians of the sacerdotal elevation of the soul to divinity."

A greater, more complete vision could hardly be found. Theurgy proposes to take a man, strip him gradually so to speak of all the inessentials, finally penetrating to the Soul within. Then this Soul within is exalted and uplifted, ever so gradually, till it finds its own Sovereign Lord, the Beloved. Lifting it ever higher and higher, while yet human and in a body of flesh and blood, the man is elevated beyond the heavens, entering into spiritual congress and fellowship with the Powers which are the Universe,

the Sources which give life and sustenance to the whole of manifested existence. Ever beyond them it soars and ascends, tran-
scending even the Gods who came forth at the first blush of the
golden dawn, until with an incomparable ecstasy of silence it
returns to the Great Source of All.

7

Angels, Holy and Unholy
The Gnostic Alternative to
Mainstream Angelology

STEPHAN A. HOELLER

William Blake, on the concluding plates (22-24) of his *The Marriage of Heaven and Hell*, presents us with a startling image. A devil enveloped in a bright flame and an angel seated on a cloud are engaged in a discussion. The devil, after opening his discourse by asserting the divinity of humankind, and subsequently being rebuked by the angel, proceeds to state with great eloquence how Jesus, "the greatest man," disregarded the Law and acted always on the basis of his own spiritual impulse and intuition. The angel, shamed and convinced by his opponent's argument, stretches forth his arms and, embracing the devil's flame, is consumed, only to arise in a transformed manifestation. Commenting on this image, the noted Jungian psychologist June Singer writes:

In one evanescent moment the Devil, boldly with eyes afire, or subtly disguised, clasps a shining Angel in his embrace. Opposites which struggled within the spirit of man while he walked the earth are united now in one vast paroxysm. Contraries are no longer set one against the other. Differences are resolved into a cloud that dissipates upward. A small mound of dust remains upon the ground.[1]

Angels of light, struggling with and ultimately becoming reconciled with fallen angels of darkness—where did the poet find precedent for such imagery? According to his friend Crabb Robinson, William Blake derived many of his ideas from certain ancient heterodox sources, for "he repeated the doctrines of the Gnostics with consistency." The Gnostic religion, condemned as a heresy since the third and fourth centuries, acted as a source of inspiration to many members of the creative elite of Western spirituality. It is a matter of record that this alternative spirituality had much to say on the subject of angels, whether celestial or infernal.

ANGEL WITH THE KEY OF THE ABYSS *Albrecht Dürer*

"Humans act as resonating agents between transcendence and terrestrial confinement. . . . Inspired and urged on by wise and helpful angels from above, and shackled and enslaved by tyrannical and unwise angels from below, we undergo troubled dreams . . . the knowledge that awakens us from these illusory dreams is . . . interior, revelatory experience."

Stephan Hoeller

Foundations of Gnostic Angelology

Gnostic spirituality distinguishes itself from orthodox Judaism, Christianity and Islam chiefly by way of its cosmogony and theogony, which are based on the doctrine of emanation rather than on that of creation. The material universe and the beings which populate it, visible and invisible, so declared the Gnostics, were not created by a personal and singular deity. They were emanated or poured forth from an original spiritual unity which thus divided itself into a plurality. Among the large number of spiritual entities and worlds which issued from the original source, some remained in close contact with their transcendental point of origin. These are angelic beings of light, who inhabit regions of transcendental glory and beauty, and who are benignly disposed toward those humans who aspire toward conscious union with the ultimate source of all. Other cosmic spirits, however, became estranged from their ultimate source. Having forgotten their true descent, they came to look upon themselves as separate, self-existing rulers (Gr. *archontes*) in their own right. One of their number, a fallen or alienated angelic being, even became so arrogant as to blasphemously assert that he is the only god, and that there are no other gods before him. It is of this lesser or intermediate godling, who is in reality no more than a great angel whose mind became darkened by arrogance and alienation, that the creation myth of Genesis speaks as God the creator.

The *system* (Gr. *cosmos*) within which material creation is contained was fashioned not by the true God or ultimate unitary reality, but rather by alienated angelic intelligences, possessing inferior spiritual powers. Familiar as they were with the story contained in Genesis, the Gnostics pointed to the use of the first person plural in that account: "Let us make man in our image, after our likeness." "Behold, the man has become like one of us, knowing good and evil." The agency that expelled humankind from Paradise, after having first confined Adam and Eve therein, was seen as a collective force of tyrant-angels.

Gnostic angelology is thus founded on the myth of a precosmic as well as cosmic division of being, which is reflected in the existence of celestial angelic hierarchies which are allied to and serve the first and original source of being. The division is further shown by the presence in the cosmos of imperfect angelic spirits, who in their ignorance have arrogated powers to themselves which they are able to exercise only unwisely and at the peril of all beings who aspire to spiritual freedom.

99

Stephan A. Hoeller

Angels and the Human Predicament

The human being stands in a unique relationship to the cosmic duality. Owing to a special act of grace on the part of the feminine aspect of the true deity (known usually as Sophia), humanity possesses within itself a spark of the highest spiritual consciousness. Within each human being there is a slumbering spark of ultimate holiness and power. Humankind may be personified as Adam, who lies asleep in a stupor of unconsciousness, his powers of self-awareness stupefied by the system of illusion created by the tyrant angels. The indwelling potential of freedom present in unconscious humanity indicates, however, the possibility of an awakening from the stupefaction.

Humans act as resonating agents between transcendence and terrestrial confinement. Until salvific revelatory experience awakens us to our true calling of spiritual freedom, we experience the universe as a vast prison. Systems imposed upon us by the tyrant angels bring enslaving laws and rules. These appear at times in the material guise of the laws of nature and at other times as psychic laws proclaimed by religion and society. Humanity is thus subject to the dark tyranny of the angels who rule the cosmic system, while at the same time it is prompted and assisted by angels of light, who are not subservient to illusory systems but serve the true reality of ultimate being. Inspired and urged on by wise and helpful angels from above, and shackled and enslaved by tyrannical and unwise angels from below, we undergo troubled dreams as we strive to shake off our intoxication induced by the deceptions perpetrated by the tyrant angels. The knowledge that awakens us from these illusory dreams is not arrived at either by moral rectitude or by cognition by philosophical means, but through interior, revelatory experience. This *Gnosis* (knowledge) is not an accession of information of scientific data or metaphysical and theological theory but a transformative modification of the entirety of the human being.

It is well known that the primary meaning of the word "angel" is "messenger." This messengership, said the Gnostics, is expressed by the hierarchies of benevolent angels in two ways: first, by conveying revelatory impulses, designed to fan the fallen spark of the human spirit into the blaze of Gnosis; and second, by uniting the human soul with a kind of celestial self, frequently referred to as the "twin angel" or in more recent parlance "guardian angel." The awakening of an individual human soul unto Gnosis is not merely a personal experience; it is a cosmic event. Since the universal and divine effort is directed toward the restoration of the unity and wholeness of being, accomplishing such wholeness in an individual human helps repair the cosmic flaw and the works of the "heresy of separateness." The salvation of the world is the Gnosis of the human being. It is in this sense that we must understand the saying of Jesus (who, as a messenger of the transcendental Father, was himself at times called an angel by the Gnostics) contained in the *Gospel According to Thomas* (Logion 22):

Jesus said to them: When you make the two one, and when you make the inner as the outer and the outer as the inner and above as the below, and when you make the male and the female into a single one, so that the male will not be only male and the female not be only female, when you make eyes in the place of an eye, and a hand in the place of a hand, and a foot in the place of a foot, and an image in the place of an image then shall you enter the Kingdom.

The Mystery of the Guardian Angel

One of the most endearing teachings of Roman Catholic doctrine is undoubtedly the one concerning the guardian angel. From early times onward the fathers and mystics of the Church taught that every human being is associated with a special and individual angel, and that this angel guards the spiritual life of the soul and presents it in the end to the Godhead at the gate of heaven. The Church Father St. Ambrose stated what became normative advice to all believers: "We should pray to the angel who is our Guardian." The great medieval mystic, St. Bernard of Clairveaux, admonished his monks in the following manner:

In whatever place you may be, in whatever secret recess you may hide, think of your Guardian Angel. . . . If we truly love our Guardian Angel, we cannot fail to have boundless confidence in his powerful intercession with God and firm faith in his willingness to help us. . . . Many of the saints made it a practice never to undertake anything without first seeking the advice of their Guardian Angel.[2]

Even more portentous are the references of numerous Roman Catholic authorities concerning the role of the guardian angel in connection with the condition of the human soul, whether it be purgatorially earthbound or beatifically ascending to heavenly freedom. Thus John Henry Cardinal Newman writes of the guardian angel's consoling words addressed to the soul in purgatory, which might just as well apply to the purgatory of earthly existence:

> Farewell, but not forever, brother dear,
> Be brave and patient on thy bed of sorrow;
> Swiftly shall pass thy night of trial here,
> And I will come and wake thee on the morrow.[3]

And, triumphantly does the guardian angel exclaim, on the occasion of the soul's entry into heaven, in another poem by Cardinal Newman:

> My Father gave
> In charge to me
> This child of earth
> E'en from his birth.
> To serve and save.
> Alleluia,
> And saved is he.
>
> This child of clay
> To me was given,
> To rear and train
> By sorrow and pain
> In the narrow way
> Alleluia,
> From earth to heaven.[4]

These examples may suffice to indicate the nature and significant role attributed to the guardian angel by the largest branch of Christendom. It is important to note by the same token that the teachings concerning the guardian angel are rooted in a fascinating early Gnostic mythologem concerning the "twin angel," briefly noted earlier. Gnostic documents reveal that within the framework of the psychology, or more exactly the pneumatology, of these early, mystical Christians, it was generally understood that every human personality was attached to a celestial spirit, the twin angel. Great personages of exceptional qualifications had frequent and conscious contact with this overshadowing angelic genius, while ordinary mortals hoped to encounter and achieve union with it at the end of their earthly journeys.

In the Gnostic codex, usually called *Pistis Sophia*, a charming tale is told by Mary, the mother of Jesus, concerning a visitation received by him at a young age. The visitor, who was a spirit that looked exactly like Jesus, inquired where he might find "Jesus, my brother." When Jesus and his "twin" met, they embraced and became one. In the life-story of the Persian Gnostic prophet

Mani (215-277 A.D.) we read that when Mani was twelve years old he had a vision of his "twin," a godlike angel, who came from "the High God, King of the gardens of light," and was bidden to withdraw from the religious sect to which he belonged and prepare himself for a future spiritual mission. At the age of twenty-four, his twin angel appeared once again to Mani and instructed him to go forth and proclaim his prophetic mission and message. When Mani was about to undergo martyrdom in prison, the twin angel appeared to him for the third time and, uniting with him, bore him up to heaven. In captivity and under torture, Mani insisted that he had no human teacher but received his whole doctrine from his "twin," whom he described as a God-sent angel who in a mysterious way was associated exclusively with himself.

Bridal Chamber and Union with the Twin Angel

The Gnostic teachers of the first three centuries did not perceive the twin angel as relevant only to a few outstanding messengers of divine light, such as Jesus and Mani. The noted Gnostic writer, poet and prophet Valentinus (c.a. 100-175) and his school perfected a mystery rite wherein persons of all walks of life could obtain contact with and ultimately be united with their own twin angels. This rite, called the "bride chamber" (or bridal chamber) represented the highest and ultimate initiatory step in the progress of the soul of the Gnostic while still in earthly embodiment. The human soul of the candidate for the bridal chamber was envisioned as the bride of the twin angel, and the passing of human consciousness from the worldly plane into the realm of spirit was seen as a wedding feast. The Church Father Clement of Alexandria, describing the Gnostic sacrament of the bride chamber, wrote: "The pneumatics [those who have become committed to the spirit] then lay aside their souls, and at the same time as the woman receives her bridegroom, each of them receives his bridegroom, the angel."[5]

According to the *Gospel of Philip*, a crucial treatise within the Nag Hammadi collection discovered in 1945 in Egypt, the bride chamber is the culminating fulfillment of the mysteries, or sacraments instituted by Jesus for the liberation of human souls (Logion 68):

The Lord did everything in a mystery; a baptism and a chrism and a eucharist and the redemption and a bride chamber.

And, recounting the words of Jesus, delivered at the time of the Last Supper, the same Gnostic gospel states (Logion 26):

He said on that day in the Eucharist: Thou who hast joined the perfect, the light, with the Holy Spirit, do unite the angels with us also, the images.

It is clear that the highest flowering of Gnosticism, as represented by Valentinus, looked forward to the union of the human soul with its supernal, angelic counterpart, and that, moreover, it also believed that Jesus himself was a facilitator and advocate of this union. Echoes of this sublime mystery affecting the union of the human and the angelic may be found in such late Gnostic and related disciplines as the Cathar sacrament of the *Consolamentum* and the "Knowledge and Conversation of the Holy Guardian Angel" known to practitioners of the High Magic of the Renaissance.

In modern terms this union may be approached as a union of the personal ego with the Self known to Jungian psychology, although such psychological explanations can never be said to exhaust the sublime meaning of the mystery at hand. The Gnostic mythologem of the angelic counterpart of every human soul, and the essential need for the union of the human with the angelic, are matters worthy of the continued consideration of psychologists and of students of mystical religiosity.

When William Blake conceived of his image of the union of an angel and a devil (as noted at the beginning of this essay), he undoubtedly realized the intrapsychic implications of his image. It has often been noted in traditions of neo-Gnostic alternative spirituality that the fallen Luciferian hosts are in fact none other than the multitude of human souls, separated from their divine source. As long as we are unable to unite with our twin in heaven, we suffer the agonies of the infernal legions who languish for aeons deprived of the vision of God. Inspired by the early example of the Gnostics, the esotericists of the Western tradition have always held that alienation rather than sin characterizes the human tragedy. However, this alienation is not beyond remedy, and the lower and the higher, even the demonic and the angelic in human nature, may be brought into an abiding union by *gnosis*. This is the great promise of Gnostic teaching and more particularly of Gnostic angelology. In an age when the deterioration of the quality of life and the excesses of technology often lead us to believe that our habitat is not far removed from a sulphurous inferno, this ancient metaphor may appear increasingly appropriate. Be this as it may, the human-demonic and the angelic-divine within us and within the fabric of the universe still await their bride chamber, and look to the day when all shall be infinite and holy, and when the seamless garment of the Fullness shall be restored.

Notes

1. *The Unholy Bible;* Blake, Jung and the Collective Unconscious (Boston: Sigo Press, 1986), p. 1.
2. Quoted in *St. Michael and the Angels* (Rockford, Illinois: Tan Books, 1983), p. 36.
3. Ibid., p. 41.
4. Ibid., p. 40.
5. Clement of Alexandria, *Ex Theodoto* 64, 1.

ABRAHAM'S SACRIFICE Rembrandt
"Angels have faith in the possibilities of every human being because they can see into the eternal core of our existence and behold there the unique, divine intention which lies behind every individual."

Jim Hindes

8

The Hierarchies:
An Outline of
Rudolf Steiner's Teaching

JAMES H. HINDES

Born in 1861, Rudolf Steiner was an Austrian philosopher who made a name for himself in Germany as a man of letters, author of several books on philosophy and the editor of Goethe's scientific writings. In 1901 at the age of forty he began to lecture and write on esoteric subjects, having found an audience in the Theosophical Society. In 1912 he separated from the Theosophical Society and began lecturing in the newly formed Anthroposophical Society. In numerous books and thousands of lectures, most of which were transcribed and then published in book form, he described the activities of spiritual beings and the hierarchies of angels in amazing detail.

My intention here is merely to sketch the main outlines of his teaching on the hierarchies. Somewhat more space is given to his description of the Archai and the Archangel Michael because of their significance for today.

According to Steiner there are nine ranks of beings (often referred to, in groups of three, as the first, second and third hierarchies) above humanity and below the Trinity. There are at least two possible sets of names: those of the Christian esoteric tradition (with its Greek or Hebrew and English forms) and the names coined by Steiner.

First Hierarchy:		*Names given by Rudolf Steiner*
Seraphim		Spirits of Love
Cherubim		Spirits of the Harmonies
Thrones		Spirits of Will

Second Hierarchy:		
Kyriotetes	(Dominions)	Spirits of Wisdom
Dynamis	(Mights or Virtues)	Spirits of Movement
Exusiai	(Powers)	Spirits of Form

Third Hierarchy:

Archai	(Principalities)	Spirits of Personality or Time
Archangels		Fire-Spirits
Angels		Sons of Life or of Twilight

To understand how these nine orders of angelic beings are related to God, the One—also known as the Trinity or Three in One—we can think of how the human self is related to the body. In a sense the self stands above and rules the body with all its limbs. But at the same time the I lives within the body and permeates the limbs. This is especially the case when we are fully awake and focused in order to accomplish something in the world. Shaking hands, for example, means more than a mere encounter between skin and skin. In such encounters the hand is an expression of the whole human being. Sometimes a glance or the look on a person's face can express the I. The body with its individual parts is not the human being but serves to reveal him or her. Similarly, according to Steiner God uses the orders of the angels as body and limbs to create and maintain the world, in the same way that a person makes use of arms and hands to work on earth.

The First Hierarchy

The work of the Seraphim, Cherubim and Thrones is the most difficult to imagine. Steiner (1970a, p. 58) says:

Beholding with the soul, we actually see how the first stage of the realization of the divine plan is achieved in the down-flow of the fire-substance by the Thrones. The Thrones appear to us as beings endowed with the power to transpose into a primary reality what has been first conceived by the Cherubim. This takes place because the Thrones allowed their own substance of primeval cosmic fire to flow into the space allotted to the new cosmic system. We can picture it quite clearly by saying that an ancient solar system disappeared, died away. Within this ancient system the ranks of the Seraphim, Cherubim, Thrones attained their highest perfection. Now, in accordance with the indications of the lofty Trinity, they chose a sphere within cosmic space and said that here we can make a beginning. At this moment, the Seraphim received the aims of this new solar system. The Cherubim worked them out, and the Thrones gave forth primeval fire, their own substance, into the appointed sphere. This will help us grasp the primal beginnings of our solar system.

Every variety of substance in the universe was provided by the Thrones. Beginning as a kind of spiritual "light-materiality," these substances became concentrated and intensified through the ages. The impenetrability of the hard earth as we know it is the end result of that evolution. The spiritual origin of all matter is hinted at in the theories of modern physics when the subatomic constituents of matter are described as nothing more than mathematical structures, essentially mental. Time also came into existence through the Thrones. Steiner (1953a, pp. 15-16) says:

It can now be observed that out of this rigidity, this timeless character of the infinite sea of courage with its beings whom we call Spirits of Will came the beings of other hierarchies. . . . Through the sacrifice made by the Spirits of Will to the Cherubim, time is born. . . . These are the spirits of personality, known to us as Archai.

The Second Hierarchy

The second hierarchy, the Kyriotetes, Dynamis and Exusiai, give the universe a wisdom-filled and meaningful form. Their work is not limited to the inner life of human beings as is the case with the third hierarchy. The name given by Steiner to this hierarchy's first rank, Spirits of Wisdom, refers to the wisdom-filled structures found in the external world of nature.

The Kyriotetes are full of wonder as they behold the sacrifice of the Thrones. They transform this sacrificed spiritual substance into the forms and shapes of the solar system and the planets. Alone, the Kyriotetes cannot create existence, but they can awaken the life therein. For the beings beneath them, they send out a spiritual light in which truth, wisdom and the good are still undifferentiated. They stand far above the possibility of evil.

The Dynamis or Spirits of Movement regulate the circling of the planets and all the movements governed thereby. Their inner life is characterized by a productive resignation or submission to world destiny. The Exusiai or spirits of form are referred to in the Bible as the Elohim. Relating his own teachings to the description given in the Bible, Steiner (1959, p. 57) says:

After the Elohim through their higher organizing powers had brought light into existence, they then appointed to his post *Yom*, the first of the time spirits, or the Archai. Thus the spiritual beings whom we call Spirits of Personality, or Archai, are the same as those called in Genesis Time-Intervals, Days *Yamim*. . . . They carry out what the Elohim direct from their higher standpoint.

The Exusiai continue the shaping of spiritual substance begun by the Kyriotetes and create the clear forms of the solar system.

They do this with the planets seen as wholes and with all sense-perceptible matter. Crystal structures, the basis for all matter, originate with these beings. If we think of all the possible forms and shapes of fluid and air-flow with vortices, as well as solid creations, then we glimpse the new and multiplex plane of forms created by the Exusiai.

Together with the Dynamis, the Exusiai bring about the spin of the earth; i.e., the rhythm of day and night. This alternation, combined with the fact that they continue to work within the physical and spiritual light, makes it possible for us to be conscious of ourselves as selves. For the development of the spiritual kernel of the human being known as the "ego" or "I" begins with our consciousness of things, external objects, which allows us to awaken in this world. In this sense the Exusiai or Elohim are the fathers of the divine human ego, which provides the basis for our earthly sense of self. They have made our bodies to stand upright and given us the countenance in which God seeks his image. It was the Elohim who said, "Let us make man in our own image, after our likeness." In our souls, and minds, they create clear and definite concepts, such as are found in mathematics and logic.

Abraham was led by a spiritual being from the ranks of the Elohim. Steiner (1981, p. 178) says:

Elohim ... belong to the hierarchy of Powers or Spirits of Form. ... Elohim is the collective name for the beings of the sun; ... they chose the sun as their dwelling—not as their sphere of work. Christ, the highest of the Elohim, is their regent. However, he does not belong to the hierarchies but to the Trinity. In Christ we have a being which is so mighty that he influences all the parts of our solar system.

Although the Elohim dwelled on the sun, the work of one of them, known as Yahweh on Earth, was reflected, spiritually speaking, off the moon and then into the new nation and religion. The purpose of that nation was to prepare as perfect a body as possible for God, in the person of the Logos, the Son God, to incarnate in the body of Jesus of Nazareth on the Earth. The guiding folk spirit of the ancient Hebrew nation, the Archangel Michael, acted as the countenance of Yahweh, who was himself the countenance of Christ.*

---

*This descent of the logos through the Hebrew religion and people is described in detail in the twelve lectures on *The Gospel of St. Matthew* given by Steiner at Bern in September, 1910.

The Third Hierarchy

The third hierarchy, Angels, Archangels and Archai, are close to humanity and can work into and through human beings. Steiner (1961a, p. 112) says:

The Angels are therefore actually the leaders of men, their guides, preparing them, and there exists an intimate connection between what gradually develops in man and the task of these Angel beings.

Angels are traditionally pictured with wings, indicating that they have freedom of flight in spirit, while human consciousness is bound to earthly things. Although any given angelic being may display masculine or feminine characteristics at different times, such beings are, of course, neither male nor female. The Greek word *angelos*, from which the word "angel" is derived, means "messenger." Angels fly up to God and bring messages down to earth. Because they also survey great periods of time, they know the meaning of all the events in a person's destiny from a higher perspective. This knowledge enables them to guide.

Angels are also described as musicians. Music can help us understand how spiritual forces work into earthly conditions. Music (not to be confused with the movement of air molecules), like the meaning of spoken words, is "above" physical matter, which it uses as a vehicle. Though invisible and not even physical, nevertheless music can be experienced in the physical world. An audience can be awakened, calmed, harmonized, comforted and strengthened by a symphony. Music can provide nourishment for the soul.

In the Apocalypse, angels are described blowing trumpets, a picture that is particularly revealing. Notes are created on trumpets by making metal, one of the hardest substances, vibrate. Angels have the power to make earthly beings "vibrate." Creative spiritual impulses constantly flow like music into the world. At times harmonious, at other times dissonant, spiritual forces "sound forth" into human lives, giving new impulses and shaping reality.

Like musicians in an orchestra, angels are constantly active. The spiritual forces which come forth from them are tuned to one another like the tones from the instruments in an orchestra. This "heavenly music" sets the world and human souls vibrating with inner movements, which are experienced as insights, soul-moods, impulses of will and inspirations.

James H. Hindes

Guardian Angels

Steiner holds that every individual human being has his or her own angel, sometimes called a "guardian angel." In our time it is particularly inadequate to say that an angel's task is to "protect." Our earthly consciousness simply does not allow us to judge what constitutes "protection" from a *spiritual* perspective. It may appear that a guardian angel failed to protect someone when actually the angel may have worked very hard to arrange a painful yet awakening experience.

As human beings, we can remember only a fraction of the sense perceptions, feelings and thoughts we have had in our lives. However, events which have escaped our memory continue to live in the encompassing, unlimited consciousness of our guardian angel. He sees through and understands all our depths and shallows, as well as all the stations of our lives.* He remembers the hopes, desires, ideals, battles, doubts and darkness to which we have given ourselves and with which we have struggled. His task is to balance the necessities and possibilities of destiny, which have resulted from our experiences, actions and wishes. In order to do this he needs a complete overview of our past lives, our present life and a view of what powers and tasks lie in the future. Angels create and shape what meets us in our lives; they lead us to events and experiences we need and to the people we must meet. They "inspire" within us moods, thoughts, insights and impulses that further our development.

Our angel can see what events are necessary every day as a consequence of preceding deeds and experiences. Every time we leave opportunities unused or take side paths, he must step in to correct and help. Yet angels have faith in the possibilities of every human being because they can see into the eternal core of our existence and behold there the unique, divine intention which lies behind every individual.

There are two gates to the realm of angels. Through one we can move toward them; through the other they can come to us. At night before sleeping we can look back over the day, recalling events, seeking to find the wisdom behind them. Our gratitude for what comes to meet us strengthens the connection with our angel and makes it easier for him to help. Prayer before sleeping prepares our souls for the inspirations we can receive during

---

*Use of the masculine pronouns is for convenience only as angels are neither male nor female.

sleep. The other gate opens in the morning upon waking. Depending upon the condition of our soul upon falling asleep, we will be more or less able to become conscious of the "plan for the day," of the gifts from the spirit waiting for us. These two gates correspond to the gates of birth and death and to the two sides of angels. Child-like purity, innocence and openness of heart reflect one side of angels, while the wisdom of age, austerity, the majesty of the breath of eternity reflect the other. Popular culture has lost any sense of the majesty of angels. With few exceptions, they are portrayed as cute and innocent beings of light.

Our actions can help or hinder the work of angels. Steiner (1967, p. 233) says:

You see, here a new element enters when we speak of Angels. And, in fact, it all depends on the individual human being—depends on his attitude, on his entire world of feelings concerning the spiritual world—as to whether or not his Angel accompanies him when he leaves his physical and etheric bodies behind and goes into sleep. He goes with children, however, with people who have achieved a certain maturity, it does, indeed, depend upon the attitude of the individual whether or not the individual has a relationship in his soul with his Angel. And if this relationship is not present, if he only believes in material existence, if he has nothing but thoughts about matter, then the Angel does not accompany him. . . . You see we come here to an area where the human attitude or frame of mind is decisive for an important experience within human life: whether or not a human being can participate during sleep in the presence of his Angel.

One cannot say, well, if there are Angels we do not need to believe in them in our waking state for they will certainly take an interest in us when we sleep.—No, they do not accompany us if we deny their existence during the day.

Merely being aware of their existence opens the soul to their influence.

In a sense our guardian angels are closer to us than we are to ourselves. Because they participate in our feelings, thoughts and will impulses, their own destiny is intimately bound up with ours. They do not live in lonely heights but have, so to speak, bowed down to accompany us. And because human destiny is so often filled with the darkness of passion and tragedy, this angelic "con-descension" can only mean a great sacrifice for them.

Angels guide communities as well as individuals. Marriage, a kind of "community of life," provides a vehicle for the "incarnation" of an angelic being. The quality of a marriage will be influenced by the couple's consciousness of the moral and spiritual side of life, which in turn determines the amount of influence an angel can exert. Clubs, associations, schools and of course, church congregations also have spiritual beings, from the ranks of angels, indwelling and uniting the consciousness of their members. Some angels are guardian spirits of great political leaders and actually have a responsibility for whole communities; they must work in a fashion similar to that of Archangels, whose responsibility is to guide whole nations.

Archangels

Expressed pictorially, Archangels have larger wings and more eyes. They can survey not only the destiny of a single individual but the biography of a folk, nation, people or language. Archangels are concerned with the history of a nation, what it can give humanity and how it must develop in order to do so. Steiner (1953b, p. 116) says:

You know that what is called folk-soul, race-soul, has become a somewhat abstract idea to-day. Many think nowadays that the individual soul of man that dwells in his body is the actual reality. And if one speaks of German, French, Russian national-souls, people look on that as more or less an abstraction, as a comprehensive concept, embracing the characteristics which the individual members of these nations possess. To the occultist this is not so at all. What one calls the folk-soul is to him an absolutely independent entity. It is only that in our present earth-existence the folk soul is purely a spiritual being, perceptible only to one who can ascend to the astral plane; there you could not deny it, for there it is present as an actual living being.

Just as we have sense perceptions, experiencing colors, shapes, etc., Archangels have as their field of perception the souls of people belonging to a particular folk or nation. This is a wide, exceptionally differentiated "landscape," in which the inner selves of human beings shine forth as individual centers of light. And just as we work within our field of perception, so do Archangels work in their field, in the souls and spirits of human beings. If we imagine a being great enough to encompass and perceive the souls of 250 million Americans, for example, and simultaneously send them thoughts, attitudes and impulses, we have an idea of the magnitude of consciousness of an Archangel. But they do more. From higher spiritual worlds they receive the souls that are to be born into a people, permeate these so that "Germans," "Englishmen," "Russians" or "Americans" develop with the characteristic soul qualities of that people. Then they release the souls after death and hand them over to a higher power that has nothing to do with nationality.

An Archangel carries within his consciousness everything belonging to the destiny of a people. To help a nation achieve its intended ends, he inspires individuals and groups in specific ways. What they then accomplish under his guidance advances a whole people toward its goal. Of course, the unfolding of a nation's destiny does not happen automatically. Human weaknesses and incapacities interweave with divine guidance to create error and false paths for nations, just as much as for individuals. There is ample room for tragedy of every kind.

Individuals and groups constantly rise up from the ranks of a people to become vehicles for specific tasks of a "folk spirit." In the past a widely respected and revered royal court could serve as an important tool for the Archangel, provided, of course, the kings and princes (or those guiding them) possessed a genuine connection to the spiritual world and folk spirit. Politics is not the only field in which a folk spirit can be served. Especially today the inspirations of Archangels can be found in the works of artists, writers, philosophers and teachers. In addition, individual deeds can signify more than mere personal destiny. Higher beings can work through individuals, despite personal weaknesses.

Adversary Powers

Angels sometimes play a role as adversary powers. At different stages in the evolution of the earth, various orders of angels, beginning with the Dynamis, "stepped out" of the normal order of evolution.* This is the "Fall" that preceded the Fall of Adam and Eve. These fallen beings continue to exist and influence the earth and humanity. Their influence, however, works against the intentions of the other angelic beings. Working primarily from two different directions—called Luciferic (too much light) and Ahrimanic (too much darkness)—these fallen spiritual beings originated evil and became the adversaries of human evolution. However, their activities, although representing an evil which must always be opposed, can also be seen as serving God's ultimate

---

*See *Occult Science, An Outline,* Chapter four, and *The Spiritual Hierarchies and their Reflection in the Physical World,* lecture ten, for a detailed description of the evolution of the adversary beings.

purpose. They provide the resistance which human beings must overcome in order to achieve the goal of evolution on earth: true freedom and love. Steiner (1970a, p. 139) says:

> How should man be integrated into the ranks of the hierarchies? After the archangels and angels, the arch-messengers and messengers, we shall have to place among the hierarchical ranks the Spirit of Freedom or the Spirit of Love. Counting from above downward, this is the tenth hierarchy, which, though still in a process of development, nevertheless belongs to the divine hierarchies.

Freedom and love are specifically the mission of the human race, the tenth hierarchy. The Good is not mere innocence. It is an active power created by the struggle against adversaries who would enslave human beings for their own purposes.

Steiner says that the destinies of nations and individuals must also reckon with the intentions of evil beings. The concrete events that occur in our destiny, both personal and national, result from three forces: angels and archangels working in a positive sense to inspire and lead; evil beings striving to fulfill their own purposes; and the decisions of human beings with their strengths and weaknesses. The final result of this confluence of forces is increasingly in our hands. In Steiner's view our consciousness is decisive.

In the realm of nations, the adversaries seek to create feelings of chauvinism, false patriotism and irrational prejudice. The division of humanity into different races came about when certain "abnormal" Spirits of Movement or Dynamis, who had "stepped out" of their normal progression of development, worked upon humanity from the vantage point of Spirits of Form or Exusiai, rather than from the higher station where normal development would have brought them. Certainly it is easy to see how the existence of different races has provided the adversaries with opportunities to awaken evil in human hearts.

Steiner said that the concept of race was not to be confused with that of folk, people or nation. A people can consist of more than one race and a race can be split up into more than one folk or people. In the future, race will become less and less significant as a factor in human evolution. Steiner (1953b, p. 145) says:

> The ancient connection of race and blood will be increasingly lost. Mankind becomes free of physical ties in order to form groups from the aspect of the spirit. It was a bad habit . . . to speak of races as if they would always remain. The concept of race loses its meaning in the immediate future.

Archangels and Language

Some Archangels are responsible for the development of languages. Languages do not always coincide with nations or people. The German people have a language in common with Austrians and German-speaking Swiss but belong to a different nation with a different destiny. The Swiss, on the other hand are a people with several different languages. Other examples can be found around the globe. Folk spirits must coordinate their work with that of the Archangels and certain Exusiai, who also guide languages. Steiner (1970c, p. 44) says:

We must not ascribe the birth of language solely to these beings who subtly work into the folk temperament and who, as beings two stages above man, imprint their formal configuration upon a people. The beings who are responsible for language are beings of great creative energy for they are in reality Powers, i.e., Spirits of Form. They exercise effective influence upon the earth because they have remained on earth, whereas their colleagues, the normal Spirits of Form, work in the "I," work from the sun into the cosmic spaces.

Every language has its own unique "deep structure" which enables its speakers to perceive and therefore be concerned with certain aspects of reality rather than others. We can see how throughout history spiritual beings have used languages to educate human beings in different fields. Plato could have thought and written only in ancient Greek, Shakespeare in English, Goethe in German.

Archai

Angels are concerned that we find our individual destinies, which will lead us to our own unique true I or higher self. Archangels integrate us into the context of a nation of people and equip us with the characteristics of that people. The Archai, however, make us into *human* beings. They are not concerned with the development of any single individual or with a particular nation, but with the advancement of humanity as a whole. They work to integrate unique individual and national contributions into all humanity. The Archai also exert a determining influence on the great communities of faith that stretch over many lands and centuries.

The Archai have no influence on the physical body of the human being. The powers of the three lower orders of angels

117

do not reach that far. A lower group among the Archai influences large civilizations existing simultaneously in disparate parts of the earth. Working in the half-conscious will, the Archai influence those general human actions that proceed from the realm of habit. In this way they create the social order, the essential character of manners and morals and the stations of life with their occupations. Occupation and social position give the human soul "character" and make it into a personality on earth.

Archai not only influence the common habits of a country or civilization; they also involve themselves in widespread so-called "public opinion." To the extent such opinion is prejudiced, filled and guided by lies and half-truths, evil Archai are involved. Our century has seen entire peoples made the target of slander in this way. Some fallen Archai stimulate passions of the blood or bind an individual's thoughts to a single egotistical group. The source of black magic is to be found in Archai who are even more evil, having the goal of sending their will, so to speak, through unguarded doors into the souls of their victims.

Archai and Zeitgeist

Archai govern the succession of great epochs of humanity's cultural development. For example, the fundamental "tone" of the Middle Ages was different from that of ancient Greece and Rome and completely alien to that of ancient Egypt or of any earlier civilization. If we use an orchestra as analogy, it is as though with every civilization a new kind of music comes forth from the realm of the Archai. Musicians and perhaps even instruments change.

Steiner named the Archai *Zeitgeister*, Spirits of the Time. He says concerning Archai (1961a, p. 119):

How men conduct their lives according to the spirit of the time, how they found states, found sciences, cultivate their fields—everything of human origin, the progress of civilization from beginning to end stands under the guidance of the Archai. They lead man insofar as he has to do with others.

As an example of an Archai at work in history, Steiner (1970c, p. 62) gives the following:

In studying a people we regard the Archangel as its guiding principle. Then follows the influence of the spirit of the age who gives his directives to the Archangel of the different nations and these in turn give them to the Angels who transmit them to the separate individuals. Because, as a rule, we see only what is obvious, so in this concerted action the activity of the Archangels is seen to be the most important element. Circumstances, however, may arise when the spirit of the age has to issue more important, more momentous directives, when he is compelled, so to speak, to take over some of the authority of the Archangel, because he must detach a portion of the people in order that the task of the age, the mission of the spirit of the age may be fulfilled. In such a case national groups split off from the rest; the spirit of the age visibly gains the upper hand over the influence of the Archangel. A case in point occurred when the Dutch people severed its connection with the kindred German people. Holland and Germany shared originally an Archangel in common; the separation occurred because the spirit of the age detached a portion of the people at a given moment and then transferred to this portion what have become the vital interests of the modern spirit of the age. Dutch history is simply a reflection of this process.

According to Rudolf Steiner the *Zeitgeist* inspiring our age is the Archangel Michael. He has been elevated from the level of Archangel and invested, as it were, with higher powers in order to pour his unique forces into the development of all humanity, not just one nation. The Archai regularly call upon the specific talents of certain Archangels who then work in sequence to give humanity the benefit of their unique gifts, much as an orchestra employs talented soloists with certain abilities to exert a major influence on the final polyphony.

There are seven Archangels who work in turn. Three of their names are relatively well known: Michael, Gabriel and Raphael. The other four are Zachariel, Anael, Samael and Oriphiel. Steiner gives the following dates for their most recent reigns:

Michael	600-200 B.C.
Oriphiel	200 B.C. - 150 A.D.
Anael	150-500 A.D.
Zachariel	500-850 A.D.
Raphael	850-1190 A.D.
Samael	1190-1510 A.D.
Gabriel	1510-1879 A.D.
Michael	since 1879 A.D.

In 1879 Michael took over from Gabriel and will continue to direct human evolution until the third century of the next millennium.

Gabriel and his age were concerned with the process of incarnation. He strove to bring humankind down into the solidity of earth. As the Archangel of incarnation, Gabriel appeared to

Mary to announce the birth of Jesus and to Zacharias to announce the coming of John the Baptist. It was a Gabrielic impulse which led to the exploratory voyages, the scientific and technical discoveries, the cultural, economic and political events in the "age of discovery." Step by step humanity conquered the earth, molding it to satisfy human desires and needs. In the centuries since, human beings, who should be citizens of two worlds, have become citizens of one alone.

Just as momentum keeps a ball rolling even after the motive forces have ceased, the age of Gabriel has continued into our time. But other forces are beginning to make themselves felt. The belief in unlimited material development is coming into question, and the attitude that physical comforts and personal happiness are crucial elements of a meaningful life has been shaken. Such soul moods are the work of Michael, who has a new agenda for humanity. The timbre of the human soul is changing. People alive today experienced the presence of Michael in the spiritual world before birth. From him they received basic attitudes toward life, discernible in the psychology of an entire generation. Sometimes these impulses can be expressed only in fragmentary or distorted ways. One such distortion is the complete rejection of *everything* resulting from the age of Gabriel, of all old forms.

Gabriel is concerned with birth, with coming to earth; Michael is concerned with death, with leading from the earthly to the spiritual. He is often portrayed with scales on which the good and evil souls have done is weighed after their death.

Michael's task is to free humanity from the one-sided materialistic culture we have created in the past centuries. The energy and initiative developed during the conquest of the earth should now be turned to things spiritual—but *without* abandoning the earth, for the power to find the spirit consciously can be acquired only by life on earth. The achievements of Gabriel must not be denied; they are needed for the future. But now the world of the spirit must also be discovered and explored. However, Michael's inspirations are encountering powerful resistance from a materialistic establishment. The weight of orthodoxy, especially in scientific fields, chains our minds to a worldview in which matter alone is reality.

Wherever "limits to growth" appear, Michael is striving to draw our attention to the existence of a spiritual world. He does this in two ways: through calamities and crises which occur in the social, political and physical realms, and by sending spiritual impulses into the souls of individual human beings. The word "apocalyptic" applies to our age, but we must remember that the original meaning of the word is "to remove the veil." Behind the veil is a world of spirit which can become perceptible because of the "shaking up" which occurs to souls in an age of many external catastrophes.

Michael does not ask for obedience but for initiative, openness to new ways of thinking and the courage to judge spiritual experiences for oneself. This does not mean that all the old forms are now outmoded but rather that individuals have personal responsibility to choose in freedom what seems right for them. To aid this new development Michael sends into our consciousness greater light. Steiner (1956, pp. 157-8) says:

When man again grows able to realize the life of ideas within him, even when not supporting himself and them upon the world of sense—then, to the eyes of the enquirer an answering light will stream again from the cosmos beyond the realm of earth. And this is to make acquaintance with Michael in his kingdom.

Man must find the power to shed light through his world of ideas and when unsupported by the clamorous world of the senses. In this living inner realization of the self-dependent—and, in their self-dependence, luminous—world of ideas, will awake the feeling of man's connection with the non-earthly, outer cosmos. A foundation will thus be laid for festivals of Michael.

But Michael does not force this light on us. He waits for us to turn to him. Steiner (1956, p. 27) says:

From this point in the world's evolution, Michael merely shows his road, so that mankind may walk on it in freedom. And this is what distinguishes this particular regency of Michael's from the previous regencies of all other archangels—indeed from all those of Michael himself until now. These other regencies worked as active forces within man, and did not merely show him their own workings; so that man in those times could not be free in his.

The new impulses from Michael express themselves in the form of three ideals which angels are working to awaken. Consciously or unconsciously, they stand behind many of the feelings which stir within human souls today. First, there is a new desire to meet other human beings, not only externally but to actually encounter their inner, true, eternal selves, so that human encounters become something like a sacrament. Second, there is the instinctive feeling that every form of religious life should be based on freedom. This is also experienced as a greater appreciation of other people's points of view. Steiner (1961b, p. 152) says:

Among the most significant impulses of the time spirit, Michael, [is] to pour clarity, absolute clarity into human souls. . . . Michael is the spirit who works in the most eminent sense, with the freedom of man.

Third, human beings are felt to be capable of grasping in *thought* the spiritual realities of the world. The experience of *knowing* spiritual truth is added to the experience of faith. In the worldview of Rudolf Steiner, these three ideals are considered to be intrinsically Christian. Indeed, Michael is above all a servant of Christ, who can be found through all three of these ideals.

It is not hard to recognize how these three ideals manifest in the world today. It is also clear how many forces have mobilized to counter them. Sometimes they are twisted into their opposite. Much of the bitterness and apathy which have overtaken parts of the younger generation result from disappointment that these ideals have not yet taken root. The resistance of institutions and modes of thought appropriate to the age of Gabriel has hindered and in some cases distorted the arrival of Michaelic impulses. But as always, the old will give way as the spirit of progress continues; but this now also applies to the inner life. An idea sent by Michael is characterized by the life it awakens in our hearts and wills. Michaelic thoughts are not abstract but want to be felt, willed and ultimately, "real-ized" on earth; for a spiritual idea when thought by a human being on earth, when grasped in the mind as an ideal, has the power to elevate something earthly into higher realms.

Steiner's Michaelic Work

Rudolf Steiner understood his own work to be in the service of Michael. Above all, Anthroposophy is a path which can lead a *modern* human being to knowledge of higher worlds. The results of Steiner's research are important, but the process is crucial. The basis for all his esoteric work was, according to him, to be found in his early (1894) work on epistemology, *The Philosophy of Freedom*. In this book, and in others from the same period of his life concerned with Goethe's theory of knowledge, he showed the way to an experience of knowledge available to all those willing to think and desiring to know for themselves. Comparing his own work with the spiritual wisdom of an earlier age, Steiner (1956, p. 140) said:

Anthroposophy cannot be a revival of the Gnosis; . . . The work of Anthroposophy is, by the light of Michael's agency, to evolve out of the spiritual soul a new form of understanding of Christ and the world. Gnosis was the old form of knowledge, preserved from earlier times,—the one best able, at the time when the mystery of Golgotha took place, to convey this mystery to men's understanding.

This background is necessary to understand how important it was for Steiner that his listeners and readers not simply hear his descriptions as a revelation to be accepted or rejected. We all have the responsibility today to know for ourselves. Of course, it may be necessary or even desirable to accept another's results as a tentative guide; thoughts and images which are correct can also serve to awaken within the listener or reader the capacity to acquire such knowledge. Simply entertaining another's thoughts is a way to test them.

Steiner's descriptions, then, were not intended as revelation in the dogmatic sense but to stimulate listeners to think on such matters in detail. Such descriptions provide concepts which help us see things which otherwise might not have been perceptible. Anthroposophy is meant to be enabling: dynamic not static, stressing Becoming rather than Being. This is seen in the nature of Steiner's understanding of angels. Spiritual beings are themselves evolving; they progress by helping men and women, communities, nations and humanity as a whole, to evolve.

Furthermore, Steiner intended his teaching to help us work consciously with spiritual beings. Knowing what angelic beings seek to achieve, and how, enables us to work *with* them and hence facilitates humanity's progress toward its goal.

Above all, Steiner considered that he was meeting an essential need of the age by sharing the results of spiritual science and of showing the path to spiritual knowledge. He saw his work as inspired by Michael, as Michaelic.

Bibliography

All works are by Rudolf Steiner.
1953a. *The Inner Realities of Evolution.* Trans. anon. London: Rudolf Steiner Publishing Co.
1953b. *Theosophy of the Rosicrucians.* Trans. M. Cotterell and D. S. Osmond. London: Rudolf Steiner Publishing Co.
1956. *The Michael Mystery,* Volume II of *Letters to the Members of the*

Anthroposophical Society. Trans. E. Bowen-Wedgwood. 2nd edition, revised by George Adams. London: Anthroposophical Society, 1956.

1959. *Genesis, Secrets of the Bible Story of Creation*. Trans. Dorothy Lenn with assistance from Owen Barfield. London: Anthroposophical Publishing Company.

1961a. *The Influence of Spiritual Beings upon Man*. Trans. anon. New York: Anthroposophic Press.

1961b. *The Mission of the Archangel Michael*. Trans. Lisa D. Monges. Spring Valley, NY: The Anthroposophic Press.

1963. *Occult Science—An Outline*. Trans. George and Mary Adams. London: Rudolf Steiner Press.

1967. *Menschenwerden, Weltenseele und Weltengeist, Erster Teil, Der Mensch als leiblich-seelisch Wesenheit in seinem Verhaeltnis zur Welt*. G. A. 205. Dornach: Verlag der Rudolph Steiner-Nachlassverwaltung. The quotation is the author's own translation.

1970a. *The Spiritual Hierarchies and Their Reflection in the Physical World, Zodiac, Planets, Cosmos*. Trans. R. M. Querido. New York: Anthroposophic Press.

1970b. *Theosophy: An Introduction to the Supersensible Knowledge of the World and the Destination of Man*. 4th edition. Trans. M. Cotterell and A. P. Shepherd. London: Rudolph Steiner Press.

1970c. *The Mission of the Individual Folk Souls in Relation to Teutonic Mythology*. Trans. A. H. Parker. London: Rudolf Steiner Press.

1972. *Building Stones for an Understanding of the Mystery of Golgotha*. Trans. A. H. Parker. London: Rudolf Steiner Press.

1981. *Geistige Hierarchien und ihre Widerspiegelung in der physichen Welt, Tierkreis, Planeten, Kosmos*. G. A. 11. Dornach: Rudolf Steiner Verlag.

1984. *The Essential Steiner, Basic Writings of Rudolf Steiner*. Edited and introduced by Robert A. McDermott. New York: Harper and Row.

9

The Cult of
the Guardian Angel

MICHAEL GROSSO

The belief in guardian angels is very old. They were probably first thought of as spirits of the dead, similar to the Japanese *kami*, the Roman *manes*, or the Germanic *valkyries*. A Zoroastrian tradition, which influenced the Bible, refers to *fravashis*, benevolent, protective spirits whose services require ritual offerings. Mysterious servants and ministers of God are a regular feature in the Old and New Testaments. But it would be a mistake to think of angels as relics from bygone ages. There is in fact a revival of interest in them nowadays.

Of course, from the standpoint of the modern worldview, the idea of angels, guardian or otherwise, is tough to take seriously. Nevertheless, any idea that persists for so long, and that crops up again and again under different disguises, must be saying something important about ourselves.

The Catholic Cult of Guardian Angels

Biblical Origins. Although the belief in guardian angels is strong in Catholic tradition, it lacks solid biblical credentials. It is not a matter of dogma that everyone has a guardian angel, but, as St. Jerome once said, the idea is "in the mind of the Church."

Several passages in the Old and New Testaments and the apochryphal story of Raphael and Tobias are the basis for the belief. The cult of guardian angels is the collective outgrowth of thousands of years of unconscious psycho-mythical evolution.

Let us look at some of the seed images.

In Exodus (23:20) Yahweh declares to Moses: "I myself will send an angel before you to guard you as you go and to bring you to the place that I have prepared. Give him reverence and listen to all that he says." Here the protective function is tribal:

DANTE'S PARADISE *Gustave Doré*
*Empowered by his love for Beatrice, Dante beholds the angels, "living
lights, waxing in splendour," as both are initiated into a participation
of heavenly things.*

"If you listen carefully to his voice and do all that I say, I shall be enemy to your enemies."

Psalm 91 is a wonderful panegyric to God's protective power: "I rescue all who cling to me, I protect whoever knows my name, I answer everyone who invokes me, I am with them when they are in trouble." Thus Yahweh addresses the psalmist. But a few lines above we read: "He [Yahweh] will give his angels charge of you, to guard you in all his ways." In this psalm, angel and god are indistinguishable. Later there is a separation, a hierarchy crystallizes, and the angel becomes a personification of God's helping function.

In the Book of Tobit, the archangel Raphael guides the young hero Tobias on a dangerous journey and reveals magic formulas that protect him from the demon Asmodeus and restore his father's sight.

In Matthew 18:10, we find the authority for believing that each of us has a guardian angel from birth: "See that you never despise any of these little ones, for I tell you that their angels in heaven are continually in the presence of my Father in heaven." Our guardian angels exist timelessly and spacelessly in the presence of the Most High. The angel is thus an intermediary, a "messenger," who brings good tidings from the Supreme Light. The guardian angel is an *imago dei*—an image or form of divine power.

Saint Paul's Letter to the Hebrews (I:14) calls angels "spirits whose work is service sent to help those who will be the heirs of salvation." In the context of this passage, Paul is anxious to distinguish between Christ and the angels, and warns against the dangers of a cult of angels. It is easy, I think, to see what he fears: the angel might easily turn into a gnostic tool for personal spiritual adventure, thus freeing the individual from reliance on the Church and even from reliance on Christ as the exclusive *imago dei*.

From the standpoint of the early Church, the peril of angels is the peril of gnosticism, of spiritual anarchy. We, however, in our new openness to the polytheism of higher consciousness, are less apt to recoil before angels as forms of free access to the Transcendent.

The Contemporary Opus Sanctorum Angelorum. The Church sanctions many attitudes, practices, and movements that it does not necessarily raise to the rank of dogmatic necessity. Popular movements that grow outside or parallel to the dogmas of the Church, as the case may be, are likely to reflect some deep psychic need.

127

Now, in the monotheistic, transcendent world of Judeo-Christianity, the cult of the guardian angel may be seen as an attempt to overcome the remoteness and impersonality of God. In a way, much of Catholic Christianity reflects a struggle to overcome the distance from deity that we find in the great Near Eastern religious traditions. Christ, the incarnation of the remote Father, is an obvious example. But it does not stop there. The impulse of Catholic Christianity is to find new ways to shrink our distance from deity.

So we find the cult of saints, the cult of Mary, along with the cult of guardian angels. Each of these, in its own way, strives to hew more intimate paths to the feet of divine reality. Like the mono-poly-theism of Hinduism, Catholic Christianity offers more than one path to the Transcendent.

There are currently within the Church several lively movements devoted to the angels. One is called the *Opus Sanctorum Angelorum* (the Work of the Holy Angels). This movement (*Opus* for short) was sanctioned by Pope Paul VI in 1968. Earlier, in 1950, Pope Pius XII urged renewed devotion to the angels, especially in the trying times to come. Tradition associates the advent of angels with the Second Coming—with endings and new beginnings.

Another source of inspiration for the *Opus* is the reports of angel appearances in the twentieth century. Padre Pio (1887-1968), a mystic known for his stigmata, seems to have lived on intimate terms with what he called his "celestial companion." Perhaps even more important for the *Opus* are the claims of an angel appearing in 1916 in Fatima to three shepherd children as a prelude to their 1917 visions of the Virgin Mary. (The figure of Mary, like the figure of the guardian angel, plays an increasingly large role in the spiritual consciousness of Catholic Christianity.)

Broadly stated, the goal of the *Opus Angelorum* is the work of conscious "collaboration among the angels and men, for the greater glory of God, the salvation of humanity and the regeneration of all creation."[1] The *Opus* is a movement toward the collective marriage of humanity with the angelic order. Guided by priests who have already been enrolled in the *Opus*, there are three degrees or stages in its rite of divine conjugation.

The Promise. First, candidates make a promise to their guardian angels. All those who love their angels and want to follow their guidance are entitled to make the Promise. Candidates kneel in the presence of a priest and promise God to love their "holy companions" and respond to their commands when heard through the voice of conscience.

The Consecration to the Guardian Angel. After a year of preparation, candidates partake of a ceremony during which they hold a lighted candle in the presence of the Blessed Sacrament. After speaking the ceremonial Consecration, candidates record it in their own handwriting. The following reproduces part of the statement:

Holy Guardian Angel, who have been given to me from the beginning of my life as my Guardian and Companion. I, poor sinner, desire to consecrate myself to you. . . . I promise to acknowledge you always as my holy Guardian and to promote the veneration of the holy angels as help which is given to us in a very special way in these days of spiritual combat for the Kingdom of God.

The candidates ask to become *like* the angels in their perfect love and will. The consecration, in short, is a ritual of assimilation to the angel.

The *Opus* is a work for "these days of spiritual combat." This is an allusion to the possibility that we are nearing endtime. But also to consecrate oneself to one's guardian angel is to certify one's task as spiritual warrior. Saint Michael the Archangel is an archetype of the spiritual warrior. As a boy, I often heard these solemn words of the priest at Mass—part of a prayer to Saint Michael: "Be our protection against the wickedness and snares of the devil . . . and do thou, O prince of the heavenly hosts, by the power of God, thrust into hell Satan and all evil spirits who wander through the world seeking the ruin of souls." The spiritual warrior understands that the world, both outer and inner, is full of snares and pitfalls. Satan is a magnificent homage to the Shadow, a reminder that we must take up our swords as warriors in the struggle for spiritual liberation.

The Consecration also includes this plea: "I beg you, holy angel of God, obtain for me a love so strong that I may be inflamed by it." The task of cooperating with the angels is thus the dual one of becoming sacred warriors *and* divine lovers.

The older tradition of the Church Fathers mirrors this balance in its belief that each of us has not only a good angel but also a bad one. Thus Origen wrote: "All men are moved by two angels, an evil one who inclines them to evil and a good one who inclines them to good. . . . If there are good thoughts in our hearts, there is no doubt that the angel of the Lord is speaking to us. But if evil things come into our heart the angel of the evil one is speaking to us."[2] The transpersonal forces, in which we as soul-makers find ourselves powerfully embedded, are bipolar—dark and light. When we invoke our guardian angels, we must also be ready to grapple with our demons. The forms and energies that drive our thought processes are not merely our own; we are entangled in the other, the alien, whether we realize it or not.

The Consecration to All Angels. The last stage of the *Opus* is a consecration to the whole realm of angels. Now, according to the Church Father Athenogoras, "the Demiurge and Creator of the world, God, through the medium of his word, has apportioned and ordained the angels to occupy the elements, the heavens, the world, and whatever is in the world" (*Suppl.*, 3, 45). Thus, since the angelic order encompasses all ranges of being, from the human to the cosmic, the ultimate goal of the Work of the Angels is none other than to live in sacred communion with all things.

Now, while this grand cosmic goal may be the climax of our spiritual adventure, the immediately fertile core of the angel doctrine is more practical.

First, all human beings, saints or sinners, Christians or pagans, enjoy the service of a guardian angel. The concept, in short, is archetypal: it applies to the psyche universally. The guardian angel is portrayed as existing "face to face" with God—in direct communion with the ultimate forces of the creative mind. In short, there is in every human being an unconscious inlet to the highest creative energies of the spirit. The doctrine of the guardian angel is a recognition of this psychic fact.

More specifically, the *Opus* teaches that the guardian angel is supposed to "ward off danger to body and soul; prevent Satan's suggestion of evil thoughts; remove occasions of sin; enlighten and instruct; offer our prayers for us; correct us if we sin; help us in the agony of death; conduct us to God or purgatory at death."

This is a remarkable list of functions. To mobilize them, however, we need "to venerate and pray to our Guardian Angel; reverence his presence; have confidence in his care; feel gratitude; follow his admonitions; show tender devotion to him."[3]

An Imaginal Model of the Guardian Angel

According to Catholic tradition, angels are conscious persons, marked with a high degree of intellectual and voluntary power; they are not bound by the limitations of physical nature.

It would be hard to make a case for the literal existence of such beings. The theologian or rational fundamentalist may feel the need to do so. But perhaps the wrong approach here could make our entire subject matter evaporate into a mist of useless uncertainties.

Any overly rational attempt to demonstrate the precise existence of angels would enfeeble their psychic and spiritual utility. With angels, one suspects, to analyze is to kill. So a Cartesian analysis of angels seems inappropriate.

But there is another way we can approach our subject. The great alternative to Descartes in modern philosophy is Vico, philosopher of the imagination.[4] Vico's anti-Cartesian battle cry was *verum factum ipsum*, the true is the same as what we make true. Angels, in short, are matters of the practical imagination.

Angels may not exist the way theologians say they do; but what does certainly exist are images of angels. In a Vichian vein, we can say that angels exist insofar as we imaginally co-create them.

I stress the word "co-create," for like Jung, Vico believed in certain universal images common to whole peoples, even to all humanity. A guardian angel is such a universal image, but its existential "truth" depends on how we make it true. We have to bring it to life in our own experience.

So, what does exist, without question, are imagings of angels. The existence and ministry of angels thus depends upon the depth and duration of their imaginal life in our souls. Once we look at it this way, it becomes clear why the Church—an ancient organization unconsciously devoted to fabricating powerful imaginal constructs—holds certain views that we, from our progressive and libertarian perspective, are likely to consider absurd and offensive.

However, the absurd rules and offensive dogmas are necessary to sustain the imaginal life of the angel and other archetypes. "I believe because it is absurd," said Tertullian, an early Church Father. What a slap in the face of rationalism! But Tertullian was more concerned about the imaginal health of the psyche than he was about the platitudes of reason. He knew that for the sake of soul-making we sometimes have to make a clean break with the whole system of worldly reason and plunge headfirst into the forging, fabricating world of the imagination.

Belief, faith, trust—which to the Freudian are an index of infantilism—are to the Vichian the atmosphere where imagination is free to soar.

Angels are true (*verum*) to the extent that we make (*factum*) them true. That is our premise. It contrasts sharply with traditional religion *and* with modern science.

Tradition, however, instinctively understands the relationship between faith and imagination. For, without attempting a detailed analysis, I think it is possible to explain by means of imagination the concept of faith, which tradition exalts.

What does it mean, for example, to say I *believe* I can swim thirty laps but that I can *imagine* myself swimming thirty laps? To say that I believe in God or in my guardian angel is to say that I entertain *some set of images of what is possible.*

Even if the images are very abstract—God imaged as the Light of Being or the Source of Unconditional Love or the Highest Good—we are still dealing with *something* placed before our imaginal eyes. "Blind," unhesitating faith in X may thus be seen as an attempt to maintain a "clear" unwavering image of X. The clearer and more unwavering the image, the greater, on Vichian principles, its creative power. Blindness of faith thus translates into clarity of imagination.

Some might object to the stress on unreflective loyalty and obedience. In the consecration to the guardian angel, one promises unswerving obedience and loyalty to Mary, to all the Saints, and to all the teachings of Mother Church. To the nonbeliever—and maybe to some believers—this smacks of a stifling authoritarianism.

However, the *Opus* is not about intellectual exploration or about civil rights. It is an experiment in co-creating angels. In other words, to get results certain psychological conditions, internal and social, need to be present. The laws of the creative imagination, as Vico so well understood, are "barbaric"; that is, they do not require the refined critical and liberal sensibilities of the "age of men." In Vico's view, the most creative phase of a civilization comes at the dawn of a cycle—what he called the "age of gods."

The Parapsychological Component of the Model

So far, I have suggested that the guardian angel is a psycho-imaginal construct we endow with life by treating it with unswerving belief, love, loyalty, devotion, prayer and gratitude. We bind ourselves to the angel by a promise, a vow. It is a kind of marriage or co-creative process.

The dogmas and practices of the Church, from a psychological viewpoint, are all meant to intensify the psychic reality of these imaginal entities. By giving them a psychic life of their own, we forge a link to our higher selves, the archetypal forces of the unconscious. Everything takes place as if we are supposed to believe in the independent existence of the guardian angel. That belief is important, for it lets us drop the controls of the ego and thus surrender to the dynamics of higher consciousness.

But the guardian angel is supposed to guard, assist, direct and enlighten us in a variety of concrete ways. The Bible is full of stories that show the practical, and often apparently miraculous, abilities of angels. With modern mystics like Padre Pio, there are extraordinary stories inspired by the ministry of angels. Among devotees of the *Opus*, we hear similar claims. In short, the cult of the guardian angel is said to produce real effects.

In a remarkable book titled *Send Me Your Guardian Angels* by Father Alessio Parente, a close confrere of Padre, there is a collection of stories about the unusual activities of guardian angels.[5] Some of the stories are about spiritual assistance; others are about help we would describe as paranormal. Consider a few examples of the latter.

Padre Pio often told people when in distress they should send him their guardian angels (whence the title of Parente's book). In one case, a man was about to be drawn into a robbery with a group of shady friends; he "sent" his guardian angel to the Padre for help. A police car appeared out of nowhere and foiled the plan.

Of course, the skeptic would dismiss this as mere coincidence. Others might consider invoking the guardian angel as a way to increase the probability of meaningful coincidences. Many tales of angelic aid suggest invoked meaningful coincidence.

Others—as reported in Parente's book—if true would definitely involve the paranormal. For example, a woman reported that her car was about to strike an object. She called on her guardian angel, and the car, she alleged, inexplicably jumped over the obstacle. Padre Pio, in stories with testimony less easily discounted, was said to have his guardian angel help him translate Greek—a language he did not know.[6] (Parapsychologists call this "xenoglossy"; Ian Stevenson has analyzed some contemporary cases.[7])

Can parapsychology help us understand the psychic power of the guardian angel construct?

I assume the extraordinary claims about guardian angels refer to *something* real and significant. Any idea that leaves such a clear residue of belief must be grounded in reality. This, of course, does not rule out the possibility of delusion, though the widespread cross-cultural reports over centuries tend to discount delusions as an explanation. I believe that if we take seriously all that we know about the soul—its archetypal *and* parapsychological dimensions—the "guardian angel" might be an idea in the psychic science of the future.

The following remarks are meant to suggest how this might be so. My aim is not to argue for any particular claim of angel-mediated miracles, but to show in general how such claims might be true.

The Creative Power of Belief. One of the well-confirmed findings of modern parapsychology is that belief in and expectation of the paranormal increase its occurrence. The guardian angel is supposed to have virtually unlimited powers over space, time and matter—powers to heal and bring us into harmony with the Supreme Principle. Believing in a being with such powers would be a powerful way to release our own extraordinary potentials.

This could account for the rules of devotion to the guardian angel as taught by believers in the *Opus*: the more we devote ourselves with love and loyalty to the guardian angel, and believe in its powers, the more our belief will activate our latent powers. Anything that destroys the delicate balance of belief will destroy the angel's capacity to do the job for us.

The business of angels is truly a venture in cooperation. We have to give something to our angels if we expect them to give in return. Disbelievers are saying they are unwilling to cooperate in this type of venture: they won't give anything away unless they have tangible and Cartesian proof that they will get something back.

The Spontaneity of Angels. As the spirit blows where it will, so do angels ride the winds of spontaneity. Angels—because they are our soul powers—can do all sorts of marvelous things. They carry our prayers to God and our good intentions to the world; they rescue us from all kinds of danger. Because they are not bound by the material world, they are inherently unpredictable.

Now, one of the best indicators of psychic ability in people is their spontaneity. Researchers have found from many types of studies that the less rigid one's mindset, the more likely it is that a paranormal force or idea will break into experience.[8] The more "unworldly" our minds, the more detached from habitual patterns of response, the greater is our openness to the promptings from a higher reality principle. The fewer the mechanical restraints —the more spontaneous our mode of being in the world—the more likely it is that extraordinary things will occur in our lives.

Angels and Release of Effort. Another supporting angle comes from parapsychology. Researchers say that any wrong effort, any anxious self-doubting sense of the ego trying to "make it" happen, gets in the way of producing paranormal occurrences. Thanks to the guardian angel, we can release ourselves from the wrong kind of ego-involved effort. The guardian angel may ultimately be our own psychic potential, but we have to turn the controls over to something beyond us, something not restricted by the fears and self-doubts of the ego, if we hope to realize that potential. By placing it all in the hands of the guardian angel, we release ourselves from inner obstacles that block cooperation with our unconscious powers.

All this tallies with the great spiritual traditions. From the Lord's Prayer (*Thy* will be done) to the Taoist idea of *wu wei* (action through nonaction), the consensus among spiritual masters is that to come into full ownership of our being we have to abandon ourselves to divine providence. We cannot serve two masters; we have to let go of the personal will. Belief in the guardian angel is a way of freeing the power of the transpersonal will.

Personifying Angels. At a certain stage of the *Opus Sanctorum Angelorum,* devotees are invited to name their own guardian angel. This is critical in co-creating the angel. It is a way of personifying and thus shaping a channel to the inner potentials symbolized by the guardian angel. In the Bible only four angels are named: Michael, Gabriel, Raphael, Uriel. The vast legions of angels said to crowd every nook and cranny of being remain unnamed. This is a curious hint of the angel's unfinished nature. By naming our angels, we add to the *opus* of bringing them into full psychic life. We begin with a promise to our higher self and end with naming and personifying it, with a birthing of the soul.

The Group Dynamic for Co-creating Angels. Do we, then, by naming the angel bring something new into being? Some remarkable experiments of Kenneth Batcheldor may shed light on the genesis of angels.

Batcheldor was an English psychologist interested in paranormal group dynamics. In a series of papers, he demonstrated how a group of ordinary people, by learning a special psychological skill, could levitate objects and produce other remarkable physical phenomena.[9] In fact, Batcheldor held that the kind of phenomena produced was based on *what the group expected and believed was possible.*

Several researchers from Toronto extended Batcheldor's work. They set out to create a "ghost," using the English psychologist's special group techniques. They published their astonishing findings in a book, *Conjuring Up Philip*.[10] I see in this work tremendous implications for a truly creative imaginal psychology.

"Philip" was an invented personality whose story was made up and then experimentally "believed in." Though only an imaginal entity, he took on a life of his own, producing highly localized sounds in a variety of physical substances, levitating objects, and responding intelligently to questions in line with his fictional personality. The experiments were done in full daylight, at times on television, and were observed by impartial witnesses. The group has not yet succeeded in creating an apparition of "Philip," but enough *has* been conjured up to add to the reality of the Tibetan idea of *tulpas* or the theosophical idea of thought-forms.

The important thing I want to say is this: there now seems enough empirical evidence to prove it is possible for a group of individuals, by inventing a myth (a story in images) and practicing a special group dynamic (believing, expecting, being spontaneous, and so forth), *to create an independent psychic entity with the ability to "do" things we can only call "paranormal."*

This research has implications for the theory of angels. (It actually has implications for all "supernatural" or imaginal entities, including God.) It may be that believers in angels—especially groups like those devoted to the *Opus Sanctorum Angelorum*—unconsciously use the same psychological techniques as Batcheldor and his followers did. They create a story, personify a psychic entity, and surrender themselves to believing in the power of this story and entity. Batcheldor and his Canadian comrades obtained results. Why shouldn't believers in guardian angels also get results?

The Return of the Angels

The idea that each of us has a guardian angel is deeply rooted in the psyche. It has gone through many changes, but the archetypal form abides. For the belief in a way to the higher self, a bridge between our everyday minds and some greater Mind at Large, has persisted to modern times. In fact, nowadays we're witnessing an interest in assorted psychic entities that are functionally very similar to the old guardian angel.

The idea of angels—images of mediation, beings that act as links between ourselves and a higher reality—may be detected in several areas of contemporary experience. One example is the widespread phenomenon of "channeling," based on nonphysical guides. The cult of UFO contacteeism is another. The near-death experience, which has come under recent scientific scrutiny, also contains important analogues to angel phenomenology. The light beings, for example, so often described in the near-death experience, certainly resemble the archetypal guardian angel. Apparitions of Mary, present since the dawn of Christianity, are mounting to epidemic proportions, especially since the nineteenth century. One of Mary's cognomens is "Queen of Angels." She herself is called the Angel of Peace, and her splendid apparitions are often preceded by visions of angels.

While I would not want to ignore the many important differences among these phenomena, I believe they are part of a general eruption of archetypes in our times. Owing to the immense success of the scientific revolution, the Western psyche has cut itself off from its animating psycho-spiritual roots, and wanders around hungry for contact with new and renewing realities, craving the numinosity of archetypes and the radiance of meaning. Hence the many manifestations of archetypal reality.

The modern psyche is suffering from what Vico called "the malicious decay of rationalism," intelligence turned alien to the needs of civil society. Science itself has become "malicious" and threatens inadvertently to destroy the planet. These phenomena of light—these angels and luminous near-death emissaries and solar brotherhoods and Virgin Marys dressed in the white radiance of eternity—are signs of a returned barbarian times. "Barbarian" for Vico meant primal imagination. In these new barbarian times, the gods and goddesses, the demons and fairies, the griffins and guardian angels we have trampled under the feet of scientific rationalism are returning with a vengeance.

As this happens, opportunities for transforming ourselves in the image of our divinely human potentials—opportunities for soul-making—will multiply, with the help of our guardian angels.

Notes

1. J. Finauer, *Divine Gift for Our Time*. In R. J. Fox, *Opus Sanctorum Angelorum* (Washington, NJ: AMI Press, 1983).
2. J. Danielou, *The Angels and their Mission* (Westminster, MD: Christian Classics, Inc., 1987).
3. Both quotations are from a mimeographed sheet passed out at a

meeting devoted to the *Opus* in the Church of Saint John's in New York City, April, 1987.

4. *The New Science of Giambattista Vico.* T. G. Bergin, Max H. Fisch, Trs. (Ithaca: Cornell University Press, 1968).

5. Fr. A. Parente, *Send Me Your Guardian Angel* (San Giovanni Rotondo: Our Lady of Grace Capuchin Friary, 1984).

6. M. Grosso, "Padre Pio and Future Man," in *Critique*, Spring, 1989.

7. Ian Stevenson, *Xenoglossy: A Review and Report of a Case.* In *Proceedings of the American Society for Psychical Research*, Vol. 31, February, 1974.

8. See especially John Palmer's monumental study of ESP "Extrasensory Perception: Research Findings." In *Advances in Parapsychological Research 2: Extrasensory Perception* Stanley Krippner, ed, (New York & London: Plenum Press, 1978), pp. 59-245.

9. Several of the more important papers in this series remain unpublished. Among the published, the most useful is K. J. Batcheldor, "PK in Sitter Groups" in *Psychoenergetic Systems*, 1979, Vol. 3, pp. 77-93.

10. I. M. Owen, M. Sparrow, *Conjuring Up Philip* (New York: Pocket Books, 1977).

10
Humanity and the Cosmic Hierarchies

G. A. FARTHING

According to esoteric science the universe is a living entity composed of hosts of living beings. These hosts, which provide the structure, qualities and governance of the universe according to everlasting law, are divisible into seven main types according to their characteristic qualities, these in turn having their correspondences at every level of being. Although distinctively named and described, these various groups of living beings constitute a Unity in which every component is intimately related to every other. Each hierarchy is composed of those below it, while in its turn it is a component of the one above it. There are therefore hierarchies of beings superior to humanity, from among whom came the guides and teachers of the early races, and those below, from whom humanity has derived the very qualities of its being.

The great religious traditions recognize these hosts under a variety of names—Spirits, Angels and Archangels, the Elohim and Sephiroth, Amshaspends, Cosmocratores and Prajapatis of the different systems. The writings of H. P. Blavatsky, especially *The Secret Doctrine*, are a major source of esoteric science in our times and contain rich material regarding these invisible hierarchies. In *The Secret Doctrine* also are found many names that refer to these lofty powers, the designation of each often signifying the function of the particular order or hierarchy or its place in the total scheme. Thus we find Lipika, Ah-hi, Dhyani-Chohans, Mind-born Sons, Sons of Light, Builders, Planetary Spirits and so on.

Esoteric science postulates worlds invisible to our physical senses that surround and interpenetrate the earth plane. Vehicles are necessary for life to operate in the modes of thinking and feeling. Therefore, there are subtler vehicles, normally invisible, by means of which thinking and feeling take place, in both humanity and Nature around us. Each of these vehicles, whatever its level, has constituents that are alive. These lives that compose the inner vehicles are organized on a hierarchical basis and constitute an organized whole. We have, then, the concept that Life operates not only through the lives at our level of being but through lives in the invisible worlds, and these latter form beings that operate at those invisible levels. Of such lives are the devas and Dhyan Chohans and the lesser lives of the Elementals (to be discussed).

These 'lives' actually comprise the planes of Nature postulated in esoteric science. They correspond directly with the principles of the human constitution. That is, just as humans have a body on the physical plane, so the feeling, thinking, intuiting and spiritual aspects of human life have vehicles on corresponding superphysical planes of Nature. Thus, the physical body is only one aspect of the sevenfold human being, whose inner aspects repeat the hierarchical pattern which reflects the structure of the cosmos. Each plane of the sevenfold universe is peopled by lives, as varied in the degree of consciousness they display and in the functions they fulfill in the cosmic scheme as are the hierarchies of lesser lives in the human body.

One of the aims that H. P. Blavatsky set before herself in presenting *The Secret Doctrine* to the public was "to assign to man his rightful place in the scheme of the universe" (1.213). What that place is becomes evident as we understand the evolution of consciousness through the hierarchical structure of the universe. For the human-stage is that stage in the total process in which spirit and matter are in equilibrium—a stage symbolized by the interlaced triangles of Solomon's Seal, the one representing matter, pointing downwards, the other representing spirit, pointing upwards, the direction of future progress. Man, in the words of one writer, is that being in whom highest Spirit and lowest Matter are joined by Intelligence (Besant, *Pedigree of Man*, p. 22).

Esoteric science or Theosophy further postulates that the process of evolution is continuous through the kingdoms of Nature. Life is given increasing expression as we rise through the kingdoms, until we arrive at the human stage, which is said to be the apex of the evolutionary process on this earth. In addition to this vertical direction of expansion by sentience and capability, there is another factor to be considered in our hierarchical picture, a horizontal direction that consists of imparted qualities.

There is enormous variety in Nature. For example, we see an infinite variety of colors, shapes, modes of operation, rates of growth, textures of materials, etc. All these variants are according to archetypal patterns. We are told that these patterns have their origins in the natures of the seven great beings that manifest as soon as the cosmic process of genesis or coming into being starts. Each of these can be thought of as head of a 'ray' shining down through all the planes of being. Each ray imparts the quality of its head to every thing and being on all the levels. All things share these qualities, or have them inherent in their natures, but not equally: one or more qualities predominate. These rays are sometimes symbolized by colors: violet, yellow, green, blue, red, orange, white (the synthesis of them all).

Each of these rays in itself represents a hierarchy of beings on all planes of existence, and these ray characteristics reflect various human principles. The ray types are symbolized in the nature of each of the planets of our solar system, and every being in the system is 'born' under the influence of one of these planets. This means that planetary influence predominates in its nature. But the influence of all the other planets is also to a degree represented in every being. This is most easily seen in the human kingdom where our characters are made up of an admixture of these planetary influences, with one predominating.

A number of quotations from *The Secret Doctrine* are given below to illustrate or justify some of the points made. (All references are to Volume I of the first or second edition.) These quotations refer to post-human beings called Dhyan Chohans. Concerning the origins of the universe, at a time when everything was in a homogeneous state before any differentiation had taken place, H. P. Blavatsky refers to one of the Stanzas of Dzyan, on which *The Secret Doctrine* is based (I. p. 21):

Stanza IV shows the differentiation of the 'Germ' of the Universe into the septenary hierarchy of conscious divine powers, who are the active manifestations of the one supreme energy. They are the framers, shapers and ultimately the creators of all the manifested Universe, and the only sense in which the name "Creator" is intelligible; they inform and guide it; they are the intelligent Beings who adjust and control evolution, embodying in themselves those manifestations of the one law which we know as "The Laws of Nature."

Referring again to this Stanza (Stanza IV.S.D. I. p. 93):

This Sloka gives again a brief analysis of the Hierarchies of the Dhyan Chohans ... or the conscious intelligent powers in Nature. To this Hierarchy corresponds the actual types into which humanity may be divided; for humanity as a whole is in reality a materialized though as yet imperfect expression thereof.

Again, on p. 106 there is a significant passage:

... the question will surely be asked, "Do the Occultists believe in all these 'Builders,' 'Lipika' and 'Sons of Light' as Entities, or are they merely imageries?" To this the answer is given as plainly. "After due allowance for the imagery of personified powers, we must admit the existence of these entities, if we would not reject the existence of spiritual humanity within physical mankind. For the hosts of these Sons of Light and 'Mind-born Sons' of the first manifested Ray of The unknown ALL, are the very root of spiritual man."

Again, a footnote to S.D.I. 1.9 refers to "the seven hierarchies or classes of Pitries and Dhyan Chohans which compose our nature and bodies." And on p. 221 the idea is reiterated:

This sixth group [creative hierarchy] moreover, remains almost inseparable from man, who draws from it all but his highest and lowest Principles, or his spirit and body, the five middle human principles being the very essence of those Dhyanis.

These passages imply that our human vehicles are manifestations of Dhyan Chohanic life. As P. G. Bowen, a student of H. P. Blavatsky's, says of mankind, "All the Hierarchies of Heavens exist within him."

The intricacies of the subject of these hierarchies, the part they play in both the structure and operation of Cosmos, and their role in the creation and constitution of humanity are referred to in the Summing-Up of Part I of Book I of *The Secret Doctrine*. Selecting some passages relating particularly to hierarchies, we have (p. 274):

The whole cosmos is guided, controlled, and animated by almost endless series of Hierarchies of sentient Beings, each having a mission to perform, and who—whether we give to them one name or another and call them Dhyan Chohans or Angels—are "messengers" in the only sense that they are the agents of Karmic and Cosmic Laws. They vary infinitely in their respective degrees of consciousness and intelligence.

The Secret Doctrine makes it clear that members of these hierarchies cannot respond to our petitions. On page 276 in the Summing-Up, we read:

To appeal to their protection is as foolish as to believe that their sympathy may be secured by any kind of propitiation: for they are, as much as man himself is, the slaves and creatures of immutable Karmic and Kosmic law. The reason for it is evident. Having no elements of personality in their essence they can have no personal qualities, such as attributed by men, in their exoteric religions, to their anthropomorphic god.

Thus, these beings are not distinctively individual as are human personalities, though there are unique characteristics for each hierarchy. On p. 274 we have:

Individuality is the characteristic of their respective hierarchies, not of their units: and these characteristics vary only with the degree of the plane to which those hierarchies belong: the nearer to the region of Homogeneity and the One Divine, the purer and the less accentuated that individuality in the Hierarchy.

All these beings that together constitute the planes of nature are themselves individually, and their hierarchies collectively, represent stages in the evolutionary process. Prior to the human stage, they are irresponsible agents of the Law which operates throughout the universe. They are termed "Elementals," and are associated with the mineral, plant and animal kingdoms, as well as constituting three pre-mineral kingdoms in superphysical realms.

Similarly, there are three groups of post-human entities, Dhyan Chohans, "Lords of Light," defined as "the divine Intelligences charged with the supervision of Kosmos." H. P. Blavatsky points out that they correspond to Archangels recognized in the Roman Catholic system. Each of the three groups has its particular place in the hierarchical structure and its particular function. She says in S.D. I, p. 106:

[Those of the first group] build, or rather rebuild, every "system" after the "Night" [pralaya, when all manifestation goes into a dormant state]. The second group of the Builders is the Architect of our planetary chain exclusively; and the third, the progenitor of our humanity—the Macrocosmic prototype of the microcosm.

All these beings must go through the human stage in their evolution. The Summing-Up on p. 279 says:

As from the highest Archangel (Dhyan Chohan) down to the last conscious "Builder," all such are *men*, having lived aeons ago, in other Manvantaras [periods of manifestation], on this or other Spheres: so the inferior, semi-intelligent and non-intelligent Elementals—are *future* men. That fact alone—that a Spirit is endowed with intelligence—is proof to the Occultist that that being must have been a *man*, and acquired his knowledge and intelligence throughout the human cycle. . . . The whole order of nature evinces a progressive march toward a *higher life*. There is design in the action of the seemingly blindest forces.

G. A. Farthing

In a quotation from some other work not specified (but quoted in S.D.I, p. 276), we read that humans can come to know the great devas or Chohans:

Man can neither propitiate nor command the "Devas" .... But, by paralyzing his lower personality, and arriving thereby at the full knowledge of the *non-separateness* of his Higher Self from the One Absolute Self, man can, even during this terrestrial life, become as "One of Us."

Finally, on p. 280 *The Secret Doctrine* explicitly states what our attitude should be towards these Dhyan Chohans or Heavenly Hosts that constitute much of our nature:

All are entitled to the grateful reverence of Humanity, however, and man ought to be ever striving to help the divine evolution of *ideas*, by becoming to the best of his ability *her co-worker with Nature* in the cyclic task.

Thus can we cooperate with these great beings in the building of ourselves and of Nature.

11
Dark Angels

JOHN ALGEO

Angels are bright beings of heaven. They are glorious creatures, fair to behold, with haloes and auras. They are the shining ones, the devas, the divine messengers of God. Artists have shown them—radiantly handsome, with golden hair, beautiful faces, large eyes focused on an eternal vision, voices that echo the harmony of the psaltery, lilies in their arms, their feet poised above the earth. They are powers and virtues, mighty beings of pure goodness. They are creatures of light.

But what about the others? The dark angels?

There are dark angels too. In the grand ecology of the universe, everything has its opposite. "To light a candle," said the mage of Ursula LeGuin's *Earthsea*, "is to cast a shadow." *Evil* is the inescapable complement of *live*. The *devil* has *lived* backwards. So what about the dark angels? What about Satan, the Adversary of God? What about the serpent in the Garden of Eden? What about the Tempter, the evil spirit at our side? What about Wormwood and Screwtape?

The Dark Side of Light

An old kabbalistic motto holds that *Demon est Deus inversus*, 'The devil is God upside down' or 'The devil is God's complement.' The Irish poet William Butler Yeats took, as his mystical name in the kabbalistic Order of the Golden Dawn, the initials of that Latin motto, *D.E.D.I.* Those letters, however, also spell the Latin verb *dedi*, which means 'I have given' and thus punningly suggests that the diabolic is a divine gift.

Yeats probably learned the motto from Helena Petrovna Blavatsky, who had been his teacher and had used it as the subject of one section in her great book, *The Secret Doctrine*. So what is the secret doctrine about this motto and the dark angel of whom it speaks? Blavatsky says of it:

This symbolical sentence, in its many-sided forms, is certainly most dangerous and iconoclastic in the face of all the dualistic later religions—or rather theologies—and especially so in the light of Christianity. [*SD* 1:411]

She adds that Christianity certainly did not invent the figure of Satan, for such a concept has always existed. The name *Satan* in Hebrew means 'adversary'; he is consequently a personification of the inevitable balancing forces that must exist in nature: the shadow by which we recognize light, the night that separates the days, the cold without which we have no sense of heat.

To say that the Devil is the inverse, the complement, of God is dangerous, however, because liable to be misunderstood, especially by those whose thinking is molded by dualism, who see spirit and matter, soul and body, the righteous and the reprobate, the saved and the damned as eternal opposites. Those who think in simple dichotomies have great difficulty in seeing the underlying unity beneath all diversities. They find it hard to conceive that Demon and Deus, the dark and bright angels, are equally messengers of the Absolute One. They find it hard to give the Devil his due.

Yet in our relative world of mayavic reality, all things have their opposites. To know anything is to know it by contrast with something that it is not. Knowledge implies opposition. Without low, there is no high. Without far, there is no near. Without pain, there is no pleasure. Without death, there is no life. Without the dark angels, there are no bright ones. Without Demon, there is no Deus. In eternity, none of those exist. In time, none can exist without its complement. So for the Elohim to be, Satan must also be.

"Homogeneity," says Blavatsky, "is one and indivisible" and "heterogeneity in its dualistic aspect, is its offspring—its bifurcous shadow or reflection," so "that divine Homogeneity must contain in itself the essence of both good and evil" (*SD* 1: 411-12). There are two aspects of this doctrine that are equally important and, indeed, are complementary, without either of which the doctrine "is certainly most dangerous" because liable to misunderstanding and perversion.

The first aspect is that what we call evil and good are both derived from the divine absolute:

One cannot claim God as the synthesis of the whole Universe, as

Omnipresent and Omniscient and Infinite, and then divorce him from evil. As there is far more evil than good in the world, it follows on logical grounds that either God must include evil, or stand as the direct cause of it, or else surrender his claims to absoluteness.... Everywhere the speculations of the Kabalists treat of Evil as a *force*, which is antagonistic, but at the same time essential, to Good, as giving it vitality and existence, which it could never have otherwise. [*SD* 1: 413]

This first aspect of the Wisdom teaching about good and evil holds that both of those qualities are equally present in the divine source of all things. That teaching is found also in the great religious documents of all ages and climes. In the *Bhagavad Gita*, Krishna identifies himself with everything in the universe, bad and good: "I am the gambling of the cheat, and the splendor of splendid things, I." And in the prophesy of Isaiah (45.7) the Almighty is quoted as saying: "I form the light, and create darkness: I make peace, and create evil: I the *Lord* do all these things." The God of our good is likewise the God of our evil.

The second aspect of the doctrine is that evil is not an independent reality, but merely the complement, the shadow of good:

There is no *malum in se* [self-existent evil, anything inherently evil of its own nature]: only the shadow of light, without which light could have no existence, even in our perceptions. If evil disappeared, good would disappear along with it from Earth. [*SD* 1:413]

So (1) evil is a reality, derived from the source of all reality, but also (2) evil has no independent existence, being simply the complement by which we recognize good. Those who accept the first aspect but deny the second are dualists or atheists or cursers of God. Those who deny the first aspect but accept the second reject the evidence of their own senses and maintain against all reason that pain and sorrow do not exist.

But the Occultists . . . who recognize in every pain and suffering but the necessary pangs of incessant procreation: a series of stages toward an ever-growing perfectibility... view the great Mother [Nature] otherwise. Woe to those who live without suffering. Stagnation and death is the future of all that vegetates without a change. And how can there be any change for the better without proportionate suffering during the preceding stage? [*SD* 2:475]

To solve "the great problems of life, pain, and death," we must experience them. To use the idiom of those today who pump iron: "No pain, no gain."

The doctrine of the Wisdom Tradition thus holds that there

is but one inexhaustible source of reality from which all things come and apart from which nothing is. And it further holds that intelligent forces derived from that source bring into existence the universe we know, and in so doing they necessarily operate with dualities of many kinds, including those we call good and evil. The process of achieving good involves the strain of suffering evil.

The Dark Creative Forces

Some of the intelligent forces or angels, as we also call the creative agents in the cosmos, work to make the substance of the universe dense, to immerse consciousness in matter, and to isolate separate individual existences. These forces devoted to density, unconsciousness, and separateness are the dark angels whose goal is the emergence of the many from the One, the involution of matter, life, and spirit. They are the centrifugal, creative forces that bring the many forth from the One.

Other forces work to refine substance into subtler states of existence, to increase consciousness, and to connect separate selves into a network of cooperation and sympathy. The forces dedicated to subtlety, consciousness, and reunion are the bright angels whose goal is the conscious, voluntary reintegration of the many into the One, the evolution of the universe to its Omega point. They are the centripetal, regenerative forces that return the many to the One.

Blavatsky describes the world process as proceeding on three parallel lines: physical, intellectual, and monadic or spiritual. Those three lines lead respectively to the development of substance, consciousness, and unitary awareness.

On the physical or substantial line of development, matter at first becomes increasingly dense until it reaches some nadir of density, some singular state of inconceivable compaction, as in one of the black holes of the universe where physical law, as we know it, does not hold. From that point of maximum density, matter evolves into complex but also more rarefied states—the matter we know being more empty space than substance and therefore already very subtle. The future of matter is an increasing etherialization.

On the intellectual or conscious line of development, awareness is progressively restricted as it moves through the elemental kingdoms, until it reaches its nadir in the mineral state, where its responses are limited to those restricted ones we call chemical reactions and the like. Thereafter it evolves through the vegetable and animal kingdoms, in which responsiveness to the environment and to other beings becomes increasingly acute, as plants respond quickly to the physical conditions around them and animals to other beings. When awareness reaches the human kingdom, interior reflection and self-consciousness flourish. Humanity is well along the road to increased awareness of the universe, but before us still lie vistas of perception and knowledge that we can yet scarcely imagine.

On the monadic or spiritual line of development, the Oneness of the source is progressively divided into smaller and smaller, more and more restricted and limited units. Ultimately, to be sure, there is only one Monad (a term from Greek that means 'unity'). But as that Monad is reflected in evolved matter and the developed kingdoms of life, it is continually refracted, so that it seems to itself to become increasingly limited and fragmented. Thus the One apparently divides into the many.

This process has also been described as one of "group souls" that individualize. In the mineral kingdom, vast areas and types of substance are ensouled by one aspect of the Monad. In the vegetable kingdom, the domain of each ray of the Monad is much restricted but still encompasses whole species of plants. In the animal kingdom, the Monad is even more restricted, expressing itself through an ever decreasing range of physical forms. Among the higher animals, a single group soul (which is one separate ray of the Monad) may express itself through only a few separate bodies at a time. Finally in the human kingdom, the monadic line of development reaches its nadir, for each human being is a distinct individuality, a persisting bit of separateness from the primal unity of existence.

In this sense, we humans, far from being the crown of evolution, as we are wont vaingloriously to imagine ourselves, are actually the nadir of spiritual development. As the most individual of all beings, we are the most separate from the divine Unity, and thus the farthest of all beings from our common source. In us the monadic development reaches its lowest point. Our future is to reestablish connections, to forge the links that will bind us back to the Unity, to become One—consciously, deliberately, of our own free will. At the Omega point of evolution, we are to merge without losing our identities, to recreate the Unity, but then a Unity that knows itself and has chosen its state.

Through the outgoing phases of these three lines of development —the densification of matter, the limitation of consciousness, and the individualization of spirit—the dark angels are the governing forces. They guide the involution of the universe. They make it solid, unresponsive, and fragmented. They bring the world into being. They are the creators.

But once the nadir on each line of development has been reached and the forces turn backward to evolve out of those limitations, the bright angels become the guides of evolution, and the work of the dark angels becomes evil in the sight of those who are evolving. The work of the dark angels continues, however: black holes are still compacting matter throughout the cosmos; consciousness still flows into the mineral forms and so is restricted; living creatures still move toward the spiritual separation of individuality. The impulse of the dark angels—the involution of matter, consciousness, and spirit—is all around us. But the human path now lies in a different direction, and so for us their work has become evil—not evil in itself, not *malum in se*, but evil relative to our direction.

As human beings, we value the work of the bright angels, because we are well along the paths of refined substance and increased consciousness, and we have turned the bend on the path of spiritual unity—although we have just made the turn, so the old forces of separateness are still strong within us. But however much we sympathize with the upward path of evolution and the work of the bright angels, we should not scorn the other. The work of the dark angels—to solidify matter, to funnel consciousness into it, and to make separate, distinct centers of identity —must come first. The work of the dark angels is necessary to the total ecology of the universe. Without them there would be nothing to evolve, and the bright angels would have no role to play.

The Dark Angel Within

However, while we respect the work of the dark angels, we must take care not to become a part of it. Our destiny, our dharma, is elsewhere. Yet there is still a temptation within us to follow the dark path. That temptation does not concern the densification of matter, for black holes are far from our condition in time and space. Neither does it much concern the limitation of consciousness, for we evolved from mineral unresponsiveness eons ago. Only exceptionally and pathologically do human beings sink back to animal or vegetative states of unconsciousness, and then it is no more than a temporary regression, not lasting beyond the bounds of a lifetime, and seldom as long as that.

Spiritual regression, however, is another matter. We have only just made the upward turn in monadic evolution; we are newly emerged from the nadir of spiritual isolation and separateness. Before our individualization, the dark angels were our friends and guides. We have old ties with them that are not easily unknotted. We sympathize still with their forces; we resonate still to their discordant melodies. They are still within us.

One of the teachings of the Wisdom Tradition is that we are composite beings—not simply souls with bodies, but compounds of principles evolved separately over the eons and brought together to make up our natures. The elements that compose us are like distinct rays of light of various colors and intensities that are focused together to illuminate a scene in a play. The lights become one illumination, but they are projected from several lamps and reflect the nature of those lamps.

The creation myth of Blavatsky's *The Secret Doctrine* has an episode in which the progenitors of humanity are discussing our making and what must go into us to produce a complete humanity (Anthropogenesis stanza 17; *SD* 2: 105). The Earth gives our gross physical body, the Solar Spirits give our life energy, the Lunar Ancestors give the model of our personality, the Heat of the Sun gives our desires; but humanity needs also "a mind to embrace the Universe," and none can give humanity that intellect, until the Sons of Wisdom add their light to the others. This creation myth has various interpretations, but one of its significant meanings is that we are composites of evolutionary impulses that are historically independent of each other, though they have combined in us.

Our prehuman development was directed toward making us spiritually independent, to bring us to the unique isolation which is the human state—the condition of individualization. The dark angels made us human by building up the individual Ego. We are the creatures who are alone. As we evolve from the human to the superhuman kingdoms, we will move from spiritual isolation to spiritual connectedness, integration, interdependence. However, our natures have been molded by the dark angels of spiritual isolation and separateness. And the effects of their labors are yet strong within us.

The biblical myth of the Fall can be seen as alluding to this human individualization and its consequences. In that myth, Adam and Eve, who are protohumanity, are led by the serpent (the dark angel) to eat the fruit of the Tree of Knowledge. The knowledge that the fruit imparts is of their own separate identities. In their disobedience to the divine prohibition against eating, they assert their separate wills—they become choosing individuals. That is the Original Sin, whose punishment is expulsion from the unity of the Garden of Eden into the diversity of the fallen world. And the first man and woman retain and pass on to their descendants the consequences of their separation—a fallen nature and a susceptibility to the wiles and temptations of Satan, the adversary, the personification of spiritual separateness.

Within the stark simplicity of the myth of the Fall and Original Sin lies a great truth. We inherit the effects of our past, and an action that may have been necessary—a quest for knowledge, a coming of age, an attainment of independence—can have consequences which, if unchecked, are inappropriate for our further development. Good things of the past may become bad things of the future.

The dark angels guided us to human independence and have still a place in our lives, for they are the impulse to self-survival. They are ego-exalting. They are self-assertive. Human society has not yet reached a stage at which we can do without such motives to action. And indeed, although in mature humanity those motives must become transformed into something less violent and more considerate of others than they have been in the adolescence of our species, we will never be able wholly to do without them. For the world can progress only as all of us in it are pulled between the twin poles of good and evil—of unity and separateness. As Blavatsky put it:

In human nature, evil denotes only the polarity of matter and Spirit, a struggle for life between the two manifested Principles in Space and Time, which principles are one *per se*, inasmuch as they are rooted in the Absolute. In Kosmos, the equilibrium must be preserved. The operations of the two contraries produce harmony, like the centripetal and centrifugal forces, which are necessary to each other—mutually inter-dependent—"in order that both should live." [*SD* 1: 416]

To preserve the equilibrium and produce the harmony within the human constitution, all forces need to be balanced—including those of the dark angels. Their forces have been called collectively the Dweller on the Threshold, and Jungian psychology personifies them as the Shadow. In Christianity they are spoken of as one's personal devil.

The devil within may not, like C. S. Lewis's Wormwood, get letters from his uncle Screwtape, or have quite as distinctly human a personality, or be as fully committed to the Christian variety of dualism; but the personal devil is more than a literary convention. Each of us has impulses, habits, and proclivities that cluster and can be imbued with a personality something like Wormwood's. The dark angels are cosmic powers that guide the involution of the universe, but they are also psychological forces from our past that shape our responses to the present.

The dark angel is a part of ourselves with which we must come to terms. As the impulse to separate ourselves from others, it is the mirror image of the bright impulse to unite with all life. Our Omega point is to realize both impulses harmoniously—as separate individuals to unite with all other separate individuals in a single pattern of compassion and benevolence. Thus the bright angels and the dark angels are both necessary to us. And what is most necessary is that we learn how to deal with both in their proper times and places and according to their proper powers.

At the end of her discussion of the kabbalistic motto, Blavatsky describes an image of:

the "Magic Head" in the *Zohar*, the double Face on the double Pyramid: the black pyramid rising against a pure white ground, with *a white head and face within its black triangle;* the white pyramid, inverted—the reflection of the first in the dark waters, showing the *black reflection of the white face. . . . Demon est Deus Inversus.* [SD 1: 424]

III
Angels
and Archetypes
—the Imaginal Realm

In the language of archetypal psychology, the Soul is imaginal: it generates archetypal images that are metaphorical, rich in meaning rather than specific in content or form. Angels are expressions of these archetypes, imaginal essences individualized in the self-luminous "matter" of the archetypal world. They are numinous powers which dominate the psyche and manifest in human behavior and in all earthly events and things.

Archetypal psychology advocates a new polytheism based on the idea, found also in esoteric philosophy, that unity of Being unfolds itself into innumerable forms. This mystic polytheism does not hold angels as objects of belief or worship, but celebrates them as revealers of a hidden Divine Being. Being is not fragmented but wholly present in each manifestation, individualized fully in the angel of each thing. Angels, in this view, are within our space-time world, and we experience them in our deepest feelings. Without angels, we are impoverished, not fully human. Only as we dwell in the company of angels do we approach nearness to God.[1]

Human spiritual unfoldment is an adventure through inner space, the mysterious arena of the psyche or soul. Various religious and psychological traditions suggest that the psyche has a "structure." Some describe ordered levels of subtle energy-matter, a scheme in which all grades interpenetrate each other, are present simultaneously, and are in ceaseless, cyclic motion. Interestingly, scientists speculate that the atomic world may be a composite of overlapping parallel worlds, and suggest that an implicate order gives rise to physical reality. The material world may be the outermost expression of a dynamic Unity of increasingly subtle levels.

According to esoteric philosophy, humans are inherently spiritual beings who are evolving powers of perception and action through the entire universal spectrum. The human psyche embodies, reflects, and is inseparable from cosmic

Soul-Spirit. Though predominantly psychospiritual beings, we focus a fraction of consciousness through the material band. Our physical existence is profoundly meaningful, however, for our evolutionary work is to bring the full, formative power of our inner nature to physical life. What we do in this respect reflects immediately into the refined angelic spheres.

Depth psychology affirms that the world of phenomena is rooted in pure psyche. We live in a psychological cosmos whose images in every sphere are statements about this soul world. Grounded in earthly sense impressions, and temporarily misled by them, humans are only marginally aware of the thought/ feeling dimension. However, the primary field for awareness and action is slowly shifting to this less tangible sphere of human creativeness. Soon we will develop full awareness and constructive intent in these subtle worlds, learning to cooperate with beings such as angels who embody psychospiritual force.

In the religious as well as psychological sense, the path of holiness is movement toward wholeness, individual and collective. Angels embody an extraordinary integrity and unity. They are fully present, totally awake in their own sphere, thus figures of undeniable authority and power. As we are attentive to whichever angel dominates the field of awareness in the moment, we feel no separation from each other or from things spiritual.

Angels are expressions of Divine Law, agents of an unseen depth of Being. They radiate within and through all things, waking us to hidden possibilities, willing us to rise to our creative potential. As unseen powers and principles, the gods are restless only when we are ignorant of their forms and ways. We can choose whether to be driven by angels, or to enter into conscious liaison with them.

The imprint of the eternal is everywhere. We have only to vision a little more deeply to see it. Mystics of all traditions suggest the way of meditation or the way of interior prayer. In psychological terms, meditation is simply a position from which one knows things as they are. It requires clear, pure intent, discrimination, and detachment. Interior prayer as a way of life means a courageous rapport with whatever face of God, whatever Angel of the Presence, is immediately before us.

Unlike trance states, meditation sharpens awareness on many levels at once. One may participate in the phenomenal world with full realization of its eternal nature. In this state of clarity, there is no longer fixation on form. The contemplative mind sees unending creative possibilities in every poem, every individual, every society, every event. Phenomena are soul or angel immanent, outworkings of an infinitely creative process. Thinking about angels yields to direct experience, gravity gives way to spontaneity and play.

1. Roberts Avens. *The New Gnosis.* Dallas: Spring Publications, 1984, 124.

12
Theologia
Imaginalis

DAVID L. MILLER

The Case of the Missing Corpse is not only a theological problem for the historical Mary on the first Easter morning. It is also the mystery story for any Mary within every self. A certain emptiness is sensed in the cave of one's being. Things are grave in the Garden. The rock has not held. Life lacks body. But then something very strange occurs. In spite of, or perhaps just because of, the absence of a literal body, things appear to take on more "body" than ever heretofore. A sort of deconstruction seems to belong together with soul-construction. Seven clues may help with this Case of the Missing Corpse.

(1) It is well known, especially to those who have had the experience, that a truly excellent wine has a peculiar property. As it is being savored, the liquid is spirited away, being, as one says of such wines, "dry." Yet, in the breathtaking moment of the spiriting-away, a curiously powerful bouquet stays, and one has a sense of the wine's "body." The experience is something like that about which Rainer Maria Rilke writes. He is speaking about the transformation that occurs when a piece of fruit is eaten, for example, "a full round apple, pear and banana, gooseberry. . . ." The fruit dies, but . . . "read it from the face of a child tasting them"—

> Is something
> indescribable slowly happening in your mouth?
> Where otherwise words were, flow discoveries,
> freed all surprised out of the fruit's flesh.(1962:41)

(2) Or, there is the matter of the Cheshire Cat who disappeared. The smile remained! It is like Aeneas's experience of his father, Anchises, reported in the fifth book of Virgil's work. Aeneas reaches out (like Mary grasping for Jesus?) and finds the father to be a shade, an *eidolon*, an image. But just this shadow nuances

When the morning Stars sang together, & all the
Sons of God shouted for joy

GENESIS William Blake
Humanity, trapped in the cave of the senses, is separated
temporarily from the heaven world by the "God" of reason,
and the ceaseless illusionary play of good and evil. The song
of the Morningstars draws us to the spiritual heights, symbol
of the eternally creative Imagination.

a life, as if life has life from the vanishing image, from an imaginal sense.

(3) Perhaps Samuel Beckett can also provide a clue. In his book on Proust there are these lines: ". . . decomposing the illusion of a solid object into its manifold component aspects . . . transforms a human banality into a many-headed goddess" (34).

(4) Or, there is the stunning instance that Beda Allemann makes of Kafka's parable on Prometheus (1967:103-114). Allemann notes, first, how metaphor is of crucial and fundamental importance to language and experience. It gives powerful expression by way of a sensual element. Things appear lifelike and connected. But then one comes to notice that metaphor stands between life and our sense of it, so that a certain immediacy is compromised by the sensuous mediation. Meaning is mediated through image or figure, but we would rather have what we take to be the real thing, straight and direct. Allemann, therefore, looks to a third possibility between mediated meaning and immediate experience. Kafka's parable provides the example of a perspective that is somehow neither metaphor (in the classical Aristotelian sense) nor nonmetaphor. Yet its function is immediate while its nature is mediatorial, just as all language is fated to be.

Kafka first tells the story of Prometheus and his being bound to the rock and his liver being eaten by the eagle of Zeus. This is, of course, the traditional image, the mythic metaphor. But then Kafka modifies the story. In the next lines (a) Prometheus in pain presses himself into the rock; then (b) he is forgotten by the Gods and the eagles; and finally (c) everyone grows weary of the whole affair—Gods, eagles, and us. Still, "at the end, the pure fact of the inexplicable rock remains!" Allemann calls this remainder "absolute metaphor," "radical metaphor," and "anti-metaphor." It is a telling which vanishes in the telling itself. One is left thrown back upon oneself by the parable. The experience is emptying, but it nonetheless allows for many meanings now to fill one fully by their presence.

(5) This brings to mind Wallace Stevens, who once wrote: "A poem is a pheasant," as if to say that image and metaphor are fundamental to poetic meaning (1977:168). After all, a poem is not literally a bird. But later he wrote, "Poetry is a pheasant disappearing in the brush" (1977:173). This connects with his other saying, "the great poem is the disengaging of [a] reality." Something is released after the "bending of the bow" of language (Heraclitus and Robert Duncan), after the tensing of the meaning of language

by way of metaphor.[1] Or, as Stevens also said, "it is not in the premise that reality is a solid," but more like "a woman writing a note and tearing it up" (1972:351).

(6) Elsewhere Stevens used the figure of the Angel to make this point. He was writing on the Angel of Reality, as he called it. This is a Necessary Angel, since, as the Angel himself says, "in my sight you see earth again," as through an image or metaphor. No imagination, no life. But the Angel-image vanishes, like Kafka's Prometheus and the Cheshire Cat and the literal wine. It is a "figure half seen,"

> an apparition apparelled in
> apparels of such lightest look that a turn
> of my shoulder and quickly, too quickly, I
> am gone. (1972:354)

The Angel as poetic image is one of "the intricate evasions of as" which help us disengage our various idolatries and literalisms (1972:348). Yet, these as-forms give substance nonsubstantialistically.

> I do not know which to prefer,
> The Beauty of inflections
> Or the beauty of innuendoes,
> The blackbird whistling
> Or just after. (1972:20)

But Stevens's Angel seems to know which to prefer. In a letter to Victor Hammer on December 27, 1949, the poet wrote: "The question of how to represent the Angel of Reality is not an easy question. . . . I have already suggested that one way of handling the thing would be to evade any definite representation but to depict the figure the moment after it had vanished leaving behind it tokens of its effulgence . . ." (1966:661).

(7) Stevens's Angel is reminiscent of Rilke's. This latter poet, in *The Duino Elegies*, was worrying how to will the transformation of visible things into invisibility. The poetic act, this poet felt, involves one with a "terrible Angel," one whose way is to let go of things in order that they might be retained at a deeper level of sense (1963:21,29). The letting-go involves one in a giving up of grasping things from a perspective of ego ("I," "me," "mine"). It implies a praising of things in words.

> Are we, perhaps, here just for saying: House,
> Bridge, Fountain, Gate, Jug, Olive tree, Window,—

possibly: Pillar, Tower? . . . but for saying,
   remember,
of, for such saying as never the things themselves
hoped so intensely to be.

.   .   .   .

   These things that live on departure
understand when you praise them: fleeting, they look for
rescue through something in us, the most fleeting of all,
Want us to change them entirely, within our invisible
   hearts,
into, oh, endlessly—into ourselves! (1963:75,77)

The Angel is the image of this experience (like sipping the wine, the truly good wine!). Rilke writes about it to his Polish translator: "The angel of the *Elegies* is the creature in whom that transformation of the visible into the invisible we are performing (in poetry) already appears complete. . . . The Angel of the *Elegies* is the being who vouches for the recognition of a higher degree of reality in the invisible.—Therefore 'terrible' to us, because we, its lovers and transformers, still depend on the visible" (1963:87).[2]

If we can begin to get a sense from these clues, it would seem that the Case of the Missing Corpse has to do with the mystery of a sense of "body" coming precisely with the letting-go of notions of literalness with regard to body. And this has something to do with Angels . . . Terrible Angels! One might imagine that Jacob knew this all too well as he wrestled. If so, then the real Deconstructionists may be, not literary critics or theologians, but Angels ascending and descending whatever ladders may be.[3]

Who are these Angels?

Perhaps anything can be an Angel, were one to wrestle it.

Yet, the question of who the Angels are is not an easy one, not only because of the wrestling, but also because the vanishing nature of Angels has received some help from theologians. Angels, it seems, are not encouraged. It is well known that the Sadducees (as opposed to the Pharisees) were opposed to belief in Angels. Eusebius and Theodoret were likewise wary, afraid that such belief would lead to veneration and idolatry. The Council of the Christian Church at Laodicea condemned "those who give themselves up to a masked idolatry in honor of Angels."

In our own time, in spite of Peter Berger's "rumor" that Angels are appearing once again, a considerable case has been mounted, if not against Angels, at least against angelism. The context of this attack is Religion and Literature Studies. Jacques Maritain articulated the notion of angelism in his book, *The Dream of Descartes* (1944). The idea was adopted and underscored by Allen Tate (1953:56-78; 1955:93-145) and by William Lynch (1960). But the most recent advocate of this point of view has been Nathan Scott, who amplifies it in his work, *The Wild Prayer of Longing* (1971).

Scott argues that a proper modern imagination, connected properly to an incarnational theology, will refuse the experiment of angelism. It "will not forget that we are made out of dust" and "foolishly suppose we can fly away from earth." The Angelic Fallacy of the imagination "rejects out of hand the too, too solid stuff of *things* and *facts*—wants to create a kind of absolute poetry that will in no way be dependent upon the received material of nature and history." Scott notes theologically that "the Angelic Fallacy is one which has been evacuated of anything resembling a sacramental vision of existence." He echoes Maritain, Tate, and Lynch in noting that angelism locates the real simply in the subjectivisms of "man's dreaming and imagining and myth-making" (1971:19-21; 1961:27).

There is a conundrum here. We were considering the Case of the Missing Corpse, and two poets, Stevens and Rilke, pointed to Angels as a clue to the recovery of body. But now we note that some literary thinkers and theologians are pointing an accusing finger in this Case toward the very same figure, that of the Angel, as precisely an image of body-loss. Is it not odd that poets in our age, more than theologians, speak for the Angels? No wonder the Angels come no more, or, if at all, only in rumor.

"It is clear why the Angels come no more," writes Jack Gilbert,

> Standing so large in their beautiful Latin,
> How could they accept being refracted
> So small in another grammar, or leave
> Their perfect singing for this broken speech?
> Why should they stumble in this alien world?
>
> Always I have envied the angels their grace.
> But I left my hope of Byzantine size
> And came to this awkwardness, this stupidity.
> Came finally to you washing my face
> As everyone laughed, and found a forest
> Opening as marriage ran in me. All

> The leaves in the world turned a little
> Singing: The angels are wrong. (41)

So, the theologians accuse the imagination of modern poetry of being too poor for a full-bodied theology, and the poet accuses theology of lacking in grace and grammar, singing and size, sufficient for a real-world imagination. At least both are agreed on the problem—what here is being called the Case of the Missing Corpse. Both, too, are agreed that Angels figure in the mystery, one way or another.

Nor are Stevens, Rilke, and Gilbert the only poets indicating the importance of Angels. There are witnesses by Stefan Georg, Honore Balzac, Paul Claudel, Georges Bernanos, Nikolai Leskov, Stephen Spender, and Robert Duncan. Jean Valentine's latest book of poems, *The Messenger*, carries the Angel-figure in its title as well as in its verse, *angelos* having meant "messenger" in Greek.

Emily Dickinson spoke of "Angels bustling in the hall." Jorge Luis Borges, writing about Angels, noted about Swedenborg: "As the English are not very talkative, he fell into the habit of conversing with devils and angels . . . every angel is a heaven" (215). Friedrich Hölderlin, echoing Swedenborg's habit, wrote:

> Much spoke I to him, for whatever poets meditate or sing,
> Is of value chiefly to the angels and to him. (131)

In an earlier handwritten edition of this poem Hölderlin had penned the word "Gods," but he later changed it for publication to "angels," as if in order to speak theologically, one must speak through Angels.

Donald Barthelme has a story in his book, *City Life*, which is about Angels. It begins: "The death of God left the angels in a strange position." The story ends:

I saw a famous angel on television; his garments glistened as if with light. He talked about the situation of angels now. Angels, he said, are like men *in some ways*. The problem of adoration is felt to be central. He said that for a time the angels had tried adoring each other, as we do, but had found it, finally, "not enough." He said they are continuing to search for a new principle. (140)

It seems to be when poets search for a "new principle" (the principles perhaps having been abandoned by theologians) that Angel-talk emerges.

Italo Calvino makes the point in his book, *The Castle of Crossed Destinies* (61):

I am the angel who dwells in the point where lines fork. Whoever retraces the way of divided things encounters me, whoever descends to the bottom of contradictions runs into me, whoever mingles again what was separated feels my membraned wing brush his cheek.

In a poem called "The Jacob's Ladder," Denise Levertov expresses a similar experience (37):

The stairway is not
a thing of gleaming strands
a radiant evanescence
for angels' feet that only glance in their tread, and
    need not
touch the stone.

It is of stone.
A rosy stone that takes
a glowing tone of softness
only because behind it the sky is a doubtful, a doubting
night gray.

A stairway of sharp angles, solidly built.
One sees that the angels must spring
down from one step to the next, giving a little
lift of the wings:

and a man climbing
must scrape his knees, and bring
the grip of his hands into play.
The cut stone
consoles his groping feet. Wings brush past him.
The poem ascends.

For Calvino and Levertov it is precisely the Angel who gives a sense of body. The poem is Angel to our very real sense of things. As Stevens says of poems and of Angels, they are "necessary" (1951:83), and to notice that we always and ineluctably "live poetically upon the earth," as Hölderlin did note (246), is to suggest that we live angelically, wrestling the terrible Angels, scraping our knees, descending into contradictions, groping with our feet, doubting, dreaming, imagining worlds that are, gripping for "the angel at the center of this rind" (Stevens, 1951:83).

If indeed Angels can give body to meaning, whatever this may mean, then theology may very well be taking place more in poetry (which has not neglected Angels) than in theology itself (which has). Or, to put the matter differently, a theology not lacking in body may have as one of its options, if not angel*ism*, perhaps then an "angelic thinking."

This last phrase is that of Marsilio Ficino, and, like Levertov's equation (poem as Angel), Ficino seems to have had in mind an "angelic thinking" as an imaginal thinking, a "thinking" in image and likeness, in myth and metaphor—in short, a poetic theology. *Theologia imaginalis*: a way of "thinking" about Religion purged perhaps of docetic angelism by Angels and images, rather than by men and ideas (Miller, 1980; Ficino:208-211; Kristellar:107).

The problem with human ideas is that they tend to stay around, having a marked propensity for fixation, for objectivization and externalization, wanting to be taken for truth itself, leading thinking and feeling unwittingly and witlessly (not to mention, ponderously) toward idolatry and dogma; whereas images, like Angels, tend to turn and transform as they disappear into the brush, like a pheasant. The Angels "tried adoring each other, as we do, but had found it, finally, not enough," the Angel said!

The mention of the name of Ficino is a reminder of the fact that theology and philosophy once knew the necessity of Angels as much as does poetry now. Louis Tomassin, the Orphic Christian in seventeenth-century France, said: "The world is filled with an infinity of Angels, good and bad, whom the pagans called Gods" (Walker:211).

Thomas Aquinas articulated this sense and, indeed, its necessity. Angels, he argued, are "demanded by the hierarchic character of the scale of being." Frederick Copleston has explained this point as follows. "We can discern the ascending orders or ranks of forms from the forms of inorganic substances, through vegetative forms, the irrational sensitive forms of animals, the rational soul of man, to the infinite and pure Act, God: but there is a gap in the hierarchy. The rational soul of man is created, finite and embodied, while God is uncreated, infinite and pure spirit: it is only reasonable, then, to suppose that between the human soul and God there are finite and created spiritual forms which are without body (i.e., Angels)" (48). So, in this Aquinian, cosmological perspective on theology, Angels are without body and are *logically* necessary to a human knowledge of the embodiment of spirit.

But there is another traditional view of the so-called necessity of Angels. In fact, it is just the placing of angelology in the context of Aristotelian logic about which Avicenna split with Averroes. The former, arguing neo-Platonically and ontologically, rather than rationalistically and cosmologically, sensed precisely a loss of body in the Aristotelian perspective. The neo-Platonic view, not so unlike the late Jewish angelology of Zechariah, Daniel, and Ezekiel (*angelus interpres*) and the Ebionite tradition of Christ as Angel (*Christos Angelos*) and the early-Church tradition of the Trinity as Angels (Daniélou:5-41), is reflected out of Plotinus in Proclus, out of Proclus in Dionysius the Areopagite, and out of Dionysius in John Scotus Erigena, Hugh and John of St. Victor, Alexander of Hales, Meister Eckhart, and Jacob Boehme.

Paul Tillich sided with this ontological and Platonic perspective. He explained the angelic function in a way not unlike Ficino's "angelic intellect." It gives *eidos*, visionary idea and imagination to thinking. In the lectures on the history of Christian theology, Tillich writes: "If you want to interpret the concept of Angels in a meaningful way today, interpret them as the Platonic essences, as the powers of being, not as special beings. If you interpret them in the latter way, it all becomes crude mythology. On the other hand, if you interpret them as emanations of the divine power of being in essences, in powers of being, the concept of Angels becomes meaningful and perhaps important. . . . The Angels are the spiritual mirror of the divine abyss . . . the essences in which the divine ground expresses itself" (1968:94). That is, Angels are not *logically* necessary. They are not necessary because we need them for knowing. But they are necessary simply because things *are* what they are and not something else.

Elsewhere in his work, Tillich is even more concrete about Angels. He says: "In our terminology we could say that the Angels are concrete-poetic symbols of the structures or powers of being. . . . Their 'epiphany' is a revelatory experience determining the history of religion and culture." Does this suggest that, wherever "meaning" occurs eventfully in life, we may imagine an Angel has just vanished? Tillich says: "The rediscovery of Angels from the psychological side as archetypes of the collective unconscious and the new interpretation of the demonic in theology and literature have contributed to the understanding of these powers of being, which are not beings (Aristotle's and Aquinas's 'separate intelligences'), but structures" (1951:260).

It is just at this point that Henry Corbin has made an important contribution from the side of his work on what he called "the Platonists of Persia." Corbin observed that in the Zoroastrian background to Iranian Sufism there is a Proclus-like view of Angels. On the road to the Cinvat Bridge, that is, to the "other" world, the Soul meets its Destiny, an Angel-Self, a celestial soul, a Fravarti called Daēna. When one meets the Other of the Self, it is an Angel which is one's true destiny, an image of vocation. Corbin, like Tillich, calls this archetypal. "To lose this archetypal dimension," says Corbin, "is literally to cease to have an Angel; it is to die, as a soul can die" (1957:132). One might also say this in reverse: to lose this Angel is to lose an archetypal dimension of self in life. The Angel is necessary, but not quite in the logical way Aristotle, Averroes, and Aquinas thought. Rather, it is necessary for psychological depth in life. The Angel gives image and body.

Corbin makes this point with urgency in an essay entitled "On the Necessity of Angelology." There he draws attention to Deuteronomy 5.7, where it is written: "You shall have no other Gods before my Face." Then Corbin asks:

Yes, but what is this Face? It could be a matter of that about which it is said: "You shall not see my Face, for no man sees me and lives" (Exodus 33.20). Yet, it is precisely a matter of the Face that God shows to man, his theophany, and the Angel of the Face, all the Angels of the Face, are his theophanies (in Shi'ite angelology, the Imāms say, "We are the Face of God"), these theophanies of which the transformations correspond to the state and mode of being of those to whom they are shown, face to Face.

So, when in Isaiah 63.9, we read the phrase, "the Angel before his Face," it may mean the image by which one sees the God who is *Deus absconditus* and yet manifest among men. The "secret" is, says Corbin, that the phrase "You shall have no other Gods before my Face" comes to mean "You shall have no other Gods before my Angel" (1979a:65-69).

Perhaps this is what Jacob had to face when he wrestled. In the Septuagint version of Genesis 32.31f, we read:

kai ekalesen Iakōb to onoma tou topou ekeinou Eidos Theou. eidon gar Theou prosōpon pros prosōpon, kai esōthē mou hē psychē.

And Jacob called the name of the place, Image (*Eidos*) of God. "For I have seen (*eidon*) God face to Face, and my soul (*psychē*) is saved."

In this connection it may be useful to recall Jesus' words in Matthew 18.10: "See that you do not despise one of these little ones (*mikrōn*);

for I tell you that in heaven their Angels always behold the Face of my Father who is in heaven."

Corbin connects this tradition of the Angel of the Face with the views of the Archangel Gabriel of Sohrawardi and of Zechariah, with the theology of Avicenna, with the notions of Trinity and *Christos Angelos* of the early Church, and with the neo-Platonic angelology in Proclus' *Platonic Theology*. The necessity of the Angels, in these places, comes to be seen as two-fold. (1) Without angelology there is a peril of being trapped in literalistic reality without a sense of transcendence, immobilized in *mere* secularity. (2) But there is a second peril: namely, misunderstanding the transcendence as being infinitely qualitatively distinct from life, wholly other, creating a gulf between sensibles and supersensibles, condemning life here and now to an inferiority or to an "asceticism with all its furies and self-accusing reflections" (Corbin, 1969:292).

On the neo-Platonic view, whether that of the Christian Pseudo-Dionysius or the Sufi Sohrawardi, the Angels occupy a *metaxy*, a realm in between sensible experience and supersensible idea, between head and heart. Like the *theologia imaginalis* implicit in the poets, the angelology of neo-Platonic theology discovers itself abiding neither in infinity nor in finitude, neither in idea nor in feeling, but in some intermediary world of imagination. Corbin calls this experience a *mundus imaginalis*, translating the Sufi notion of *'alam al-mithāl* (1969:7-19). The associations are also confirmed by Saint Dionysius, in the last paragraph of his work *The Celestial Hierarchy*: "It concerns the Forms of the Holy (*hierōn anaplaseōn*) . . . the Types of Fantasy (*tupōtikais phantasiais*) . . . Angels' Images (*angelikōn . . . eikonōn*) (1958:191).

The Biblical tradition, in a somewhat odd way, already implies the important intermediary connecting function of the Angels. In I Corinthians 11.10, St. Paul writes: "That is why a woman ought to have a veil (*exousian* = "authority"!) on her head, because of the Angels." Presumably this refers to Genesis 6.1-2: "When men began to multiply on the face of the ground, and daughters were born to them, the sons of God saw that the daughters of men were fair; and they took to wife such of them as they chose." So, the imaginal-angelic function is erotic in nature. It is sensuous and bodily.

Not removed far from this view is that of the Greeks, who linked *angeloi* not only to poets and birds (that is, heralds and messengers), but also to Hermes (and "hermeneutics"), to Hekate, to Nemesis, and to Artemis (Kittel:74ff). These four chthonic *angeloi* are guides in the journey to the "other" world. They are in the depths where soul's feeling really is.

Philo, in his essay *On Giants*, linked the feeling of soul (*psychas . . . daimonas*) with Hermes as Angel and Logos. In another essay, *On Dreams*, Philo wrote: *tēn tou theou eikona, ton angelon autou logou*, "the image of God is the Angel of his Logos" (Kittel:76). So it is not surprising that in Exodus 33.2, rather than Yahweh, an Angel is guide to the people of Israel. The holiness of Yahweh would have consumed them. In Judges 2.1, it is an Angel who brings the people out of Egypt, functioning thereby as Hermes or Hekate would have for the Greeks.

So, the Angel as image of something transcendent here and now may be many things!—it is hermetic word (compare I Corinthians 13:1:*glōssai tōn angelōn*, "angel tongues"), herald, *kērygma*, guide, connecting link, eros, the Face of that which we face, heart and mind at one in imagination, alter-ego, a mediator that vanishes leaving life with body, the immediacy of soul, the power and form of being itself, the gods, Self, God! No wonder Walter Nigg (1962) and Stephen Crites (1975) are so eager, in our time to recover the Angels![4] As Corbin put it: "The wrestling is not *against* but *for* the Angel."

But where does one find these Angels?

If Angels are not to be found on the Scale of Mental Acts or on the logical Chain of Being and Causation, then perhaps they are where they always were: namely, on ladders!

Is not a ladder the proper place for the imaginal Angel who functions as intermediary, since a ladder connects what is above and below, even and perhaps especially when neither "above" nor "below" is known or knowable? And a ladder can vanish like an Angel, not being engraved permanently in stone nor being a dogmatic staircase of some hierarchical edifice. After going up and going down, a ladder can be thrown away, as both Wittgenstein and the Hindu tradition have mystically noted, and even recommended.

Was it not Jacob's ladder and the Angels ascending and descending upon it about which Jesus was thinking when he spoke with Philip and Nathaniel? Jesus had gone to Galilee. The route from Bethany beyond Jordan to Cana would have taken him past Jabbok, Mahanaim, and Bethel, where heavenly dreams and mystical visions had come to Jacob-Israel (Howard:489f). Nathaniel, true to his name as an Israelite, is, like Jacob at Bethel, to see Angels. Jesus says to him: "You shall see greater things than these . . . you will see heaven opened, and the Angel of God ascending and descending upon the Son of Man" (John 1.50f).

The Angels that gave Jacob his name, his true sense of Self as Israel, now in the Fourth Gospel are seen as the procession of the Body of God. And the formula is, as is usual: ascending *and* descending.[5] It is as if a ladder is anything upon which Angels as images rise and fall. There may well have been many such ladders that are in fact the body of a savior, many which have come and gone, functioned and vanished. Shepherds as well as Kings have known. In their souls' nights, angelic images came into their dreams and then went away, as they themselves did, too. The experience changed their perspectives radically. The narrative of their stories was touched by image; history touched by imagination; horizontal by vertical; ego by archetype; life by Angel.

Others have had experiences similar to the Shepherds and Kings. There was an important ladder in the dream of Saint Perpetua, not long before her martyrdom. Saint John Climacus (whose name means "ladder"!) suffered the same vision in the seventh century. For Saint Bonaventura the entire world was a ladder—*itinerarium mentis ad deum*—for in the world he found everywhere traces and images of ultimate things. Similarly for the Jewish Kabbalists, the Sefiroth is the ladder of En Sof, the Unknowable One. According to Martin Buber, there is no rung of being on which we cannot find the entire holiness of God, everywhere and at all times (Buber:5). That is, the ladder is not hierarchically graded like the Great Chain of Being, decreasing in value and power as one moves from Being toward Nonbeing. Rather, each and every one of its rungs is a differentiation, an articulation in an individual way, an image and trace of the One in power and in polytheistic manifestation.

For Apuleius the ladder was the seven planets. In seventeenth-century alchemical tradition, the *scala lapidis* was the table of elements, each one of which is really gold. To the yogi, the ladder is the chakras of his own body. The Po people lost their ladder, their connectedness. A crippled boy tried to ascend it, as if one could get some "where" other than where one is already. So the boy's mother threw the ladder away! Not so, however, in the case of Sumatran and Mazovian mythology. There the ladder still exists . . . in the form of the feathers of every bird! (Gaster:184ff).

The medicine men of the Dyaks of Borneo—not to mention

those of Nepal, Babar, and many other places—discover their ladders of healing when they receive initiatory visions, ascending and descending with souls and daimones (Eliade:58, 123-129, 326-328, 430f, 487ff).

At the oracle-shrine of Trophonius in ancient Greece, the ladder used by an initiate was to be light in weight, so as to be very portable and so it would fit into a tight place. According to the Pyramid Texts of the mid-third millenium in Egypt, the ladder of soul was the hip of the goddess Isis herself. Not that another deity might not be a ladder. For example, one might climb on Mother Nut, her name meaning "ladder," since she springs to heaven and into the depths, as a text puts it, on the Fingers of the God, Lord of the Ladder. And, remember those ladders of the Hopi and Zuni, told about in the creation stories, and still in use.

The Cross is a ladder in medieval iconography. But so also is the zodiac, a ship's mast, sunbeams, rainbow, smoke, trees of various sorts, mountains, ropes, vines, arrows, chains, stalks . . . and for Jack a beanstalk, whereas for another it is Rapunzel's hair, or even the Virgin herself, who was described by one ancient text as *scala efferens a terra in coelum*, like Isis.

Perhaps the point is that anything may be a ladder, if one can see the Angels on it. Or perhaps there is another point, too.

When the people wanted to express what the ladder was, their language imagined it with the Indo-European root *klei-*, Greek *klima*, and Latin *clime*. Each of these carries the same imaginal sense. For example, *klimatos* in Greek means "inclination," since a ladder is leaned against something at an angle. The particular "inclination" specified by the Greek term is that of earth to sun, or a particular location on earth in relation to the North Pole. Hence, *klimatos* can indicate a "region" or the "weather" or "atmosphere" of a region, and therefore the "climate." From the root of *klimatos* the Greeks wrote *klinein* and *klimax*, meaning "ladder," because of its "slant," of course. Then, in their rhetoric books, the *klimax* of a speech was its "slant" or "inclination" or "leaning," rather than its ending.[6] It is not where one goes on a ladder that is the climax, but rather the going and coming itself, ascending *and* descending. It is this which gives the inclination or the climate of opinion, marking the region and its terrain. Therefore, the word *klimaktera* means "round" or "rung" or "step." And *klinē* means "couch," just as *klinikos* in Greek and *clinicus* in Latin is a "clinic," where the couches are and where Freud found the

171

dreams . . . neither standing forth nor lying down, just an inclination.

If Angels as images are the differentiations of being, then the goings and comings, ascendings and descendings, the ups and downs on whatever ladders there may be—all these give slant, inclination, leaning, climate, atmosphere, perspective. So, in I Kings 8.58, Psalm 119.36, and Proverbs 2.2, one may read: "Incline thine heart!" by which is meant not something *we* do, but a noticing of how our hearts are already inclined from some autonomous Source. Gérard de Nerval wrote in *Aurélia*:

> Last night I had a most delicious dream . . .
> I was in a tower so deep in the earth and so
> high in the sky, that my whole existence seemed
> to be consumed in ascending and descending. (112)

Could it be, then, that the Angels are themselves the rungs? And that the rungs are Angels?

From Ficino, the Septuagint, and Pseudo-Dionysius, we have noted the identification of Angels and images. This is expressed in other places, too. The word *ekoni* in Syriac, the term for icon or image, also means "angel." Josephus referred to Angels using the word *phantasma*, "fantasies" or "imaginings" (Kittel:80). Corbin says of the Sufi notion of *khidr* (a personal invisible angelic guide), that this "Angel is bound up with the idea that the Form under which each of the Spirituals knows God is also the Form under which God knows him, because it is the Image under which God reveals Himself to Himself through the particular person" (1969:62). The Gospel of Philip, from the Nag Hammadi texts, speaks of uniting the Angel and the image (Robinson:139). Jacob Boehme, in his work, *Aurora*, says: "As man is created in the image and similitude of God, so also are the Angels, for they are the brethren of men" (103). And so on. . . .

But if the Angels are images, images must be Angels, that is, individuations of ultimate reality, varieties of religious experience, the body of life, the "forms of things unknown," the rounds of our ladders. So, what are these images as Angels?

Could it be that they are our dreams; our daydreams, wishes, and fantasies; our moods, those images accompanying our paranoias, depressions, elations; images of our thoughts and ideas; the images of our illnesses, the body's images, a pain in the posterior or in the neck, a backache, yellow belly, headache and heart attack, indigestion, weak knees, false teeth? All these may be

Angels—can we believe it as we wrestle them?—ascending and descending, the ups and downs, the "others" of self, ego's companions, messengers, intruders, wrestlers, initiators. These may be our ladders, too, giving—as they indeed do!—inclination, leaning, disposition, perspective.[7] Jacob's dream *is* his Angel; it is his ladder, too, differentiating his being in structure and power.

Consider the ladder. The rungs ascend and descend, but they go to no particular "where," in themselves. Where we already are is the location of the ascending and descending. "The way up and the way down are the same," Heraclitus wrote (Wheelwright:90). This is paradox for a logic that imagines the climax to be some end at last attained. But for a vision whose imagination locates the presence and power of ultimacy closer to hand, it is a simple statement of experience.

Why then would one call this ladder and its rungs Angels and choirs of Angels, rather than, say, Scale of Mental Acts, Great Chain of Being, the Hierarchy of the Ordo Entis, the Levels of Life, Passages, Stages of Development, Complexes, Gestalts, Archetypes, Forms, or Ideas?

Why? Because Angels can be wrestled, conversed with, given names, move on wings, take flight, have faces which can be faced. One can hear the singing. Perhaps this is why Swedenborg fell into the habit of conversing with Angels and why Hölderlin said that for whatever poets meditate or sing is of value chiefly to the Angels. Rilke advised that we show it to the Angel and see it through the Angel (1963:75). The ladder-vision is, as Stevens said, an "angelic eye" (1972:31), that is, an imaginal perspective.

The disappearance of the Angels in contemporary theology may well signal the disappearance of the imagination from the study of Religion. But if this way is sometimes lacking in theology, Angels and their images are by no means absent from poetry, which may be one of the locations of an active theology in our time. For, after all, this essay is finally about the resurrection of the body by way of an imaginal sense of things.

A theology of poetry's Angels, not to mention those of Religion, would perhaps be a poetic theology of imagination: a *theologia imaginalis*. Such may well be as necessary as Stevens sensed and as the neo-Platonists knew. Robert Duncan uses the word "urgent" (50):

> The poem
> feeds upon thought, feeling, impulse,

to breed itself,
a spiritual urgency at the dark ladders leaping,

This beauty is an inner persistence
toward the source.

... like whatever Mary, going toward the cave of whichever Garden,
"while it was still dark."

Notes

1. Compare Joseph Campbell writing on this same point: "The bow, in order to function as a bow and not as a snare, must have no meaning whatsoever in itself—or in any part of itself—beyond that of being an agent for disengagement—from itself: no more meaning than the impact of the doctor's little hammer when it hits your knee, to make it jerk. A symbol . . . is an energy-evoking and -directing agent. When given a meaning, either corporeal or spiritual, it serves for the engagement of the energy to itself—and this may be compared to the notching of the arrow to the bowstring and the drawing of the bow. When, however, all meaning is withdrawn, the symbol serves for disengagement, and the energy is dismissed—to its own end, which cannot be defined in terms of the parts of the bow" (178).

2. Compare Rilke's other lines: "O how he has to vanish (i.e., Orpheus) for you to grasp him" (1962:25); and, "spirit . . . loves in the swing of the figure nothing so much as the point of inflection" (1962:93).

3. Harold Bloom, in an essay on deconstructionism, makes this point about the Angel, citing John Ashberry ("Perhaps an Angel looks like everything / We have forgotten") and Walter Benjamin ("The Angel . . . resembles all from which I have had to part. . . . In the things I no longer have, he resides. He makes them transparent"). And again, Bloom quoting Ashberry:

   > They seemed strange because we couldn't actually see them.
   > And we realize that only at the point where they lapse
   > Like a wave breaking on a rock, giving up
   > Its shape in a gesture which expresses that shape. (Bloom:30f)

   Compare the interpretation of the line from Emerson ("The poet turns the world to glass") in Miller, 1978:331-335.

4. Compare the implication of a perhaps not pseudonymous work of Thomas Aquinas to the effect that "the entire work of the alchemists is an endeavor to reintegrate the unsublimable residue, the sinners on earth and the fallen Angels into a whole" (Von Franz, 1966:255).

5. Compare the work of the medieval neo-Platonic Christian theologian, Raymond Lulle, on *ars ascendendi et descendendi*.

6. See note #3, and compare Bloom's use of the term "clinamen" in his

own deconstructionist criticism. Bloom translates the saying of Nietzsche, *Jedes Wort ist ein Vorurteil,* with the English, "Every word is a clinamen" (9).

7. Compare the saying of James Hillman: "Imagination is . . . both diaphanous and passionate, unerring in its patterns and in all ways necessary, the necessary angel that makes brute necessity angelic" (142).

Works Consulted

Allemann, Beda, 1967. "Metaphor and Antimetaphor." *Interpretation: The Poetry of Meaning.* Edited by Stanley R. Hopper and David L. Miller. New York: Harcourt, Brace, & World.

Barthelme, Donald, 1971. *City Life.* New York: Bantam Books.

Beckett, Samuel, 1931. *Proust.* New York: Grove Press.

Bloom, Harold, 1979. "The Breaking of Form." *Deconstruction and Criticism.* New York: Seabury Press.

Boehme, Jacob, 1914. *Aurora.* Translated by Sparrow. London: Watkins.

Borges, Jorge Luis, 1978. *The Book of Imaginary Beings.* Translated by Di Giovanni. New York: E. P. Dutton.

Buber, Martin, 1947. *Ten Rungs: Hasidic Sayings.* New York: Schocken Books.

Calvino, Italo, 1977. *The Castle of Crossed Destinies.* New York: Harcourt Brace Jovanovich.

Campbell, Joseph, 1969. "The Symbol Without Meaning." *The Flight of the Wild Gander.* New York: Viking.

Copleston, Frederick, 1962. *History of Philosophy: Medieval Philosophy.* Volume II, part 2. Garden City: Doubleday-Image Books.

Corbin, Henry, 1957, "Cyclical Time in Mazdaism and Ismailism." *Man and Time: Papers from the Eranos Yearbooks.* Edited by Joseph Campbell. New York: Pantheon. 1969, *Creative Imagination in the Sufism of Ibn 'Arabi.* Translated by Mannheim. Princeton: Princeton University Press. 1979a, "Nécessité de l'angélologie." *L'Ange et l'homme.* Paris: Albin Michel. 1979b, "Pour une charte de l'Imaginal." *Corps spirituel et terre céleste.* Deuxième édition. Paris: Editions Buchet/Chastel.

Crites, Stephen, 1975. "Angels We Have Heard." *Religion as Story.* Edited by Wiggins. New York: Harper & Row.

Daniélou, Jean, 1957. "Trinité et angélologie dans la théologie judéo-chrétien." *Recherches des sciences religieuses, XLV.*

Dionysius-Areopagite (Pseudo-), 1958. *La Hiérarchie céleste.* Sources chrétiennes, #58. Translated by De Gandillac. Paris: Editions du Cerf.

Duncan, Robert, 1960. *The Opening of the Field.* New York: New Directions.

Eliade, Mircea, 1964. *Shamanism.* Translated by Trask. New York: Pantheon.

Ficino, Marsilio, 1944. "Commentary on Plato's *Symposium.*" Translated by Jayne. *University of Missouri Studies, XIX/1.*

Gaster, Theodor H., 1969. *Myth, Legend, and Custom in the Old Testament.* New York: Harper & Row.

Gérard de Nerval (Labrunie, Gerard), 1965. *Aurélia ou le rêve et la vie.* Paris: Minard.

Gilbert, Jack, 1962. *Views of Jeopardy.* New Haven: Yale University Press.

Hillman, James, 1979. "Image-Sense." *Spring* 1979. Irving, Texas: Spring Publications.

Hölderlin, Friedrich, 1961. *Selected Verse of . . .* Translated by Hamburger. Baltimore: Penguin Books.

David L. Miller

Howard, Wilbert, 1952. "Exegesis of John." *The Interpreter's Bible.* Volume VIII. Nashville: Abingdon Press.

Kittel, Gerhard, ed., 1964. *Theological Wordbook of the New Testament.* Volume I. Translated by Bromiley. Grand Rapids: Eerdmans.

Kristeller, Oskar, 1964. *The Philosophy of Marsilio Ficino.* Gloucester: Peter Smith.

Levertov, Denise, 1961. *The Jacob's Ladder.* New York: New Directions.

Lynch, William, 1960. *Christ and Apollo.* New York: Sheed and Ward.

Maritain, Jacques, 1944. *The Dream of Descartes.* New York: Philosophical Library.

Miller, David L., 1978, "Hades and Dionysos: The Poetry of Soul." *Journal of the American Academy of Religion,* XLVI/3. 1980, "Theology's Ego/Religion's Soul." *Spring* 1980. Irving, Texas: Spring Publications.

Nigg, Walter, 1962. "Stay You Angels, Stay with Me . . ." *Harper's Bazaar,* XCVI (December).

Rilke, Rainer Maria, 1962, *Sonnets to Orpheus.* Translated by Norton, New York: Norton. 1963, *The Duino Elegies.* Translated by Leishman and Spender. New York: Norton.

Robinson, James, director, 1977. *The Nag Hammadi Library.* New York: Harper & Row.

Scott, Nathan, 1961, "The Bias of Comedy and the Narrow Escape into Faith." *The Christian Scholar,* XLIV/1 (Spring). 1971, *The Wild Prayer of Longing.* New Haven: Yale University Press.

Stevens, Wallace, 1951, *The Necessary Angel.* New York: Vintage Books. 1966, *The Letters of . . .* Edited by Stevens. New York: Alfred Knopf. 1972, *The Palm at the End of the Mind.* Edited by Stevens. New York: Vintage Books. 1977, *Opus Posthumous.* Edited by Stevens. New York: Alfred Knopf.

Tate, Allen, 1953, *The Forlorn Demon.* Chicago: Regency. "The Angelic Imagination." 1955, *The Man of Letters in the Modern World.* New York: Scribners.

Tillich, Paul, 1951, *Systematic Theology.* Volume I. Chicago: University of Chicago Press. 1968, *A History of Christian Thought.* New York: Harper & Row.

Von Franz, Marie-Louise, 1966, *Aurora consurgens.* Translated by Hull and Glover. New York: Pantheon. 1980, *The Passion of Saint Perpetua.* Irving, Texas: Spring Publications.

Walker, D. P., 1972. *The Ancient Theology.* Ithaca: Cornell University Press.

Wheelwright, Philip, 1964. *Heraclitus.* New York: Atheneum.

13

Daimons and the
Inner Companion

MARIE-LOUISE VON FRANZ

There are demons in all times and all cultures. . . . In ancient Egypt there were good spirits and evil ones. The dwarf Bes and the youthful Horus, for example, were positive demons; the evil demons were often referred to as a nameless collective, the "companions of Seth." Similarly with the Devas of Iran. In Mesopotamia and Asia Minor there were also such good and evil demons; the latter, for instance, are spirits of the dead and evil winds that bring sickness, as well as "spies," and "secret agents," whose aim it is to bring harm to human beings.

In pre-Hellenic Greece the demons, as in Egypt, were part of a nameless collectivity. The word *daimon* comes from *daiomai*, which means "divide," "distribute," "allot," "assign," and originally referred to a momentarily perceptible divine activity, such as a startled horse, a failure in work, illnesses, madness, terror in certain natural spots. There are even skills that are in a way demons. The idea of a demon as a person's constant companion emerged in the fifth century B.C. in Hesiod, and in the third century B.C. it spread very widely. Such a demon causes the individual's happiness or unhappiness; as early as the fourth century B.C., sacrifices were made to a good (*agathos*) daimon as house-spirit.

Plato does not use the word *daimon* unambiguously; usually it is synonymous with *theos* (god), sometimes with the nuance of a "near-human" being. In the *Symposium*, Diotima says that Eros is a mighty daimon and "spirits, you know, are halfway between god and man." To Socrates' question, "What powers have they then?" she answers, "They are the envoys and interpreters that ply between heaven and earth, flying upward with our worship and our prayers, and descending with the heavenly answers and commandments, and since they are between the two estates they weld both sides together and merge them into one great whole. They form the medium of the prophetic arts, of the priestly rites of sacrifice, initiation, and incantation, of divination and of sorcery, for the divine will not mingle directly with the human, and it is only through the mediation of the spirit world that man can have any intercourse, whether waking or sleeping, with the gods. . . . There are many spirits, and many kinds of spirits, and Love [Eros] is one of them."

In the Stoa and in Platonism of the middle period the shades of difference between gods and demons were more sharply drawn: the gods are the mighty powers of the universe, remote from men, majestic, for the most part aloof from the suffering and the passions of humanity. The demons, on the other hand, inhabit the intermediate realm between Olympus and mankind, especially the regions of the air and the sublunar world, and there they join the nature spirits in springs and plants and animals. In presenting his late Platonic conception, Apuleius of Madura formulates this as follows: The poets had falsely attributed to the gods what was valid only for the demons; "they exalt and favor certain human beings and they oppress and humble others. They feel therefore compassion, anger, joy, and fear and all the other feelings of human nature . . . all the storms that are so far removed from the tranquility of the heavenly gods. All the gods pass their time in an unchanging spiritual state . . . since nothing is more perfect than a god. . . . All these feelings are suited, however, to the inferior nature of the demons, which have immortality in common with the upper beings and passions with the lower beings. . . . I have therefore called them 'passive,' because they are subject to the same disorders as we are."* In a certain sense a man's spirit, his "genius," and his "good spirit" (like Socrates' *daimonion*) are themselves also *daimons* like the other spirits that inhabit the air. After death they become *Lemurs* or *Lares* (house-gods) or, if they were evil, *larvae* (ordinary ghosts).

Apuleius' great model was Plutarch (born A.D. 50), who worked out this world order: At the top of the cosmic order are the visible gods, the celestial bodies that belong to the element fire; beneath them the demons who belong to the air; still lower the spirits of the dead heroes (in water); and finally human beings, animals, and plants with their earth-nature. Our souls can climb upward or downward, according to merit. The demons are not immortal

---

*Translated from *Opuscules philosophiques et fragments* by Apuleius, edited by J. Beaujeu (Paris, 1973).

but can live for thousands of years. When they die there are often storms or epidemics of the plague. Evil demons mostly punish transgressions of taboos with incurable madness.*

The distinction made in late antiquity between gods, who are remote from all earthly suffering, and demons, who are subject to all the human passions and feelings, seems to me to be very important. The demons are, so to speak, closer to human beings, more subjective-psychological than the gods. Cicero even describes them as *mentes* or *animi*, that is, as "souls." Others call them *potestates*, "powers." The description of demons as "souls" may be found in many earlier authors but especially in later ones, in the Stoa, Poseidonius, Philo, Plutarch, Clement of Alexandria, and others.†
From the standpoint of Jungian psychology the distinction in antiquity between gods and demons means the following: The gods represent more than the archetypal ground-structure of the psyche, which is far removed from consciousness, while the demons are visualizations of the same archetypes, it is true, but in a form nearer to consciousness, which comes closer to the subjective inner experience of humans. It is as if a partial aspect of the archetype were beginning to move closer to the individual, to cling to him and to become a sort of "grown-on soul."

In Neoplatonism we have the following cosmic world-order (there are naturally a number of variants): The highest god in wise providence ordered all things. A further providence is attributed to the gods who move through the sky, the celestial bodies; they see to the growth of mortal man for the preservation of the species. A third function of providence is entrusted to the daimons, which are the protectors and guardians of special human concerns. Celsus, who was of an academic-Stoic cast of mind, even attributes to them specific functions: they provide the human species with vitally needed water, wine, bread, and air; they bestow fertility in marriage and each one watches over a specific part of the body, which is why they must be appealed to whenever a certain part of the body is in need of healing. They can grant prophecies to men, but in certain circumstances can also bring about physical evil. Such evil can best be healed through public tribute to such a demon. . . .

In the final initiation of Apuleius into the Egyptian mysteries he is called to the worship of Osiris, the son-husband of Isis. For

---

*See *La Démonologie de Plutarque* by G. Soury (Paris, 1942).
†See *Apuleius philosophus Platonicus* by F. Regen (Berlin and New York, 1971).

the man of that day Osiris represented the immortal inner personality into which a man is transformed after death. In the alchemistic tradition, therefore, Osiris was the equivalent of the "stone," that is, the resurrected body. In Egypt the immortal nucleus of the soul was also called the Ba-soul. In his essay "The Dialogue of a World-Weary Man with His Ba," Helmuth Jacobsohn has shown that the Ba represented, on the one hand, something like the unconscious personality of a man and, on the other, what Jung has described as the Self, whereas the Ka embodied something resembling a man's vitality and those elements of his personality and constitution that are inherited. The Ba was depicted as a *star* or as a bird with a human head. (We know that in the beliefs of many peoples human beings are supposed to have a number of different souls; the ancient Greeks also believed that people possess several souls—*psychai.*)

According to Plutarch, Isis and Osiris are very great "daimons" but they are not gods. Therefore they represent something which is transsubjective but which is closer to the human than are the gods, something which can be experienced inwardly in certain states of very strong emotion. Through initiation into the mysteries, a human being could become a special servitor of these daimons, could even be completely dissolved in them after death without losing his individuality; that is why in Egyptian coffin-texts the dead are evoked as "Osiris N.N." Apuleius does not tell us what happened to him during his encounter with Osiris, maintaining the silence imposed by the mysteries. We can only assume that in this experience he found an indestructible psychic ground for going ahead with his life.

We should be skeptical about attempts to relate some of these "souls" or "daimons" to the Jungian concepts of shadow, anima, animus, and Self. It would be a great mistake, as Jung himself often emphasized, to suppose that the shadow, the anima (or animus), and the Self appear separately in a person's unconscious, neatly timed and in definable order. In the reality of everyday practice it is much more likely that a person in depth psychological analysis will first meet with something psychically "absolutely other" in himself, a dark, chaotic something, appearing to him in complicated dream images in which, little by little, he begins to discover his alter ego. Some orientation begins to emerge from this chaos as certain inferior traits in this "other" begin to separate out, traits that are relatively easy to recognize as belonging to the particular person. As this process continues, the contrasexual aspects in this *massa confusa* gradually begin to be distinguishable. It is only after these, too, have drawn nearer to consciousness that it later becomes evident that a part of the great power and the divinity of these figures does not come from the person himself but originates in a still deeper and more embracing psychic center, the Self. In the series of dreams of a modern physicist, which Jung published in *Psychology and Alchemy*, there appears the image of a sublime and majestic woman whose head radiates light as the sun does. In this image the anima and the Self (sun) are still entirely one; this is rather like the appearance of Isis toward the end of *The Metamorphoses* of Apuleius. It becomes apparent only later that the anima may be distinguished from a power emanating from a still deeper level.

If we look for personifications of the Self among the daimons of antiquity, we see that certain daimons are more like a mixture of shadow and Self, or of animus-anima and Self, and that is, in fact, what they are. In other words, they represent the still undifferentiated "other," unconscious personality of the individual.

This is the case not only with the Egyptian Ba-Osiris but also with the ancient Roman idea of the *genius*. The *genii* of the ancient Romans were originally household gods of a kind. Their name is etymologically related to *gignere*—to "beget" or "engender"—so that the genius represented first of all the reproductive power of the father of a family and of the son and heir, much like the Egyptian Ka-soul of the Pharoah. The marriage bed was called *genialis lectus*; this referred not only to sexual potency but also to the qualities that today we would call psychic vitality, temperament, resourcefulness, and a lively imagination. The genius rejoiced when those who honored him ate and drank well and when their sexual experience was good (*indulgere genio*), but homosexuality and sexual perversions put him out of humor. Miserly and dry people allow their genius to waste away. That the genius represented much more than the merely sexual is shown by the fact that for the Romans even places in a landscape or fields or groves could possess their genius, the *genius loci*, which assured the continuity of their existence. Used in this way the word *genius* referred more to the psychic atmosphere or to the mood that such a place can evoke. Here we have once again that original situation in which the objective psyche appears to live altogether in outer things, that is, is experienced by human beings only in complete projection.

For the Romans the house especially possessed several genii:

Vesta guarded the hearth, the Penates protected provisions, the *Lar* guaranteed safety and good fortune, and, by no means the least important, the deceased members of the family lived on in the house with the living as anonymous *Dii Manes*.* The statuette of the genius of the father of the family usually stood by the hearth in the kitchen. It was the figure of a youth bearing a horn of plenty in which there were often phalli, or the genius was itself a phallus or a snake. (The *genius loci* was always represented as a snake.) It was not only the father of the house, however, who had his genius; the mistress also had such a guardian spirit, a feminine figure called "Juno," who embodied the power of giving birth and the maternal-feminine factors in woman.

Originally "genius" and "Juno" were quite impersonal "atmospheric" house gods, but by the third century before Christ they had become much more individualized. Not only the head of a family but every man had his own genius, every woman her Juno, and each person offered certain sacrifices to his genius at a small celebration on his birthday. It was thought that the genius was born with the particular person and was the arbiter of that individual's fortunes. Horace describes him: "Companion who rules the star of birth, god of human nature, mortal in each man, of changing countenance, white and black." † Later the genius was thought to be immortal. At the same time that the genius became more individualized, his image—probably as a result of the growing familiarity with the Greek spirit—was extended in the third century B.C. The *genius loci* became the genius of the city, of schools, of the Senate. The genius of Jupiter, visualized as a phallus, protected the storehouses. The genius of a god, so employed, embodied at the same time his moral and psychic essence.

The Italic ideas about the genius were altered in still another way through the encounter with the Greek spirit. They merged with the philosophic concepts of the Greek thinkers that centered on an immortal spiritual psychic nucleus. In the *Timaeus* (90B-90C), Plato sets forth his theory that every human being has a divine daimon that is the noblest component of his psyche. Whoever seeks wisdom and seriously concerns himself with divine and eternal things nourishes his daimon, whereas worldly trivialities abase and mortify him. A more intensive interest was thereby

---

*See *The Genius Figure in Antiquity and in the Middle Ages* by J. C. Nitzsche (New York and London, 1975).

† See *Epistolae* 2, 2, 187ff.

awakened in the Platonic school in those mysterious "voices" that, as we know, Socrates was in the habit of admonishing. This Socratic daimon was regarded as an example of that divine daimon of which Plato writes. The extent to which this daimon or these daimons were thought of as endopsychic varies.

Some of the Stoics taught the existence of such a daimon in double form: one is a divine component of the psyche (*Nous*), but the other is a spark of the fiery world-soul that has migrated into human beings; this latter daimon—or this part of the daimon—guides a man from without through his whole life. In the opinion of Plutarch (died A.D. 125), only a pure man can hear the voice of this daimon, a completely bodiless being who is the mediator of supernatural, "parapsychological" knowledge to the human being he watches over. The Neoplatonists thought of this genius-daimon as immortal, as one who becomes an actual divinity after his mortal sojourn. Whereas the Italic genius originally died with his bearer, in the later view he lives on after death as a *Lar* (benign spirit).

As a result of the Stoa's spiritual-ascetic orientation in late antiquity, and of Neoplatonism, the Italic genius lost his earlier component of physical vitality, the pleasure principle, which originally had been innate to him. In *De genio Socratis,* a work by Apuleius, there is mention of two genii who live in human beings; one is the immortal ethical guardian and inner friend of a specific person, and the other (who lives in the *genua,* "knees") embodies sensual desire and covetousness and is evaluated negatively.

The idea of the genius also merged quite early with the astrological idea of a personal *fate* shaped by the date of birth (hence Horace: ". . . who rules over the birth-star"), because sacrifices had always been made to the genius on one's birthday. In his *Saturnalia,* Macrobius describes this in detail. In his view every human being is a combination of *four* daimons: of Eros, as we have become acquainted with him; of a particular destiny (a fate ordained by God); of a daimon whose nature is stamped by the position of the sun in his horoscope; and finally by a *Tyche* (fortune) that is dependent on the position of the moon. The daimon knows the future and is at all times in touch with the world-spirit, with the Logos or spermatic pneuma of the universe. *In him masculine and feminine are merged,* so that he is thus an androgynous symbol of wholeness, no longer merely genius or Juno but an archetypal image that, like the *lapis* in alchemy, unites the opposites of masculine and feminine in *one* figure.

Apuleius describes Socrates' genius (*daimonion*) as follows: He is "a private patron and individual guide, an observer of what takes place in the inner person, guardian of one's welfare, he who knows one most intimately, one's most alert and constant observer, individual judge, irrefutable and inescapable witness, who frowns on evil and exalts what is good." If one "watches him in the right way, seeks ardently to know him, honors him religiously," then he shows himself to be "the one who can see to the bottom of uncertain situations and can give warning in desperate situations, can protect us in dangerous situations, and can come to our rescue when we are in need." He can intervene "now through a dream and now through a sign [synchronistic event], or he can even step in by appearing personally in order to fend off evil, to reinforce the good, to lift up the soul in defeat, to steady our inconstancy, to lighten our darkness, to direct what is favorable toward us and to compensate what is evil."* It is well known that in late antiquity a primitive element of religious experience in the philosophic-religious theories was much stronger than in the classic period, perhaps through contact with the more primitive outlying border areas of the Greco-Roman culture. I know of scarcely any account from antiquity that gives a better description of the experiences of the Self than this short summary by Apuleius—with the exception, naturally, of Apuleius' great teacher, Plutarch, who followed exactly the same line.

As in the case of the other daimons, this daimon, which embodies the individual's larger, more comprehensive personality, was in late antiquity also like a mountain the bulk of which lay in the transpersonal realm of the psyche, extending only a small tip into the human being's personal sphere. With the Christianization of the ancient cultural world, however, it was for the most part the transpersonal aspects that were retained, his aspect as the messenger of the gods being assimilated to the idea of the angels; and the other aspects, that is, the parapsychological knowledge, the vitality, and lustfulness of the genius, were attributed to the devil and his tribe. But a faint intimation of the individuality of this figure lived on in the idea that the individual may have a particular guardian angel or patron saint. The reason for this apparently regressive development lay in the fact that the figure of Christ had attracted to himself all the positive qualities of the genius figure. *He* was exalted to *one* symbol of the Self, in a form,

---

*De Deo Socratis, chapter 16.

however, in which the collective elements far outweighed the individual elements. Gradually, as the institutionalized ritual and the confession of faith increased in importance, less and less weight was given to the Pauline inner experience of the Christ and to the visions of the early Christian martyrs. Among those within the Church, only the mystics remained loyal to that line of tradition which put the central value on the inner *experience* of Christ.

An attitude of mind lived on in the Hermetic philosophy of late antiquity and *in alchemy* which, in contrast to Christianity, sought an unprogrammed experience of the "inner companion" or of the daimon who showed the way. This daimon was usually honored in these traditions as Hermes-Psychopompos, as Poimandres (Shepherd of Men), and as *Agathos Daimon* (Good Spirit). Richard Reitzenstein, in *Poimandres*, has explicitly drawn attention to the existence of an actual Hermes religion in late antiquity, but so far his work has not been adequately recognized. In my opinion this religion had a significance that should not be underestimated. In those circles a truly religious attention was paid to the "inner companion," an attention that in the language of today's psychology we would describe as relatedness to the inner "guru," or, in Jungian language, to the Self. . . .

As Henri Corbin has proven,* the gnostic-hermetic Hermes figure lived on in Persian mysticism (for instance, Avicenna and Sohraward). There he is the emissary of the Oriental world, of the world of the sunrise, that is, of inner enlightenment, and he accompanies the visionary in his inner development and realization of the godhead. In this mystical spot of the rising of the sun a *personal* figure takes shape, a figure embodying the visionary's innermost depths. Normally this figure appears to men and women only after death, but it can be seen beforehand by the mystic in the state of ecstasy. It was equated with the Metatron, with the original Anthropos, with the Nous, and with the Holy Ghost and the archangel Gabriel. It appears to the soul in order to lead it on an inner journey to God and to enlighten it with secret knowledge about God. This angel symbolizes the individuality of the relation between God and each particular soul and yet is at the same time only the *one* same figure in all

---

*See *Avicenne et le recit visionnaire* by Henri Corbin, 2 volumes (Teheran and Paris, 1954).

souls. Here, too, as in the Hermetic philosophy, this personification of the Self is the most individual core of the individual person and simultaneously the human self, that is, the self of all humanity. Becoming conscious of this inner figure means for the soul that it becomes a *clear mirror* of this image and from that point on proceeds in its company as with an escort. This image is, as Corbin writes, the *principium individuationis*, which is individualized "in solitude by the solitary" and which each person sees in the way in which by nature he is fitted to understand it—"*Talem vidi qualem capere potui*" (I saw him as such, in the way in which I was able to understand him), as it says in the *Acts of Peter*.

The visionary journey guided by this psychic companion then leads, as Corbin explains, to a *continuing and progressive internalization* of the whole cosmos and to a gradual transformation of the seer himself into the inner teacher.

As to the attitude of consciousness needed to gain insight into *this* projection, the situation is differently modulated than that of the integration of the shadow and the animus or anima. In the case of the shadow it is largely a question of humility; in the case of the other two figures it is one of an at least partial insight into their individual qualities and simultaneously of a wise "live-and-let-live" attitude toward their overwhelming nature. When, on the other hand, personifications of the Self begin to appear, the ego is then confronted with the necessity of sacrificing itself; *it can never integrate the Self* but can only bow before it and try to relate to it in the right way. That does not mean a total renunciation of one's own freedom—even before God, man has to reserve the right to a last word, remaining fully conscious, however, that the power he addresses is always the stronger one. The encounter with the Self means, therefore, a deep and far-reaching change in the conscious attitude. It is not for nothing that the above-described inner daimon is called, among other names, the "Angel of Metanoia": he brings with him a *withdrawal* from the play of Maya, of the world's illusion, an absolute retreat from the world. No one can accomplish this by simply willing it. It is effected in him by the Self and in many cases takes place only shortly before death. Only a few thoughtful, reflective people experience it earlier. Insight into the nature, the essence, of the Self is purchased only at the price of great suffering that wipes out the worldly prejudices and preoccupations of the ego, thereby forcing it into a change of attitude. Every deep disappointment or disillusionment is, in this sense, a step forward along the way of individuation, if it is accepted with insight and not with resignation or bitterness.

In the encounter with the Self there emerges a goal that points to the conclusive ending of all projections, namely, to death. In his *Memories, Dreams, Reflections,* Jung reports a dream about this: He sees himself walking along a road through a sun-bathed landscape. He comes to a small roadside chapel and enters it. Instead of a statue of the Madonna or a crucifix, there is a beautiful flower arrangement on the altar. Before the altar sits a yogi in the lotus position and in deep meditation. "When I looked at him more closely, I realized he had my face. I started in profound fright, and awoke with the thought; 'Aha, so he is the one who is meditating me. He has a dream, and I am it.' I knew that when he awakened, I would no longer be."

The yogi is the same archetypal figure as the inner Hermes-Psychopompos described above, except that here he appears in Far Eastern dress. The dream points to the fact, as Jung himself also mentions, that there is a meaning here of which those in the East have always been much more conscious than we have: namely, that in the end the whole world is only a projection, a reality "arranged" with mysterious purpose and which, if the Arranger so wills it, can disappear again, to make place for a great awakening to another reality unimaginable by us.

14

Temperance:
Heavenly Alchemist

SALLIE NICHOLS

Every blade of grass has its Angel that bends
over it and whispers, "Grow, grow"!

Talmud

In Trump fourteen, an angel with blue hair, wearing a red flower on her forehead, pours liquid from a blue vase into a red one. The theme of this card connects Temperance with Aquarius, the water carrier, the eleventh sign of the zodiac. Aquarius rules the circulation of the blood and has been correlated with the circulation of ideas. It traditionally symbolizes the dissolution of old forms and the loosening of rigid bonds, heralding a liberation from the world of phenomena.

Aquarius usually is pictured holding only one urn. As for the two containers pictured here, Paul Huson, in his *The Devil's Picture Book*, makes some interesting comments. He reminds us that in the Egyptian zodiac of Denderah, Aquarius was identified with Hapi, the god of the Nile, whose waters were the source of life, both agricultural and spiritual. Like her Egyptian counterpart, then, the Angel Temperance blends two opposite aspects or essences, producing life-giving energy. Huson also points out that a similar idea was dramatized by the second-century Gnostic, Marcos, who celebrated the Eucharist by using two chalices instead of one. "By pouring the contents of one into the other," Huson says, "he mixes water with wine, the water being equated in his scheme with Sophia, 'divine wisdom,' which had fallen to earth and been whirled about in the dark empty spaces, and the wine with the fiery spirit of the Savior Christ."[1]

The Angel Temperance is a crucial figure in the Tarot sequence, inspiring much of the action that follows. Whether we think of the red and blue opposites she intermingles as symbolizing spirit and flesh, masculine and feminine, yang and yin, conscious and unconscious, or whether their interaction is thought of as "the marriage of Christ and Sophia" or "the union of fire and water," makes little difference, for all of these are implied. The liquid which flows between the two jars is neither red nor blue but is pure white, suggesting that it represents a pure essence, perhaps energy.

Of course two elemental opposites such as fire and water cannot at first confront each other directly. Such a confrontation at this point would no doubt be catastrophic. It might end either in violent take-over by uncontrolled fiery elements or in equally disastrous quenching of the flaming spirit by a tidal wave from the unconscious. Before the red and blue elements can safely meet in daylight awareness, a preparation must take place in the dark recesses of the psyche. It is this ceremonial over which the Angel presides.

As in any conflict situation, a creative first step toward resolution is to find an arbiter—someone whose wisdom and understanding can encompass both sides. The winged Temperance, who holds with equal concern both the red and the blue, is such a figure. Her wings tell us that she is superhuman—able to rise above petty, mundane matters. She inhabits a realm beyond mortal reach. No human figure is pictured in this card, indicating that whatever is happening here is taking place in the hero's unconscious, without the awareness or participation of the ego.

Angels have long been seen as winged messengers from heaven, meaning psychologically that they represent inner experiences of a numinous nature which connect man with the archetypal world of the unconscious. These winged visions appear in our mundane lives at crucial moments, suddenly bringing new insights and revealing new dimensions of experience.

In biblical accounts, angels traditionally appeared in order to make an annunciation or a revelation of transcendental import. Usually an angel's message is one of concern not only to the individual who sees the vision, but to the collective group as well. Such visionary experiences mark dramatic turning points, personally and culturally. Sometimes they presage a miraculous birth (as in the Annunciation to Mary) or trumpet a call to rebirth (as in the Last Judgement), a theme which will appear later on in the Tarot series.

The Angel Temperance does not announce herself with blinding light or clash of cymbals. Rather she stands before us quietly as an enduring presence. Unlike the Angel of Judgement pictured in card twenty, who will burst through the barrier which separates the celestial from the terrestrial to appear in a blaze of glory in the skies, the Angel Temperance, as befits her name, stages no dramatic entrance. In fact, she makes no entrance at all. She is simply there, absorbed in the business of pouring. One feels that this winged being is not newly descended from heaven, but has been standing here a long time waiting for the hero to become aware of her.

According to ancient belief, each living person, animal, and plant had its guardian angel. Perhaps this is the hero's good angel. If she bears a message for him, it is conveyed by her actions which seem to say: "Patience—Faith. There are powers operating in the universe and in yourself which are beyond your everyday experience. Trust these deeper currents of life; let yourself flow with them."

For Meister Eckhart, angels represented "ideas of God." According to Jung, an angel personifies the coming into consciousness of something new arising from the deep unconscious. He once defined angels more specifically as "personified transmitters of unconscious contents which announce that they want to speak."[2] The Angel Temperance, as we see, has not yet made a pronouncement. But if the hero wishes to hear the Angel's message, he could probably initiate a dialogue with her. Such a dialogue establishes a living relationship to the answering "other" within.

This method of dramatizing one's connection with an inner figure (which Jung calls "active imagination") was apparently used by the alchemists too. They called it *meditatio*. Ruland the Lexicographer defines *meditatio* as "an inner dialogue with someone who is invisible, as also with God, or with oneself, or with one's good angel."

After quoting Ruland thus, Alan McGlashan adds these words, "and with one's dark angel."[3] This is a pertinent addition, for (as Jung has pointed out) angels, like all archetypes, are creatures of questionable morality. In the Tarot card which follows this one, The Devil, we shall in fact come face to face with the most questionable and darkest of these, Prince Lucifer, the fallen angel.

But the Angel Temperance may be safely trusted, for she wears a flower on her forehead whose five-petaled circular shape suggests a mandala, symbolic of the quintessence. This living mandala is placed at the spot of the third eye, traditionally the area of supreme consciousness, and in Jungian terms the spot of individuation. Statues of Buddha always bear some sign on the forehead. It is the sign of awakened consciousness, the symbol of the twice-born.

Although the hero's awareness of his Angel is still buried too deep for his conscious mind to penetrate, nevertheless he begins to understand intuitively that he, too, is marked. He has emerged from his confrontation with death as one twice born; he feels his own awareness flowering into new life. Having glimpsed this angelic being, he now feels chosen—singled out from the multitude.

To be visited by such an angel is a remarkable experience. The poet Rilke put his experience with such archetypal beings into these words:

> Who can have lived his life in solitude
> and not have marvelled how the angels there
> will visit him at times and let him share
> what can't be given to the multitude,
>
> the all out-scattered and disintegrated,
> who into cries have let their voices loose?[4]

Such a compensatory message of healing and unity as Rilke describes usually comes to us at times when we are most alone— when our lives, inner and outer, seem the most fragmented. It is at these moments, when the ego feels insecure, that figures from the deep unconscious can move into our range of awareness.

The hero now finds himself in such a condition. That this moment marks a psychological turning point is also evidenced by the fact that Temperance is the final card in its horizontal row on our map, indicating that a dynamic change in the flow of libido is about to take place.

The terrors and insights he experienced in confronting the skeleton of the previous card have left the hero feeling shaken and lonely, disoriented and set apart. He cannot return to his old ways and habits; his life as he formerly lived it lies in ruins. His conscious personality is temporarily shattered. Although the shell of his old security is now irreparably damaged, through its very cracks a new light can be seen, a dim vision of potential wholeness.

Amidst the clamorous cries of the many conflicting ideas, feelings, and opinions whirling about inside him, a center of hidden silence begins to become manifest. Sometimes when he looks with the inward eye, he can catch the faint outlines of his guardian angel as pictured in the Tarot. Sometimes when he listens intently he can hear the soothing sound of his subterranean waters as they begin to flow again, and he can feel his energies quicken and spring to new life. The domain of death is finished; fresh libido is available.

Now it is time for this libido to be poured into a new container. But the change cannot be consciously willed or directed. "Psychic energy," says Jung, "is a very fastidious thing which insists on fulfilment of its own conditions. However much energy may be present, we cannot make it serviceable until we have succeeded in finding the right gradient."[5] Life's creative energies cannot be directed by sheer will power into whatever channels the conscious ego might select, however reasonable, logical, and appropriate these channels might seem to the thinking mind. "Life can flow forward," as Jung says, "only along the path of the gradient." To balance the flow of opposites so that energy finds its proper gradient requires the patience and skill of an angel. Since this kind of transformation is beyond our conscious control, it is appropriate that the hero step out of the picture, trusting his Angel to perform this part of the Great Work alone.

At any level of meaning, reconciliation of the opposites is not a matter of logic and reason. Generations of men have struggled to reconcile the search for meaning, exemplified in religion, and the search for fact, embodied in science, to no avail. The supposed dichotomy between these two basic urges in men cannot be reconciled through the intellect. Like all opposites, they cannot be resolved by logic; they can only come together at the point of *experience*. This truth is illustrated most eloquently in a filmed interview with Jung in which he was asked: "Do you believe in God?" to which he replied, "I don't *believe* . . . I know."

The Angel Temperance might personify this kind of inner knowing which will increasingly supplant "belief" and "opinion" in the hero's response to life. We might see in this card the beginning of the Aquarian Age in the psyche, leading to the rediscovery of man and his world as a whole. Originally, the word "whole" was synonymous with "holy," and the verb "to heal" meant "to make whole." It was Jung's conclusion that neuroses represent a lost capacity for the wholeness and holiness of religious experience. In Temperance, contact with the numinous is reestablished. Her two urns, like the Holy Grail and the communion chalice, have magic powers to gather together, contain, preserve, and heal. And this winged personage herself will remain as a kind of archangelic guide for the hero on his journey. She will stay with him as a constant reminder that his thoughts, his energies, and his plans are never wholly under conscious control.

The liquid in the Angel's urns seems to spring by its own vitality from some inexhaustible source, like the mythical waters of the miraculous pitcher. The pattern of the liquid's trajectory can be seen as a lemniscate opened out. The closed lemniscate, which appears as the Magician's hat in the first Trump, suggests the unitary system of primal creative energy before the separation of the opposites, the motion of the tail-biting uroboros. In Temperance the lemniscate has unfolded so that the opposites are now separated and clearly defined as two vases, with the precious liquid being transferred from the higher to the lower container, generating a new kind of energy.

The libido, thus revivified, begins to flow in another direction. After the enforced inactivity of the Hanged Man and the cruel dismemberment of Death, the hero's energy now leaps, like an electric current, from the higher to the lower potential. A fresh connection is being made between the sky-blue clarity of spirit and the bloody red of human reality. Aquarius, the sign of ideal relationship, is concerned with the interplay between perfect principle and perfect form. Since the Angel both pours and receives in one gesture, she creates a new rapport between the directive thrust of the positive yang and the quiet containment of the receptive yin. In this way, she unites the magic of the Magician with that of his female counterpart, Strength.

In The Magician and in Strength, the lemniscate is pictured as a hat. Such a hat is a kind of trademark or insignia of office. It indicates that its wearer is but the custodian of the magic powers or divine talents which it symbolizes. The Angel Temperance wears no hat. Her divine powers are invested in herself.

A good way to understand the drama of this card is to contrast it with the theme of interaction of the opposites as it is pictured in other Trumps. For example, in The Chariot, which is the card directly above Temperance in our map, the red and blue opposites appeared as two headstrong horses yoked together. Although these two seemed an ill-matched team, their mysteriously invisible reins hinted at divine guidance. In Temperance, this divine guidance comes directly from the winged Angel, its central, and sole, figure.

The symbolism of Temperance is more impersonal and abstract than that of The Chariot. It offers us a view of the situation from the aspect of eternity, putting us in touch with the Aquarian realm of pure, unitary knowledge which exists behind our world of appearances. Here energy, formerly experienced as two separate beasts, is now revealed to be one vital current. In The Chariot the task of the libido was to move the hero forward on his journey. In Temperance the libido itself undergoes transformation. The opposites, which were pictured at the beginning of the Realm of Equilibrium as the two pans of Justice's scales held apart by a fixed bar, are now shown as red and blue containers for the one unique fluid of Being. They have now become alternate forms which shape and hold this *élan vital*.

In the previous chapter, Death, brandishing time's weapon, threatened to cut short the hero's mortal existence. The grinning skeleton represented time in its most threatening aspect. By facing this monstrous reality, the hero began to be lifted into a realm beyond time, to step out of the prison of earthly limitation into the world of eternals. The Angel makes a connection between the everyday world of historical time and "sacred time," to use Mircea Eliade's term. Eliade describes this realm as "a sort of eternal mythical present that is periodically reintegrated by means of rites."[6]

In Temperance, the ritual of the pouring reconnects the hero with the sacred world he had glimpsed before as Hanged Man but has since lost. In the future there will no doubt be times when he will again find himself out of touch with his Angel and her world of immortal verities. But never again will he feel wholly bereft, for he has now experienced the sound of her waters deep in himself and baptized his petty cares in the mainstream of her creative energy.

This ritual is by no means a purely philosophical concept. The help which the Angel offers is a practical one, vital to both outer reality and to the inner journey. If we take the two vases to represent outer and inner, conscious and unconscious, the Angel, by her ritual pouring, helps the hero to reconcile these two aspects of life. As Jung emphasizes, the necessity arises daily to reconcile the world of our dreams with that of our daily lives. Otherwise these two worlds are apt to intrude on each other in a most confusing way. When the unconscious steps into our outer world to borrow as its dream symbols the events, persons, and objects of our daily experience, it threatens the accustomed order of everyday life. In a similarly confusing way, the rational ego mind can intrude into the image world of the unconscious, disturbing and disrupting its healing work.

When these two worlds get mixed up unconsciously, with no guardian angel to preside, our lives become muddled and confused, often with disasterous results. If we try to live on the outer side a drama that more properly belongs to the inner, the plot could end in tragedy. We might, for example, project the Angel Temperance onto some person of our acquaintance, handing over to this person's care and keeping all our conflicts, problems, hopes, and dreams, expecting this seemingly superior being to guard and regulate the flow of our life. If so, it goes without saying that the Angel of card fourteen would one day pop up in our deck as the Devil of card fifteen.

It is equally impractical, of course, to attempt to squeeze into our inner world events which properly belong in outer reality. If, for example, we have a problem with our spouse or neighbor, it is futile to take this drama wholly on the symbolic level, spending long hours concocting imaginary dialogues with this person or theorizing in solitary confinement about possible reasons for the other's behavior. Although some introspection is valuable, there comes a time when one must step into reality and initiate a real-life dialogue with the person in question. Quite often, when we summon the courage to do this, we find the outer reality to be much less threatening than the inner drama we had concocted. It can even happen that what had appeared in our imagination as a tragedy of antagonism turns out in fact to be a comedy of errors.

So, like the Angel, we must find two containers for our two worlds so that they won't accidentally get mixed up, and like her, we must always keep a firm hold on both. When and how to intermingle the contents of these containers is something we can only learn by trial and error.

This fourteenth card has been called The Alchemist. The theory of alchemy was that all matter could be reduced to one substance out of which, by devious processes, the base and corruptible could be distilled away, so that ultimately only the pure and incorruptible, the philosophers' gold, could be bodied forth. Perhaps something similar is beginning to take place in the deepest waters of the hero's psyche. It is as if Death's harvest of partial aspects, of outworn concepts and modes of behavior (symbolized by the assorted heads, feet, and hands of card thirteen) have been reduced to one substance, out of which a new psychic being can begin to form.

The Angel who performs this subtle alchemy is rightly called

Temperance. To temper means "to bring to a suitable or desirable state by blending or admixture." We temper steel to make it strong yet resilient. Ideally we temper justice with mercy and for the same reason. Justice appeared as the first card in the Realm of Equilibrium on our map. It is useful to compare that card with Temperance, the final card in this row. In Justice, the central figure sat enthroned, as rigid and inflexible as the vertical thrust of her sword, the opposite pans of her scales held apart by an equally inflexible crossbar. As we saw, she demonstrated the law of the opposites and how they functioned together in a complementary manner. The instruments which Justice held were man-made devices for discrimination and measurement. Although she presided over moral considerations, she sat above them; she was not personally involved. She appeared as an allegorical figure, neither a human nor one of the gods.

Temperance, although a heavenly being, looks more human than Justice. She is winged, yet she stands solidly in our reality; thus she partakes of both the heavenly and the earthly realms, connecting the two. Unlike Justice, she seems to be very much involved and deeply concerned with the process at hand. In contrast to the rigidity typified by Justice and her scales, everything about Temperance seems as fluid as the magic liquid she pours. The Angel's body sways and flows in a rhythmic dance which matches the ripple of the waters. The red and blue panels of her skirt, their colors significantly placed in opposition to those of the vases, suggest that the transfer of libido pictured here is part of a continuous process, an endlessly alternating current. It is a natural happening, taking place outdoors against an uncultivated background whose twin green plants echo the vitality contained in the twin vases. The play of waters pictured here could not be controlled or measured by even the most refined instruments of civilization. The drama of Temperance happens only by the grace of God and under the ministration of the angels.

Another recurring pattern in the middle row of Tarot Trumps is, of course, that of equilibrium, or the balancing of opposites. Throughout this row we see a continuous interplay of masculine and feminine energy. Justice pictures a woman, but she holds a sword, symbol of masculine Logos. The Hermit presents an archetypal Old Wise Man, yet he wears the flowing robes of Mother Church. The Wheel of Fortune dramatizes the cyclic interaction of all opposites, to be followed by Strength, in which a lady and her lion intermingle their two kinds of energy in harmonious symbiosis. Following this, the Hanged Man shows us someone achieving balance between heaven and earth. In Death, other opposites, such as king and commoner, male and female, are being chopped up and plowed under, preparatory to re-organization and reassimilation, a process that begins in the final card of this row, Temperance.

It is worth noting that much of the action in this second row is initiated or presided over by feminine figures. Justice, the sphinx on Fortune's Wheel, Strength, and Temperance, all clearly feminine, dominate the action. The Hanged Man is passive, unable to act. Encased and immobilized in a kind of coffin composed of Nature's trees and earth, he is held captive by the feminine. Only the Hermit and Death (both androgynous figures) portray the masculine principle in action. The gentle Hermit, armed solely with a small lamp, initiates no action; he merely sheds his soft, inquiring light on whatever is happening. Death is pictured as very active, but he is not his own master. His scythe, with its crescent shape, belongs to the Moon Goddess Astarte, mistress of time, tides, and change.

Another pattern to be discovered in this Realm of Equilibrium is the way the cards alternate in theme between the general and the specific. First the general problem is presented, then is illustrated and amplified by specific instances of its application in an alternating rhythmic pattern. First, Justice pictures the universal moral dilemma, the problem of determining and measuring guilt and innocence. Next comes the Hermit, whose lamp illuminates a more individual and human approach to the problem. Card number ten, The Wheel of Fortune, brings us back again to the universal. It poses the eternal question of fate versus free will: Are we, like the animals, forever trapped on the not-so-merry-go-round of instinctual behavior? By way of answer, the next two trumps show us two alternatives. First the lady with the lion who demonstrates how bestial nature might be tamed, and second, the Hanged Man, whose body seems as helpless as the animals on Fortune's Wheel, but whose spirit (unlike theirs) is free to find meaning in suffering. Card Thirteen brings us back again to the universal, reminding us that man and beast alike are powerless to avoid the skeleton, Death. And now Temperance cleanses our faulty perceptions, connecting us in a divine yet human way with the immutable world beyond the reach of time's scythe. In doing so, she makes a graceful transition between the world of moral problems and the world of divine illumination, which will be a theme expressed in the last seven cards of the Tarot series. But even for an angel, the process is a slow one. The work which she initiates here will only be consummated at the end of the Tarot journey.

Since Temperance is referred to as "The Alchemist," it might be worthwhile to restate some of the things we have been saying in the language of the old alchemists. In doing so, we may observe how accurately this Tarot Trump and the cards that follow it reflect the symbolic language of those pioneers who blazed the trails toward individuation.

In alchemical language, the "gluten of the eagle" and the "blood of the lion" were mingled in the "philosophical egg," or alembic, then subjected to heat. In Temperance we see pictured the beginning phase of this Great Work, the Angel's compassionate concern furnishing the heat necessary to start the "cooking" process. The next two cards (The Devil and The Tower of Destruction) will show ways in which various other kinds of heat—speaking both alchemically and psychologically—will be applied.

The action of the Angel Temperance as she works with the waters of the hero's psyche is like that of the sun, Nature's alchemist, on our earth's waters. The sun makes of our planet an alchemical retort in which the ocean waters are lifted to heaven and then, their impurities distilled away, are returned to the earth in drops of rain. This continuous circular process epitomizes the natural interrelationship between heaven and earth—between the archetypal figures of the collective unconscious and man's ego reality.

It is Temperance who first introduces this kind of fluid discourse between the heavenly and the earthly realms or, speaking psychologically, between the self and the ego—a dialogue which will be the central theme of all the cards to follow. Significantly, Temperance is the only winged being in the Tarot who descends to earth, confronting man face to face. The winged Eros of card six, it will be recalled, appeared only in the heavens, hovering unseen in the background to shoot his potent arrow and disappear. That the hero's guardian angel stands before him in earthly reality, indicates that he now experiences the reality of the unconscious in a new way. Never again will he dismiss figures of the inner world as creatures of his imagination. Although he may still think of "inner" and "outer" as two worlds, henceforth he will grant the inner world a validity equal to that of the outer world. Perhaps as he gains confidence he will be able to move toward the inner world and interact more freely with its inhabitants.

The motif of the dance is an important one in the Tarot. Dancing is an art form in which body and soul interact in an individual and expressive way. A dancer reaches out to objects and other human beings, expressing relationship on the earthly level; and he reaches his arms toward heaven, invoking the gods. There are several dancing figures in the Tarot. The Fool, as usual, begins it all unconsciously as he prances along in his happy way. The Hanged Man, whose dance is equally unconscious, can be seen as the brash Fool, come a-cropper on life's realities. The skeleton's Dance of Death is followed by Temperance's ritual dance with the living waters. We may view these two dances, if we like, as one single event. If you will look for a moment at Death and Temperance, you will see how their bodies lean toward each other in such a way that they form an ellipse.

This ellipse is a symbol for the kind of alchemical interchange between heaven and earth which we have been describing. As we shall see in the following chapters, it is a recurring theme in the bottom row of the Trumps, culminating in The World, which pictures a Dancer. If you will look at card twenty-one, you can see how the fluid movement of this final figure is almost exactly foreshadowed in the body movements of Temperance. Notice also how the ellipse formed by the swaying bodies of Temperance and Death appears in The World as an elliptical wreath surrounding the Dancer.

But the transition from the dance of Temperance to that pictured in the final card is not an orderly one. As we know, life's choreography does not proceed on steppingstones of logic. Rather it follows a spiral course which alternately swings us high and casts us down again.

We have stayed with our Good Angel long enough. It is now time to look the Devil in the eye. He stands waiting to meet us in the next card.

Notes

1. Paul Huson, *The Devil's Picturebook*, pp. 183-184.
2. C. G. Jung, Quoted by Amy I. Allenby, "Angels as Archetype and Symbol," *Spring 1963*, p. 48.
3. McGlashan, *op. cit.*, p. 29.
4. Rainer Maria Rilke, *Poems 1906-26*, Norfolk, Conn., New Directions, 1959, p. 73.
5. C. G. Jung, *Two Essays on Analytical Psychology*, C. W. Vol. 7, par. 76.
6. Mircea Eliade, *The Sacred and the Profane*, New York, Harcourt, Brace, Jovanovich, Inc. 1959, p. 20.

IV
Mystical and Magical Encounters

Unlike angel imagining, which is free of earthly attachment, mortal awareness is captive to sensory faculties and personal conditioning. We let sensory impressions limit us to habitual ways of knowing. We hamper ourselves even more by distrusting flights of imagination in our reliance on reason. Depth psychologists say that imagining may be a primary means of perception and the creative agency of the soul. Imagination brings together spirit and matter in new wholes which are expressed in art, poetry, religion and science. It is a valid means of visioning the inner life of things.[1]

Genuine visions have a unique life, reality and depth not shared by visualizations or daydreams. Divine figures in visions . . . persons, places, events . . . often shine with an interior radiance. They are seen through the imagining faculties of the soul more clearly than we perceive through physical sensing, and we may remember them in detail. Teresa of Avila evaluated the genuineness of her visions through several definite criteria: they have a sense of power and authority; they produce tranquility, recollectedness, and a desire to praise God; they impart an inner certainty that what is envisioned is true; they are clear and distinct, with each part carrying great meaning. She adds another important criterion, that true visions result in a life of improved ethics and increased psychological integration. They give strength and peace and inspire love for God.[2]

Artistic imagining parallels the mystic experience, carrying many of the same qualities. Everyday awareness is maintained, though enhanced. Artistic imagining holds an important key to the significance of angel-human interaction. Artistry not only produces elegance of form and function at the physical level; it affects "matter" in a more fundamental way. Selfless creating magically transforms the inner life of both artist and Nature. James Hillman, archetypal psychologist, suggests that matter is transfigured by wonder. When we allow something to reveal its own aspiration, we encourage ITS imagination to activate, allowing personification and a flowering of its inner life.[3]

The quality of any encounter is significant. Physicists have found that simply observing something alters its behavior in unpredictable ways. Apparently, what we choose to observe and how we relate to it alters and perhaps even helps to create (or recreate) what we see. Physicist David Bohm speculates that "what the cosmos is doing as we dialogue is to change its idea of itself . . . through us the universe decipher(s) . . . and changes . . . its own being."[4] He comments that humans may be realizing a role in Nature once reserved for the gods.

We must explore more fully the subtleties of relationship, for even casual encounters are significant. In a living Cosmos, communion is sacred dialogue. Every meeting, even with what appears inert, is with a living presence. Through the soul of things, we envision and are beheld by divine Being. We commune with angels every day, in the most mundane as well as momentous events.

As they are the inner life and light of familiar things, we speak of angels in comfortable ways. Though religion, psychology, philosophy, science, and the arts all have varied languages, they all reveal related aspects of one life. Each is limited without the others. No matter if angels are now discrete entities, then become abstract powers and potencies, and again an immediacy in our soul. They exist simultaneously in many forms, all of which express their, and our, incredible wonderful diversity.

For human-angel communion to be regenerative, we must begin to vision heaven here, to sense the eternal as it manifests for individuals. We need to watch and listen in a new way. In communion with angels we discover our individual paths, craft the wings of imagination and intuition, affirm our common destiny through self-sacrifice and love, cooperate in the creation of beauty. Together we rend the illusionary veil which separates heaven and earth.

1. Roberts Avens. *Imagination Is Reality*. Dallas: Spring Publications, 1988, 24.
2. Deirdre Green. *Gold in the Crucible: Teresa of Avila and the Western Mystical Tradition*. Great Britain: Element Books Limited, 1989, 56-8.
3. James Hillman. *The Thought of the Heart*. Eranos Lecture Series. Dallas: Spring Publications, 1987, 32-3.
4. Renée Weber. *Dialogues with Scientists and Sages: The Search for Unity*. New York: Routledge & Kegan Paul, 1986. 19.

15
Journeys

PETER LAMBORN WILSON

Black Elk

I looked up at the clouds, and two men were coming there,
headfirst like arrows slanting down; and as they came, they sang
a sacred song and the thunder was like drumming. I will sing
it for you. The song and the drumming were like this:
  'Behold, a sacred voice is calling you;
  All over the sky a sacred voice is calling.'
Black Elk Speaks

Black Elk was a cousin of Crazy Horse; he lived through the
Wounded Knee massacre of 1890, became a holy man, and worked
in Wild Bill Hickock's Wild West Show, among his other adventures.
As an old man in 1931 he told his story to a white friend, John G.
Neihardt, fearing that otherwise his great vision would be lost.
Black Elk believed he possessed a healing mission for all mankind,
and especially his own people; after a life he interpreted as a
failure, he doubted himself. But the document Neihardt produced,
and later *The Sacred Pipe* composed by Black Elk with J. Epes
Brown, constitute two of the most profound mystical and metaphysical records of this century; both have been a major force
in the revival of Native American religion.

Black Elk's teachings centre around a vision he experienced
at the age of nine: an ascent to heaven. It begins with his falling
ill, as is frequently the case with mystics still unaware of themselves,
especially shamans.

The two figures described above (Black Elk later painted them
with wings and spears, so that they look exactly like Native
American Angels) come to fetch the spirit of the paralyzed boy.
With them he soars into the clouds: 'We three were there alone
in the middle of a great white plain with snowy hills and mountains

staring at us; and it was very still; but there were whispers.'

The Angels then present the boy with a preliminary vision: a mandala composed in this cloudy space. A bay horse appears and speaks. In the West he points out twelve black horses whose manes are lightning and who snort thunder.

In the North appear twelve white horses, their manes flowing like a blizzard, and white geese soaring and circling around them. In the East twelve sorrel horses with necklaces of elk's teeth and eyes that glimmer like the daybreak star, and manes of morning light. In the South, twelve buckskins with horns on their heads and manes like trees and grasses.

The mandala grows with the addition of whole herds of horses dancing, which change into animals and birds of every kind. A huge procession follows Black Elk to a tepee made of clouds and a rainbow, where he finds the six 'Grandfathers' who have summoned him. 'They looked older than men can ever be—old like hills, like stars.'

The Grandfathers are the chiefs of the six directions (hence another mandala, representing the entire cosmos). Each of them presents the child with a gift. The West, the eldest, gives him a cup of water (the power to make life) and a bow (the power to destroy). Then he points to himself and says, 'Look close at him who is your spirit now, for you are his body and his name is Eagle Wing Stretches.' In other words, this is Black Elk's spiritual double or guardian, his spiritual 'name.'

The other grandfathers then present him with a healing herb, a peacepipe, a red stick symbolizing 'the centre of the nation's circle,' and power over the birds ('All the Wings of the air shall come to you, and they and the winds and the stars shall be like relatives'). The sixth Grandfather, spirit of the Earth, appears to be the most decrepit of them all, but suddenly he begins to grow younger till Black Elk realizes 'he was myself with all the years that would be mine at last.' (Another form of the guardian—thus Black Elk is specially protected by two powerful Archangels.)

Again the horse-mandala forms; this time four beautiful maidens dressed in scarlet appear before each herd, holding the symbolic gifts. A black horse sings a song of renewal. 'His voice was not loud, but it went all over the universe and filled it. There was nothing that did not hear, and it was so beautiful that nothing anywhere could keep from dancing.' The whole universe dances to this song, so reminiscent of the harmony of the Spheres, or the Resurrection music of Israfil or Gabriel.

Then follows another vision. Black Elk stands on a mountain at the centre of the world (it was Harney Peak in the Black Hills—'but anywhere is the centre of the world'). He sees 'in a sacred manner the shapes of all shapes as they must live together like one being. And I saw that the sacred hoop of my people was one of many hoops that made one circle, wide as daylight and as starlight, and in the centre grew one mighty flowering tree to shelter all the children of one mother and one father. And I say that it was holy.'

The two Angels now return to take the child back to his Grandfathers. 'He has triumphed!' cry the six together, making thunder. They again bestow their gifts, and as they do so they melt into the ground. At last the oldest dismisses him: 'Grandson, all over the universe you have seen. Now you shall go back with power to the place from whence you came, and it shall happen yonder that hundreds shall be sacred, hundreds shall be flames!' As Black Elk returns to earth he hears the Sun singing: '. . . with visible face I appear. My day, I have made it holy.' A spotted eagle conveys him home, and he sees his sick body waiting for him; as he enters it, he wakes. 'Then I was sitting up; and I was sad because my mother and father didn't seem to know I had been so far away.'

This extraordinary narrative is at once the most recent and the most primordial of Angelic recitals—and one of the most poetic and profound.

The Miraculous Night Journey

It is the one mighty in Power hath taught him, the Vigorous
One; he grew clear to view as he hovered in the loftiest sphere;
then he drew nigh and hovered in the air till he was distant
two bows' lengths or nearer. . . . And verily he saw him yet
another time by the lote-tree of the utmost boundary nigh unto
which is the Garden of Abode. When that which shroudeth did
enshroud the lote-tree, the eye turned not.

Koran, LI, 5-17

According to the traditional interpretation of this text, Mohammed saw Gabriel in his cosmic form (as opposed to hearing him, or seeing him in the form of a man) only on the two occasions thus described. The vision of the lote-tree refers to the Prophet's *mir' aj* (his 'ladder' or Night Ascension). The Koran gives very

MIRAJ MUHAMMAD *Sultan Muhammad*
The angel Gabriel brings Muhammad a supernatural mount, representing
the contemplative mind, and calms it before Muhammad can ride.
Muhammad travels through several heavens with Gabriel, and is then
led by Michael "through so many veils of light that the universe I
saw had nothing in common with everything I had previously seen
in these worlds."

adapted from Peter Lamborn Wilson

few details, but the Prophet himself recounted more, and later folklore fleshed out the tale even further.

It takes place just after Mohammed has been chosen as a prophet. One night three Angels come to him while he sleeps, cut open his breast and tear out his heart. With water from the sacred well of Zam-Zam in Mecca, they wash the heart and lave away all that they find within him of doubt, idolatry, paganism and error. Then they fill the cavity with a liquid of wisdom poured from a golden vessel, replace the heart and sew up the breast again.

On the next night, 'I lay asleep in my house. It was a night in which there were thunder and lightning. No living beings could be heard, no bird journeyed. No one was awake, whereas I was not asleep; I dwelt between waking and sleeping.'

Suddenly Gabriel the Archangel descended in his own form, of such beauty, of such sacred glory, of such majesty, that all my dwelling was illuminated. He is of a whiteness brighter than snow, his face is gloriously beautiful, the waves of his hair fall in long tresses, his brow is encircled as with a diadem of light on which is written 'There is no god but God.' He has six hundred wings set with 70,000 grains of red chrysolite.

When he had approached me, he took me in his arms, kissed me between the eyes and said, 'O sleeper, how long wilt thou sleep? Arise! Tenderly will I guide thee. Fear not, for I am Gabriel thy brother.'

The Angel offers Mohammed a choice of three cups: one of wine, one of honey, one of milk. The Prophet starts to take the wine, but Gabriel corrects him and gives him the milk. According to the commentators, wine is the animal 'breath,' honey the physical 'breath' and milk the mental 'breath.'

Gabriel now brings Mohammed a supernatural mount, the Buraq, a winged mule with a woman's face. The Buraq (like Garuda) represents the contemplative mind—it is restive, and the Angel must calm it before Mohammed can ride.

They soar into the sky, hover for an instant over the Kaaba, and whirl away towards the north. In an instant they have arrived in Jerusalem at the Farthest Mosque, the Dome of the Rock. Here the muezzin is giving the call to prayer. They enter and find an assembly of Angels and prophets, who welcome them.

Now, according to some versions, Mohammed abandons the Buraq, tying her to the Rock, and climbs a golden ladder which appears over the Mosque. In other versions he keeps her throughout the journey. In any case, they now rise to the first heaven.

We are already familiar with several schemes of seven heavens, corresponding to the planets. In the earliest versions of the *mir' aj* details are scanty: the travellers encounter prophets in each sphere (Adam in the first, John and Jesus in the second, then Joseph, Idris [Hermes], Aaron, Moses and Abraham), as well as presiding Angels. Later versions add more colourful details, such as Angels of mixed fire and ice, visions of the punishments of the damned, descriptions of various ranks or choirs of Angels mentioned in the Koran, etc.

In one treatment (ascribed to either Avicenna or Sohrawardi) two more heavens are added. In the eighth are found the glorifying Angels; from these beings, observing their mode of worship, Mohammed learns the words and movements of the ritual prayer which he will teach his followers. In the ninth the Lote or Lotus Tree of the Farthest Boundary marks the limit of the Imaginal World. Beyond this, Gabriel cannot go, and Mohammed sees only a vast sea of golden light. Around the Tree dwell a multitude of souls who have become Angels, and an Archangel who pours water from a vessel into a great river; this is the First Intelligence, the first created being, emanating the very stuff of the universe.

Mohammed proceeds alone into the golden sea, and finds himself in a valley.

Over against the valley I saw an Angel in meditation, perfect in Majesty, Glory and Beauty. When he saw me he called me to him. When I had come close I asked, 'What is thy name?' He said, 'Michael. I am the greatest of the Angels. Whatever difficulty thou conceivest, question me; whatever thou desirest, ask of me.' I said to him, 'To come hither I have undergone many toils and sufferings. But my purpose was this: to attain to gnosis and the vision of Truth. Show me the direction that leads to Him, so that perhaps I may attain the goal of my desire, and receive a portion of His universal Grace.'

Then that Angel took me by the hand, he made me enter and led me through so many veils of light that the universe I saw had nothing in common with everything I had previously seen in these worlds.

He hears a voice summon him: 'Come yet nearer.' He experiences intoxication and fear of the divine *tremendum*, but the Voice says, 'Fear not, be quieted, come nearer yet.' Again it commands: 'Ask!'

Mohammed speaks: 'Permit me to ask concerning all that has been shown to me, so that all doubts may end.' Then the Voice instructs him 'without a voice,' and bestows on the Prophet the highest mode of intellectual intuition, the perfection of gnosis.

Now Mohammed returns, descending through the heavens, to Mecca. As he wakes to himself in his room, he discovers that a water jug, which the Buraq knocked over with her hoof as they departed, is still pouring out upon the floor: the whole trip has taken place outside time, literally in a split second.

Dionysius and the Paradiso

Dionysius set himself so ardently
  to fix upon these orders his regard,
  he named them and distinguished them as I.
                    Dante, Paradiso VIII

Dante constructed a towering spire upon the Church and culture of medieval Europe; even to discuss the angelology of the *Divine Comedy* would require a volume by itself. One cornice of the great cathedral is Dante's treatment of the Angelic Orders described by Dionysius the Areopagite.

The *Celestial Hierarchies* compares God to a ray of primal light which can never be deprived of its intrinsic unity; and yet it 'becomes a manyness' and proceeds into manifestation. This manifestation is in one sense the light iself, but in another sense a veil covering the divine unity.

The primal ray of light, as it descends towards the extremity of creation (a hypothetical 'brute matter'), must be graded or arranged in an order, a hierarchy, 'so that we might be led, each according to his capacity, from the most holy imagery to formless, unific, elevative principles and assimilations.' It is for this reason that everything 'delivered in a supermundane manner to Celestial Natures [i.e., Angels] is given to us in symbols.' God has revealed to us the Celestial Hierarchies that we might attain 'our due measure of deification.'

In this theology the concept of *theophany* becomes all-important. A theophany is a 'beholding of God which shows the divine likeness, figured in itself as a likeness in form of that which is formless.' Through such a symbol 'a divine light is shed upon the seers . . . and they are initiated into some participation of divine things.'

The Angels are most potent theophanies; and the initiation referred to above is passed down, as it were in a chain, from the higher to the lower ranks, till mankind receives it from the Angels. Thus one might say that for man every theophany (appearance of God) is in fact an appearance of an Angel.

In Cantos XXVIII through XXX of the *Paradiso*, Dante expounds on Dionysius by actually creating images for the doctrines of the *Celestial Hierarchies*. Having reached the Primum Mobile, the outermost limit of the cosmos, Dante pauses and gazes into the eyes of his beloved guide, Beatrice. He sees reflected in them a point of light

> of so intense a beam
> that needs must every eye it blazes on
> be closed before its poignancy extreme.

This point is in fact the divine light itself, surrounded by nine circles of light which are the Angelic Orders. Thus Dante experiences Heaven *in* Beatrice, 'who hath imparadised my mind.' She is in effect Dante's personal theophany, his Guardian Angel; and this symbol of reflected light is one of the images which make up the basic imaginal structure of the poem.

Dante now turns and gazes upon the rings of light themselves, empowered to do so by the theurgic effect of his love for Beatrice. He beholds the system as a series of lustrous haloes or rainbows surrounding a central point.

Beatrice explains it to him; then as she falls silent, he sees innumerable Angels:

> thick as the sparks from molten iron sped
> so did the sparks about the circles chase. . . .
> From choir to choir I heard Hosanna rolled
> to that fixt point which holds them in their home,
> hath held them ever, and shall forever hold.

Beatrice tells him that the highest choirs derive their bliss *seeing* God:

> . . . the celestial bliss
> is founded on the act that seeth God,
> not that which loves, which cometh after this.

In other words, gnosis or knowledge is higher than Love.

Beatrice points out each of the Orders in descending rank, and comments:

> Upward these Orders gaze; and so prevails
> downward their power, that up toward God on high
> all are impelled, and each in turn impels;

thus interpreting Dionysius's teachings on the initiation of the Angels.

She now goes on to comment in a special way on the Areopagite's teachings on the Creation:

> Not increase of His own good to proclaim
>   (which is not possible) but that His own
>   splendour might in resplendence say *I Am;*
> In His eternity, where time is none,
>   nor aught of limitation else, He chose
>   that in new loves the eternal Love be shown.

In Mohammed's words: 'God was a hidden treasure, and He desired or "loved" to be known; so He created the world that He might be known.'

The Angels have from the beginning kept their vision fixed on God's face. Each Angel is a separate species, since each possesses its own mode of absorbing and reflecting the primal light which irradiates it:

> And since on the mind's vision love ensues,
>   that sweetness glows within them fiery-bright
>   or warm, according to the mode they use.
> See now the Eternal Virtue's breadth and height,
>   since it hath made itself so vast a store
>   of mirrors upon which to break its light,
> Remaining in itself one, as before.

Now, as day breaks in the wake of the Angelic vision, Dante beholds Beatrice and finds her more beautiful than he had ever known her:

> The beauty I saw not only exceeds our wit
>   to measure, past all reach, but I aver
>   He only who made it fully enjoyeth it . . .
> As the sun doth to the eyes that tremble most
>   so doth to me the thought of the sweet smile
>   whereby, shorn of itself, my mind is lost.

Thus Beatrice herself mirrors forth the Beatific Vision, which extinguishes all reason as in a blazing fire. Beatrice is an Angel; Beatrice reveals the Angelic World; and Beatrice is the theophanic symbol in which love and knowledge are united.

THE CHOIR OF ANGELS *Hildegard of Bingen*
"*Hildegard offers us in this rich icon a picture of compassion by way
of the interconnection of angels and humans. . . . Compassion is about
responding to the interconnectivity of creation by way of (1) celebration
. . . all the 'armies' form a common chorus together . . . and (2) justice-
making.*"

Matthew Fox

16

All Beings
Celebrate Creation:
Illuminations of Hildegard

MATTHEW FOX

Hildegard writes that "all of creation is a symphony of joy and jubilation." In this beautiful mandala—which is in fact nine concentric circles, one might even say, nine mandalas—she draws us into the experience of the joy and jubilation that all creatures celebrate together. Hildegard chooses nine circles to correspond to the nine choirs of angels—angels, archangels, virtues, powers, principalities, dominations, thrones, cherubim and seraphim. But it is striking that only the outer two circles are winged and angelic—the other seven circles have human countenances. Indeed, even the outer two circles are less angelic than we would expect at first glance. She describes the outermost circle as having "faces of humans" and the second outer circle as having "faces of humans in which the image of the Son of Man also shines as in a mirror."[1] She describes these two outer circles as "two armies of heavenly spirits shining with great brightness." These groups surround five other "armies in the fashion of a crown." The first of these (the third circle from the outside) displays faces of humans shining brightly; the next circle pictures faces so bright that she could not look at them; the next appears "like white marble with burning torches above their heads"; another were carrying helmets on their heads; and the fifth groups were not humans at all but were "red as the dawn."

Each of these "armies" Hildegard calls a "crown." Cirlot explains the meaning of crown in alchemical literature. "Planetary spirits receive their crown—that is, their light—from the hands of their king—that is, the sun. The light they receive from him is not equal in intensity but graded, as it were, in hierarchies, corresponding to the grades of nobility ranging from the king down to the baron."[2] Carl Jung calls the reception of "the radiant crown" the symbol for attaining the highest goal in evolution—the crown of eternal life. Within the creation theological tradition, of course, a crown reminds us of the theology of royal personhood—how God who is King has called creation to be "crowned" with dignity and responsibility. In this way, creation endures, justice is preserved, creativity insured. "You have made humans a little less than God, and you have crowned them with glory and honor," sings the Psalmist. (Ps. 8.6)

Two more armies arranged as a crown are described by Hildegard as constituting the inner circles. The first were "full of eyes and wings and in each eye a mirror appeared and in the mirror the face of a person appeared." And in the innermost group the figures "were burning as if they were a fire. They had many wings and were revealing as in a mirror all the distinguished orders of the church." What did Hildegard see these crowns, armies, planetary spirits doing? They were a chorus, a choir, singing, singing about the marvels that happen in the human heart. "All these armies were resounding with every kind of music. With amazing voices they were glorifying God magnificently for those miracles which God performs in blessed souls." They were all celebrating the divine gift of creation. Hildegard reports: "I heard a voice from heaven say to me: 'The all-powerful and ineffable God, who was before all ages but herself had no beginning nor will she cease to exist after the end of the ages—she it is who formed every creature in a marvelous way by her own will.' " Hildegard gifts us here with an unforgettable image of Dancing Sarah's Circle.[3] In this rich mandala all of creation is represented as interdependent and celebrative. Angel and human commingle, intermix, interrelate. Some angels are created, Hildegard tells us, "that they may help in the needs of humans" and others so that God's mysteries may be communicated to humans. All these blessed rings of creatures are "rejoicing in the joy of salvation," they are "bringing forth the greatest joys in indescribable music through the works of those wonders of heavenly things that God brings about in his saints."[4] Moreover, they invite us to dance a "dance of exaltation." We can join this dance, however, if we "hurl away injustice" and choose to perform justice. Thus Hildegard is also offering us in this rich icon a picture of compassion. Compassion, which is essentially about interconnectivity, is pictured by way of the interconnection of angels and humans. Hildegard lets go in this vision of the distinction or dualism between angel and human. Compassion is about responding to the interconnectivity of creation by way of 1) celebration—all the "armies" form a common chorus together—and 2) justice-making.

Elsewhere, Hildegard underscores the interdependence that characterizes our universe when she writes: "God has arranged all things in the world in consideration of everything else."[5] And again, "everything that is in the heavens, on the earth, and under the earth, is penetrated with connectedness, is penetrated with relatedness."[6] No wonder angels and humans can join so readily in a common choir—what does this say about race, religion, culture? What does this say about learning to sing with others? Hildegard says that ecumenism is a law of the universe, a way of wisdom, a return to our origins.

In delineating meanings to each of the rings of creatures, Hildegard says the following: The outer two circles celebrate how "the body and soul of humans ought to be servants of God." The outermost circle celebrates "the beauty of rationality" for the wings on the figures symbolize the intellectual powers that emanate from God to humans. The next circle reveals the mysteries of God and the incarnation of God's Son, thus the body is symbolized there. The next five circles stand for the five senses which ought to be regulated by the body and soul, the outer two rings of human powers. The first of these five crowns represents the virtues which "fight strongly" and lead people "to much strength to a good end of much brightness and blessedness." The powers are the bright ones, so bright that no one can behold them. No weakness, not death nor sin, can "apprehend the serenity and beauty of the power of God . . . because the power of God is unfailing."

The principalities, with torches and made of marble, represent "those who by a gift of God exist as leaders of men and women in their time." They must learn to "put on the sincere strength of justice" and "persevere in the strength of fairness." The dominations tell us to imitate God and God's Son by fortifying ourselves "with a strong desire for good works." The red figures are the thrones—they do not resemble human forms at all because they are so immersed in the "very many mysteries of heavenly secrets which human weakness is not able to comprehend." They are the color and brilliance of the dawn because they represent the coming of the Holy Spirit over Mary, the mother of Jesus. The inner two rings depict, first the cherubim, which signify "the knowledge of God" with their eyes and mirrors and human faces in the mirrors. And the innermost circle of red figures, "burning like a fire," are the seraphim. They represent "all the distinguished orders of the church" and they "burn in the love of God and have the greatest desires for his vision." In them, "the secrets of God appear wondrously." The innermost circle, which would be the tenth circle, is empty—it is the full emptiness, the via negativa, the hole that represents the "path of Transcendence,"[7] the mirror which is fecund nothingness. It is all things and no thing. Full potentiality. The source of all creativity. The mystery of the not-yet-created, the center where beauty is born. The number ten traditionally symbolizes "the return to unity," and the beginning of new creation. It also indicates "the totality of the universe."[8]

It is interesting to see how much like human hands the wings of the angels are. Also, how faces are smiling within the wings. And how the innermost red circles appear Aztec in form. These figures closely resemble the creator god Quetzalcoatl from the Aztec paintings found in the *Mexican Codex Borgia*.[9] Truly, the entire cosmos is invited into this living mandala, this song. We are all marvels of creation, royal persons, called to "sing justice" back into creation.

Notes

1. *Scivias*, p. 100. This illustration is the Sixth Vision of the First Part of *Scivias*, pp. 100-108. Subsequent citations in this section are from pp. 100-103.
2. Cirlot, pp. 69f.
3. See Matthew Fox, *A Spirituality Named Compassion, op. cit.*, Chapter Two, "From Climbing Jacob's Ladder to Dancing Sarah's Circle," pp. 36-67.
4. *Scivias*, p. 107.
5. Uhlein, p. 65.
6. *Ibid.*, p. 41.
7. Cirlot, p. 73.
8. *Ibid.*, p. 223.
9. David Maclagan, *Creation Myths, op. cit.*, pp. 60f.

17

Angelic Nature
From Works of
Emanuel Swedenborg

EDITED BY MICHAEL STANLEY

Swedenborg reports very many experiences of encounters with angels. But the true quality of the angelic can only be known from deep within oneself and from there recognized in another being. So also with Swedenborg. His accounts of the angelic are self-discoveries—for him, as they can be for us in studying his descriptions and accounts. In what follows we learn much of the heavenly in the 'new' Swedenborg himself, writing now with feeling and in depth on qualities which he had barely mentioned before his enlightenment.

Abstracted Thought and Speech

In the other life, especially in the heavens, all thought and hence all speech, are carried on in an impersonal sense, and therefore thought and speech there are universal, and are relatively without limit; for so far as thought and speech are associated with persons and their specific qualities, and with names, and also words, so far they become less universal, and are associated with the actual thing, and there abide. On the other hand insofar as they are not associated with persons and what is connected with them, but with realities abstracted from them, so far they are dissociated from the actual thing, and are extended beyond themselves, and the mental view becomes higher and consequently more universal. *AC 5287*

When [angels] think abstractly concerning the entity; then the thought diffuses itself in every direction according to the heavenly form which the influx proceeding from the Divine produces, and this without the disturbance of any society. For it insinuates itself into the general spheres of the societies, and in this case does not touch or move anyone in the society, thus does not divert anyone from the freedom of thinking according to the influx from the Divine. In a word, abstract thought can

217

THE ANGEL APPEARING TO THE SHEPHERDS Rembrandt
A blinding light emanating from the heavens illumines the place of vision. All else is darkness. In this unusual image, some of the animals and shepherds flee. The vision is unexpected, and too potent for the unprepared.

pervade the whole heaven without delay anywhere; but thought determined to person, or to place, is fixed, and arrested. *AC 8985*

Love

The nature of the Lord's love surpasses all human understanding and is unbelievable in the extreme to people who do not know what heavenly love is in which angels abide. To save a soul from hell the angels think nothing of giving their own lives; indeed if it were possible they would suffer hell themselves in place of that soul. Consequently their inmost joy is to transport into heaven someone rising from the dead. They confess however that that love does not originate one little bit in themselves but that every single aspect of it does so in the Lord alone. *AC 2077*

Heavenly or celestial love does not wish to exist for itself but for all, thus to impart all that is its own to others. It is in this that heavenly love essentially consists. *AC 1419*

Timelessness

I have spoken with the angels about the memory of past things, and the anxiety thence arising about what is to come, and have been instructed, that the more interior and perfect the angels are, the less care they have about what is past, and the less do they think about what is to come, and that hence also is their happiness. They say, that the Lord gives them every moment what to think, and this with blessedness and happiness, and that thus they are without cares and anxieties . . . but although they have no care about what is past, and have no solicitude about what is to come, they have still the most perfect remembrance of what is past, and intuition of what is to come, since both the past and the future are in all their present. *AC 2493*

Angels . . . do not know what a period of time is, for the activity of the sun and moon with them does not produce divisions of time. As a consequence they do not know what a day or a year is, but only what states and changes of state are. *AC 488*

Eternity . . . is manifested continually by means of time to those who dwell within time. . . . The present with the angels includes past and future together. Consequently they have no anxiety about things of the future. *AC 1382*

Freedom

The more distinctly a man appears to himself to be master of himself the more clearly he perceives that he is the Lord's, because the more nearly he is conjoined to the Lord the wiser he becomes... the angels of the third heaven, because they are the wisest of the angels . . . call it freedom itself; but to be led by themselves they call slavery. *DP 44*

Proprium (Ego)

Contrary to some spiritual teaching, the proprium or ego is never to be annihilated, but only (and repeatedly) pushed aside by the life from God by man's own choice. This is as true of the angelic state after death as it is in this life, for without proprium there is no freedom of choice. So the angels are left perpetually free to receive love and wisdom in place of the self-centredness of the old ego.

Angels are not angels from their proprium [ego]. Their proprium is exactly like that of a man and this is evil. That an angel's proprium is such is because all angels have been men, and that proprium adheres to them from birth. It is only removed, and to the extent that it is removed, to that extent they receive love and wisdom, that is, the Lord, in themselves. . . . The Lord can dwell with angels only in what is His, that is, in what is His very own, which is love and wisdom, and certainly not in the angel's proprium which is evil. Hence it is that so far as evil is removed so far the Lord is in them, and so far they are angels. The very angelic itself of heaven is the Divine Love and Wisdom. This Divine is called the angelic when it is in angels. From this again it is clear that angels are angels from the Lord, and not from themselves. *DLW 114*

Innocence

Because innocence is the inmost in all the good of heaven, it so affects minds that when it is felt by anyone—as when an angel of the inmost heaven approaches—he seems to himself to be no longer his own master and is moved and, as it were, carried away by such a delight that no delight of the world seems to be anything in comparison with it. *HH 282*

Innocence attributes nothing of good to itself, but attributes all good to the Lord . . . an angel is a wise child in an eminent sense. *HH 278*

Peace

The state of tranquillity and peace [in heaven] is from no other source than that the angel perceives that *all things inflow*, and that evil is not his, nor good his; thus he is in peace, and yet, as it were, he appropriates the good. *SD (minor) 4696*

Wisdom

Angelic wisdom involves perceiving whether a thing is good or true without reasoning about it. *AC 1385*

The wisdom of angels is indescribable in words, but can only be illustrated by some general things. Angels can express in a single word what man cannot express in a thousand words. Again, a single angelic word contains innumerable things that cannot be expressed in the words of human language. For in every single word spoken by angels, there are arcana of wisdom in a continuous connection to which human knowledges never reach. . . . The interior angels also can know from the tone together with a few of the words the entire life of one speaking. *HH 269*

Every grain of your thought, and every drop of your affection is divisible to infinity, and that so far as your ideas are divisible you are wise. Know then that everything divided is more and more multiple, and not more and more simple; for when divided again and again, it approaches nearer and nearer to the infinite in which are all things infinitely. . . . A single natural idea is the vessel of innumerable spiritual ideas . . . a single spiritual idea is the vessel of innumerable celestial ideas. Hence the distinction between celestial wisdom, in which are the angels of the third heaven, and spiritual wisdom in which are the angels of the second heaven; and also between the latter and natural wisdom in which are the angels of the ultimate [lowest] heaven and also men. *CL 329*

Joy

Heavenly joy itself, such as it is in its essence, cannot be described, because it is in the inmost of the life of the angels . . . it is as if the interiors were fully opened and unloosed for the reception of delight and blessedness, which are distributed to every least fibre and thus through the whole. Thus the perception and sensation of this joy is so great as to be beyond description. For that which starts from the inmosts flows into every particular derived from the inmosts, propagating itself always with increase towards the exteriors. *HH 409*

The joy of the angels is from love to the Lord and from charity to the neighbour—that is, when they are in the use of performing things of love and charity—and that in these there is so great a joy and happiness as to be quite inexpressible . . . heaven and the joy of heaven first begin in man when his regard for self dies out in the uses which he performs. *AC 5511*

When I wished to transfer all my delight to another, a more interior and fuller delight continually flowed in in its place, and the more I wished this, the more flowed in; and this was perceived to be from the Lord. *HH 413*

Sorrow

The angels are in sorrow about the darkness of earth. They say that hardly anywhere do they see light, and that men seize upon fallacies, confirm them, and by this means multiply falsities upon falsities . . . the angels specially lament over confirmations about faith separate from charity and justification thereby. They also lament men's ideas about God, angels, and spirits, and about their ignorance of what love and wisdom are. *DLW 188*

Perception

Those who are in heaven have more exquisite senses, that is, a keener sight and hearing . . . the light of heaven, since it is Divine truth, enables the eyes of angels to perceive and distinguish the most minute things. Moreover, their external sight corresponds to their internal sight or understanding; for with angels one sight so flows into the other as to act as one with it; and this gives them their great keenness of vision. In like manner, their hearing corresponds to their perception, which pertains both to the understanding and to the will, and in consequence they perceive in the tone and words of one speaking the most minute things of his affection and thought; in the tone the things pertaining to his affection, and in the words the things pertaining to his thought. But the rest of the senses with the angels are less exquisite than the senses of seeing and hearing, for the reason that seeing and hearing serve their intelligence and wisdom, but the rest do not;

and if the other senses were equally exquisite they would detract from the light and joy of their wisdom, and would let in the delight of pleasures pertaining to various appetites and to the body; and so far as these prevail they obscure and weaken the understanding. *HH 462a*

In every object those in the inmost heaven see what is Divine; the objects they see indeed with their eyes; but the corresponding Divine things flow in immediately into their minds and fill them with a blessedness that affects all their sensations. Thus before their eyes all things seem to laugh, to play, and to live. *HH 489*

Attitude

People in whom charity is present think nothing else than good of the neighbour and speak nothing but good, and this not for their own sake or that of him with whom they seek to curry favour, but from the Lord thus at work within charity. . . . They are like angels, residing with someone. . . . Angels stir up nothing but what is good and truth; and things that are evil and false they excuse. *AC 1088*

Power

Any obstruction [in the spiritual world] that ought to be removed because it is contrary to Divine order the angels cast down or overthrow merely by an effort of the will or a look. Thus I have seen mountains that were occupied by the evil cast down and overthrown, and sometimes shaken from end to end as in earthquakes. *HH 229*

Angels . . . have the power of restraining evil spirits. . . . They exercise their power chiefly when with man, in defending him at times against many hells, and this in thousands of ways. *AC 6344*

One single angel is more powerful than ten thousands of spirits in hell, yet not so from himself but from the Lord. And he has that power from the Lord in the measure that he believes he can achieve nothing from himself and is accordingly the least. And he is able to have such a belief in the measure that *humility and an affection for serving others* exist in him, that is, insofar as the good that is essentially love to the Lord and charity towards the neighbour is present in him. *AC 3417*

223

Michael Stanley, Editor

Harmony and Unanimity

The angelic heaven, which coheres together as a one, consists in infinite variety, no one there being absolutely like another, either as to soul and mind or as to affections, perceptions, and thoughts therefrom or as to inclinations and intentions therefrom, or as to the tone of the voice, as to the face, body, gesture, walk, and many other things. And yet, though there are myriads and myriads, they have been and are being arranged by the Lord into a single form in which there is complete unanimity and concord. This would not be possible unless all the angels, being so various, were led universally and individually by One. *CL 324*

Blessedness consists in unanimity and harmony, so that many, even very many, suppose themselves to be one . . . for from the harmony of many there exists a One from which there is blessedness and happiness. And from the concord of happiness, the happiness is doubled and trebled. *SD 289*

Abbreviations of Swedenborg's Works Cited

AC	Arcana Caelestia
AE	Apocalypse Explained
CL	Conjugial Love
DLW	Divine Love and Wisdom
DP	Divine Providence
HH	Heaven and Hell
SD	Spiritual Diary

Selected Bibliography

Acton, Alfred, *Letters & Memorials of Emanuel Swedenborg* (SSA, Bryn Athyn, 1955)

van Dusen, Wilson, *A Guide to the Enjoyment of Swedenborg* (Swedenborg Foundation, N.Y., 1984)

van Dusen, Wilson, *Presence of Other Worlds* (Harper & Row, N.Y., 1974)

Emerson, E. W., *Representative Man*

Henderson, Bruce, *Window to Eternity* (Swedenborg Foundation, N.Y., 1987)

Hite, Lewis F., *Swedenborg's Historical Position* (Mass. New Church Union, 1928)

James, Henry, *The Secret of Swedenborg* (1869)

Johnsson, Inge, *Emanuel Swedenborg* (Twayne Publishing N.Y.)

Keller, Helen, *My Religion* (Swedenborg Foundation, N.Y.)

Kingslake, Brian, *Swedenborg Explores the Spiritual Dimension* (Seminar Books, London, 1981)

Synnestvedt, Sig, *The Essential Swedenborg* (Twayna Publishers, N.Y., 1970)

Sigstedt, Cyriel O., *The Swedenborg Epic* (Bookman Associates, N.Y.)

Tafel, Rudolph L., *Documents Concerning Swedenborg* (Swedenborg Society, London, 1875)

Toksvig, Signe, *Emanuel Swedenborg, Scientist & Mystic* (Faber & Faber Ltd, London)

Trobridge, George, *Swedenborg Life & Teaching* (Swedenborg Foundation, N.Y.)

Warren, Samuel M., *Theological Writings of Swedenborg* (Swedenborg Society, London)

White, William, *Emanuel Swedenborg* (1867, 1868)

Wilkinson, James J. G., *Emanuel Swedenborg* (James Spiers, 1886)

Very, Frank W., *An Epitome of Swedenborg's Science* (Four Seas Company, Boston, 1927)

18

The
Greater Gods

GEOFFREY HODSON

The Sephirothal Hosts

The contribution of occult philosophy to the problem of the emanation and constitution of the universe is dual. It consists first of an affirmation of the existence in Nature of a directive Intelligence, a sustaining Life and a creative Will; and second of information concerning the existence, nature and function of those individual embodiments of these three Powers in Nature, called in Egypt and Greece "Gods," in the East *Devas*, and in the West "Angelic Hosts."

Occult philosophy shares with modern science the view that the universe consists not of matter but of energy, and adds that the universe of force is the Kingdom of the Gods. For fundamentally these Beings are directors of universal forces, power agents of the Logos, His engineers in the great creative process, which is regarded as continuous.* Creative energy is perpetually outpoured. On its way from its source to material manifestation as physical substance and form, it passes through the bodies and auras of the Gods. In the process it is "transformed," "stepped down" from its primordial potency. Thus the creative Gods are also "transformers" of power.

Highest amongst the objective or fully manifested Gods are the seven Solar Archangels, the Seven Mighty Spirits before the Throne. These are the seven Viceroys of the threefold Solar Emperor. A planetary Scheme[1] or Kingdom in the new-born universe is assigned to each of the Seven from the beginning. Each is a splendid figure, effulgent with solar light and power,

---

*The Intelligences referred to here are neither male nor female, but at the time this was written it was customary to denote them as masculine. Also the terms "man" and "men" are intended to denote humankind.

an emanation of the sevenfold Logos, whose Power, Wisdom and Beauty no single form can manifest. These mighty Seven, standing amidst the first primordial flame, shape the Solar System according to the divine "idea." These are the seven Sephiras concerning whom and their three Superiors, the Supernal Trinity, fuller information is offered in Part III. Collaborating with them, rank upon rank in a vast hierarchy of beings, are the hosts of Archangels and angels who "imbue primordial matter with the evolutionary impulse and guide its formative powers in the fashioning of its productions."[2]

The Gods differ from man in that in the present *Maha-Manvantara*[3] their will does not become so markedly differentiated from the One Will. The human sense of separated personality is almost entirely absent in them. Their path of evolution which, in the present Solar System, does not deeply penetrate the physical worlds as does that of man, leads from instinctive to self-conscious co-operation with the One Will. Occult science teaches, however, that in preceding or succeeding periods of manifestation they either have been or will be men. H. P. Blavatsky says:

The whole Kosmos is guided, controlled, and animated by almost endless series of Hierarchies of sentient Beings, each having a mission to perform, and who—whether we give them one name or another, whether we call them Dhyan Chohans or Angels—are 'Messengers,' in the sense only that they are the agents of Karmic and Cosmic Laws. They vary infinitely in their respective degrees of consciousness and intelligence; and to call them all pure Spirits, without any of the earthly alloy 'which time is wont to prey upon,' is only to indulge in poetical fancy. For each of these Beings either *was*, or prepares to become, a man, if not in the present, then in a past or a coming cycle (Manvantara). They are *perfected*, when not *incipient*, men; and in their higher, less material spheres differ morally from terrestrial human beings only in that they are devoid of the feeling of personality, and of the *human* emotional nature—two purely earthly characteristics. The former, or the 'perfected,' have become free from these feelings, because (*a*) they have no longer fleshly bodies—an ever-numbing weight on the Soul; and (*b*) the pure spiritual element being left untrammelled and more free, they are less influenced by *Maya* than man can ever be, unless he is an Adept who keeps his two personalities—the spiritual and the physical—entirely separated. The incipient Monads, having never yet had terrestrial bodies, can have no sense of personality or EGO-ism. That which is meant by 'personality' being a limitation and a relation, or, as defined by Coleridge, 'individuality existing in itself but with a nature as a ground,' the term cannot of course be applied to non-human Entities; but, as a fact insisted upon by generations of Seers, none of these Beings, high or low, have either individuality or personality as separate Entities, *i.e.,* they have no individuality in the sense in which a man says, '*I am myself* and no one else'; in other words, they are conscious of no such distinct separateness as men and things have on earth. Individuality is the characteristic of their respective Hierarchies, not of their units; and these characteristics vary only with the degree of the plane to which these Hierarchies belong; the nearer to the region of Homogeneity and the One Divine, the purer and the less accentuated is that individuality in the Hierarchy. They are finite in all respects, with the exception of their higher principles—the immortal Sparks reflecting the Universal Divine Flame, individualised and separated only on the spheres of Illusion, by a differentiation as illusive as the rest. They are 'Living Ones,' because they are the streams projected on the Kosmic screen of Illusion from the ABSOLUTE LIFE; Beings in whom life cannot become extinct, before the fire of ignorance is extinct in those who sense these 'Lives.'[4]

Two Streams of Evolving Life

The concept, founded upon occult research, of certain Orders of the Angelic Hosts as creative and directive Intelligences, expressions of aspects of the Divine nature and consciousness, Lords of the subtle elements of earth, water, air and fire and Gods of regions of the Earth, differs in one respect at least from that of certain schools of Christian thought. Investigation does not support the view that angels are deceased human beings. On the contrary, it reveals that human nature and human character undergo no change whatever immediately after death; that temperament, likes and dislikes, gifts, capacities, and for the most part memory, at first remain unchanged. According to the Bible, angels were in existence before the death of the first man. They were present when sentence was passed upon Adam and Eve, and one was placed with flaming sword "to keep the way of the Tree of Life."[5] There would seem, therefore, to be no scriptural foundation for the belief that death transforms men into angels. Indeed, speaking of man, St. Paul says: "Thou madest him a little lower than the angels."[6]

The Biblical account of the angels as ministers and messengers from God to man, appearing to individuals in times of need, is supported by the teaching of occult philosophy. So, also, is the vision of Jacob at Bethel, in which he saw "a ladder set up on the earth, and the top of it reached to heaven; and behold the angels of God ascending and descending on it."[7] The Order of the angels is hierarchical. On the lower rungs of the angelic ladder of life are the lesser nature spirits, brownies and gnomes, associated with the element of earth; fairies and sylphs with that of air; undines or nereids with water; and salamanders with fire. Above them, as previously stated, are angels and Archangels in an ascending scale of evolutionary stature, reaching up to the Seven Mighty Spirits before the Throne.

Countless in their numbers, innumerable in their Orders and degrees, the Gods dwell in the superphysical worlds, each Order performing its particular task, each possessing specific powers and each presenting a characteristic appearance. The whole constitutes a race of evolving beings at present pursuing an evolutionary pathway which is parallel to that of man, and which with him uses this planet and Solar System as a field of activity and unfoldment.

The Appearance of the Greater and the Lesser Gods

As will be seen from the descriptions which follow, the angelic form is founded upon the same Archetype or divine "idea" as is that of man. The outlines, however, are less clearly defined, the bodies less substantial, suggesting flowing forces rather than solid forms. Angels themselves differ in appearance according to the Order to which they belong, the functions which they perform and the level of evolution at which they stand.

Brownies, elves and gnomes appear in Western countries much as are described in folk-lore. In some Eastern and Central and South American countries their forms are more archaic, and even grotesque. Undines or nereids, associated with the element of water, resemble beautiful, and generally unclothed, female figures, femininity being suggested by roundness of form, there being, as far as I have found, differences of polarity but no sex differentiation in *The Kingdom of the Gods*. Varying in height from a few inches to two or three feet, undines are to be seen playing in the spray of waterfalls, reclining in the depths of deep pools or floating swiftly over the surface of river and lake. Fairies and sylphs, associated with the element of air, generally appear to clairvoyant vision much as represented in fairy-tale. They look like beautiful maidens with brightly-coloured wings, not used for flight since these beings float swiftly or slowly at will, their rosy, glowing forms partly concealed by gossamer, force-built "garments." Salamanders, associated with the element of fire, appear as if built of flame, the form constantly changing but suggestive of human shape, the eyes alight with fiery power. The

THE ANGEL OF JAVA, from Hodson, The Kingdom of the Gods
"A remarkable Buddhist shrine, known as the Borobudor, was built
in the island of Java some eight hundred years ago, and has become a
place of pilgrimage. Investigation revealed the presence of a very great
presiding Angel, conserver and distributor of the power of the Shrine
and source of potent spiritual forces which flow over the Island of
Java and the surrounding seas."

Geoffrey Hodson

chin and ears are sharply pointed and the "hair" frequently streams back from the head, appearing like tongues of flame, as the salamanders dive steeply into the flames of physical fires and fly through them.

Variations of these forms are to be seen in different countries of the world and in different parts of the same country. Where unspoilt, and not too highly populated, the countryside of England is rich in fairy life.

The Abode of the Gods

The Gods know the sun, physical and superphysical, as the heart and source of all power and life within the Solar System. From that heart, the vitalising energies which are the life "blood" of the solar and planetary "body" of the Logos are continually outpoured and withdrawn. In bringing the universe into existence, He, the Solar Logos, "breathes" forth His creative power, which flows to the very confines of His system, causing the material universe to appear. At the end of creative Day, He "breathes" in, His power is withdrawn and the material universe disappears, re-absorbed into THAT from which all came forth. This outbreathing and inbreathing of the solar life and energy is rhythmical. The one major creative "Word" or chord of the Solar System consists of innumerable frequencies, differences of vibratory rate producing differences of substance and form. The great race of the Gods lives and evolves amid this universe of outrushing and returning force.

Mountain Gods

On a single planet such as our Earth, Solar Archangels and angels are represented by corresponding planetary Gods. In addition to these major creative Intelligences, there are the angels presiding over divisions and areas of the surface of the Earth. They are called Landscape Angels and are partly concerned with creative and evolutionary processes in the mineral and plant kingdoms of Nature. A mountain is a living, evolving organism, a body, as indeed is the whole Earth, in which the Three Aspects of the Logos are incarnate. At least three processes are occurring within and about every mountain: the creation and evolution by the action of the Divine Will-Thought of atoms, molecules and crystals of which the mountain is built, the vivification of substance and form by the indwelling Divine Life and the awakening and development of the incarnate mineral consciousness. In each of these, Nature is assisted by hosts of nature spirits and Gods working under the direction of a responsible Official, who is the mountain God. When a peak is part of a range, the whole range in its turn will be presided over by a far more highly evolved Being of the same Order as the Gods of single peaks.

The appearance of these Beings is most magnificent. In height colossal, often ranging from thirty to sixty feet, the mountain God is surrounded on every side by outrushing, brilliantly coloured auric forces. These flow out from the central form in waves, eddies and vortices, varying continuously in colour, in response to changes of consciousness and activity. The face is generally more clearly visible than the rest of the form, which not infrequently is veiled by the outflowing energies. The features are always strongly yet beautifully modelled. The brow is broad, the eyes wide set and ablaze with power and light. Whilst in man the heart and solar plexus *chakras* are distinct, in mountain and other Gods they are sometimes conjoined to form a brilliant force-centre, often golden in colour, from which many of the streams of power arise and flow forth. On occasions these streams take the form of great wings stretched out for hundreds of yards on either side of the majestic figure.

Whilst all such Gods live their own intensely vivid life amongst their peers in the higher superphysical worlds, one part of their attention is almost continuously turned towards the mountain below, into the sleeping consciousness and life of which they continually direct streams of stimulating, quickening force. Occasionally, in order to perform its awakening functions more quickly and effectively, a God will descend deep into the mento-astral double of the mountain, its potent energies unified with the creative forces of which the mountain substance and form are products, its life blended with the indwelling Life and its consciousness one with the incarnate, Divine Mind. After a time it reappears and resumes its station high above the peak.

As stated above the Gods of single peaks are subordinate to a still greater God which, though larger and more brilliant, resembles its subordinates and performs similar functions for the whole mountain range and surrounding landscape. Such great Gods of Nature are not usually interested in man, neither do they display knowledge of human life and modes of thought. Intensely concentrated upon their task, they are generally remote and impassive, even as are the snowclad peaks. Certain of them, however, would seem to have had contact with men in earlier civilisations, to have retained interest in human evolution and to be willing, on occasion, to inspire and advise human individuals and groups responsive to their influence.

Messages from the Heights

Amongst the many mountain Gods observed in the Sierra Nevada Mountains in California, the two presently described showed interest in and knowledge of man. Of the first of these Gods, I wrote at the time of observation:

The great sphere of his[8] outer aura gleams white as sunlit snow-fields across which he moves majestically. Within the white radiance, and partially veiled by it, shine the deep greens of the cypress trees, and within these again the golden glory of the noonday sun. Then glows a rosy light of softest hue, next azure blue and last, all white and radiant, the Godlike form.

The face is moulded in strength, square-jawed and powerful. The "hair" resembles flickering, backward-sweeping flames and in the air above a crown of upward-rushing, radiant energies flashes with the brightly coloured jewels of his thoughts.

An attempt to discover something of the content of his consciousness and, more particular, his views concerning the Gods, visible Nature and the ideal relation of man thereto, produces upon me the impression of the utterance of successive principles, each followed by a profound stillness in which the idea is dwelt upon and assimilated. The God thus seems to "say":

"The globe is a living being with incarnate power, life and consciousness. The Earth breathes. Its heart beats. It is the body of a God who is the Spirit of the Earth. Rivers are as its nerves, oceans great nerve-centres. Mountains are the denser structure of the giant whose outer form is man's evolutionary field, whose inner life and potent energies are the abiding place of the Gods.

"The approach to Nature by modern man is almost exclusively through action and his outer senses. Too few among her human devotees approach her in stillness, with outer senses quieted and inner sense aroused. Few, therefore, discover the Goddess herself behind her earthly veil.

"There is a value in the active life, a power and a beauty in Nature's outer garb. Power far greater, and beauty far deeper, lie beneath her veil, only to be drawn aside by silent contemplation of her hidden life.

"The heart of Nature, save for its rhythmic pulse, abides in silence. The devotee at Nature's shrine must approach her altar reverently and with quiet mind if he would find her beating heart and know the power within the form.

"The doorway of her temple exists and is to be found in every natural form. Contemplation of a single flower may lead the seeker through. A plant displaying Nature's symmetry, a tree, a mountain range, a single peak, flowing river, a thundering cascade—each and all of these will serve the contemplative soul of man as entrance to the realm of the Real wherein Nature's Self abides.

"In contemplation of Nature's outward forms, the doorway to her temple should be approached. Self-identification with her inner Life, deep response to her beauty without and within—these are the means of entry to her inmost Shrine.

"Within, await the High Gods, the timeless Ones, the everlasting Priests, who minister throughout creative Day within the temple, which is the natural world.

"Few, far too few, have found entrance there since Greece became a ruin and Rome fell into decay. The Grecians of old dwelt in simplicity. Complexities had not yet appeared. Human character was direct, human life simple and human minds, if somewhat primitive, attuned to the Universal Soul.

"The wheel revolves. The golden days return. Nature calls again to man who, as he hears, endeavours to respond. Man has passed through the cycle of darkness which followed the decay of Rome. Yet, involved in increasing complexities, he has lost his contact with Nature's hidden life. To regain it, all that dulls the senses, everything gross, everything impure and all indulgence must be left behind. The divine heart of Life must be approached in silent contemplation and single-mindedness; thus only may that heart be found."

A second mountain God was in its turn described at the time as follows:

There comes a great white angel of the heights shining with the light of sunshine upon snow. On every side his far-flung aura gleams with brilliant hues, ordered in successive bands from central form to aura's edge, pale rose, pale blue, soft green and purple. From his head a widening stream of white and fiery force arises and from behind the form flow waves of power suggesting auric wings.

The face is strong, virile, masculine. The brow is broad, the eyes wide apart and alight with power. The "hair" is formed of flashes of flame, like fiery power shooting upwards from the head. The nose and chin are delicately yet strongly modelled, the lips full, the whole face instinct with the majesty and power of the mountain range. The form itself is veiled by streams of white, flowing energy. At intervals, throughout the form and outward-flowing power there flashes a white radiance, dazzlingly bright, as of the sunlit snows.

He answers my call for light, "speaking" as if in a deep, resonant bass,[9] vibrant as if with the power of the Earth itself:

"The Gods await the conscious reunion of the mind of man with the Universal Mind. Humanity awakens slowly. Matter-blinded through centuries, few men as yet perceive the Mind within the substance, the Life within the form.

"In search of power and wealth, men have traversed the whole Earth, have penetrated the wilds, scaled the peaks and conquered the polar wastes. Let them now seek within the form, scale the height of their own consciousness, penetrate its depths, in search of that inner Power and Life by which alone they may become strong in will and spiritually enriched.

"He who thus throws open his life and mind to the Universal Life and Mind indwelling in all things, will enter into union therewith and to him the Gods will appear."

Ceremonial as a Means of Co-operation between Angels and Humans

The ministry of the angels, a cardinal doctrine of many faiths, has long been a living reality to a great many people. Occult research supports the doctrine, revealing that, as part of that ministry, certain Orders of angels are regularly present at religious Services[10] and certain other Ceremonials; for whenever super-physical forces are evoked and directed, whether by means of thought and will alone or by the use of symbols, signs and words of power, appropriate Orders of angels at once appear as the natural agents of those forces. Their function is both to conserve and direct the forces generated by ceremonial action, prayer and adoration and to serve as channels for the power and the blessing which descend in response. This ministration is far more effectively carried out when recognised by ministrants and congregation.

Two other aspects of the subject are, however, worthy of

consideration. These are the effect upon the evolving life in Nature of Church Services such as the Celebration of the Holy Eucharist and the participation in human worship of the nature spirits and the Angelic Hosts. A digression is, however, necessary in order to present the point of view from which I write concerning the life and consciousness of Nature. Under certain conditions of heightened awareness,[11] the universal, indwelling, divine Life becomes visible, though translation of such vision into brain consciousness and words presents many difficulties. When this state is attained, the divine Life in Nature is seen as an all-pervading, glowing, golden Life-force, omnipresent as an ensouling principle in every atom of every world. Physical forms then disappear. One is within and part of an all-pervading ocean of golden, glowing Life, which consists of myriads of points of light, interconnected by lines of force, the whole being part of an apparently infinite, living web[12] of exceedingly fine mesh which pervades all beings, all things, all worlds. Each of the points is found to be a source of Life, almost a sun, within which Life-force wells up as from an inexhaustible fount. From these centres, the golden power flows along the great web, vitalising all substance. There is no dead matter. All beings and all things are seen to be filled with the indwelling Life or Fire of God.

An inspired poet[13] truly described this state of consciousness:

> Lo! Heaven and earth are burning, shining, filled
> With that surpassing glory which Thou art.
> Lost in its light each mortal weakness, stilled
> Each rapt adoring heart.

In the light of this vision, it would seem that the life of Nature is quickened every time the Holy Eucharist and certain other rituals are performed. The degree of response varies in each of the kingdoms of Nature and depends upon evolutionary development. In the mineral kingdom in which consciousness "sleeps" it is relatively dull; in the plant in which consciousness "dreams" it is greater; in the animal and in nature spirits, in both of which consciousness "awakens," it is greater still; and in self-conscious beings such as angels and men it is greatest of all. At each Celebration, the power of response throughout the five kingdoms is increased, and this aid in the attainment of heightened awareness is part of the usefulness of every valid religious Rite.

In illustration, Nature may be likened to a plant which depends upon sunlight for its growth and flowering. If, after many cloudy days, the sun suddenly appears in all its brilliance, the life-processes of the plant are greatly stimulated, as the experiments of Sir Jagadish Chandra Bose, the great Indian scientist, so clearly demonstrated. If, in addition, the sun itself could be brought down to the plant without harming it and the plant receive into itself directly and individually an added measure of sunlight, then its whole growth would be correspondingly stimulated. It has seemed to me that a similar but spiritual, quickening occurs at Holy Communion, when the Lord Christ, the Sun of Divine Love, as also the Son of God, in His own Person draws near to all Nature and through the Sacred Elements is received by man.

The Holy Eucharist

My understanding of this wider significance of Church worship was deepened by observation of the response of Nature and the participation of the angels at an open-air Celebration of the Holy Eucharist[14] in Java. The selected site of the temporary Church, which was a garden on the slopes of Arjoena Mountain, permitted a splendid view across a great plain to Mount Kawi and, in the remote distance, to Mount Semeroe.

Before the service began, nature spirits assembled near the Church in large numbers, attracted by the preparations and the intent of all concerned. As might be expected in this lovely land of luxuriant tropical vegetation, fairies and tree-spirits predominated in this assembly, whilst the great mountain Gods participated from their stations above their respective peaks. In addition, certain high Gods of earth, water, air and fire attended, as would seem to be the case at every such Celebration, when they contribute their special power and direct the participation in the Service of their subordinates and the forces of their element. This is especially noticeable at the *Offertorium*, in which all Nature seems to unite with man in the offering of the elements and in self-surrender to the Lord of Life.

As angels and nature spirits from near and far thus shared in human worship, the Celebration in Java assumed a magnitude far beyond anything visible at the physical level. At the moment of Consecration when, as always, the Power and the Presence of the Lord descended in a golden radiance, with the Host at its heart, the angels bowed low in reverence. The Life in all Nature in the neighbourhood of the Church seemed to glow more brilliantly. The consciousness of mineral and plant seemed to awake and respond, as the glory of His Presence shone from the altar as the truly magical words of Consecration were uttered. Angels joined mentally with the human congregation in fullest measure in the *te adoremus* and *adeste fideles*, their participation appearing to be far more vivid than man's, since human consciousness is dulled by incarnation. At the *ite missa est*, as is usual, the spiritual forces generated by the whole ceremony were liberated upon the world, angels accompanying them on their spiritualising mission. The Gods of Nature and the nature spirits, having received into themselves these quickening forces, later released them into those aspects of Nature with which they were variously associated.

Thus, externally, through the Rite which He instituted, and by the co-operation of angels and men, the Lord of Love keeps His promise to be with us "always even unto the end of the World." Interiorly, He needs no ceremonial to keep this promise; for in His mystical at-one-ment with the Spiritual Selves of all mankind, He pours into them His perfected and quickening Life and Light and Power. Even so, awareness in consciousness of His perpetual atoning Ministry could be aided by united worship in forms found to be elevating to those of various temperaments.

Notes

1. A septenary system of superphysical and physical planets, seven of which are represented physically by Venus, Vulcan, Jupiter, Saturn, Neptune, Uranus and the Earth. Vide *The Solar System*, A. E. Powell, T. P. H., London.
2. Vide *The Secret Doctrine*, H. P. Blavatsky, Vol. I, p. 246, Adyar Edition.
3. *Maha-Manvantara*, Sanskrit. Major *Manvantara* as of Planetary Scheme or Solar System. See footnote 2, p. 24.
4. *The Secret Doctrine*, H. P. Blavatsky, Vol. I, pp. 318, 319, Adyar Edition.
5. *Genesis* III, 24.
6. *Hebrews* II, 7, also *Psalm* VIII, 5.
7. *Genesis* XXVIII, 12.
8. Masculine for convenience only, though the male was suggested in the virility and power of the face, form and influence of this particular God, as indeed of all mountain Gods which I have seen.
9. Though such communication is purely mental, words, and even an impression of vocal timbre, are sometimes conveyed to the brain.
10. See *The Science of the Sacraments* and *The Hidden Side of Christian Festivals*, both by The Rt. Rev. C. W. Leadbeater, and *The Inner Side of Church Worship* by Geoffrey Hodson, T. P. H., Adyar.
11. Induced by contemplation of a scene or object of great beauty, enjoyment of a work of art, participation in an act of worship or meditation upon a spiritual truth.

12. Vide *The Web of the Universe*, E. L. Gardner, T. P. H., London.
13. Rev. Scott Moncrieff. *St. Alban Hymnal.*
14. The Liturgy of the Liberal Catholic Church was used; St. Albans Press, 30 Gordon Street, London, W. C. 1. The description given is not to be regarded as an advocacy of Catholicism, but only as a record of attempted observation of some of the superphysical effects of the Celebration of the Holy Eucharist. The Theosophist studies comparative religion and finds a certain group of ideas to be common to all world faiths and the exclusive possession of none of them.

A GUARDIAN, A FORMAL PRESENCE Lee Mullican
"*These Guardians, if I may suppose so, enter from a world beyond religion and religiosity. It is a world, or worlds, a universe or universes, immaterial, anti-material, that they emanate from, a world that has been there, must have been there from the beginning, and which remains there, and will remain now and in the future.*"

Jascha Kessler

19

The Orishas:
Communing with Angels in the Candomblé Tradition of Brazil

NATHANIEL ALTMAN

Every native culture has worked in one way or another with nature beings. In addition to acknowledging their connection with the elements of fire, water, air and earth, anthropological evidence regarding ancient cultures throughout the world abounds with references to sacred and ceremonial places, including mountains, lakes, waterfalls and rivers. To these native peoples, the energy beings connected with these places were as real as the rivers and rocks themselves. This special relationship between humans and nature spirits was a central part of their lives.

These people knew that the major tasks of the devic beings were twofold: first, to stand behind the evolution of all physical forms on earth; and second, to aid in the upliftment of humanity. These people were aware that nature beings could share, on subtle levels, the wisdom, love and healing that is essential to human development and growth.

As modern civilization began to create towns and cities, most of humanity has, over the centuries, gradually lost contact with the earth. As a consequence, we have almost lost contact with these subtle forces of nature. By doing this, we have cut ourselves off from an important source of guidance, wisdom and healing which can teach us how to live in harmony with the Earth Mother, with ourselves, and with every one of her children.

Some of the early traditions that were deeply involved with the subtle forces of nature still survive today. One of them is known as *Candomblé*. Brought from Africa (primarily from what is today Nigeria, Angola and the Congo) to the shores of Brazil by slaves in the sixteenth century, the religion of Candomblé is currently practiced by millions of people. Most of the Brazilian devotees of Candomblé live in the northern coastal cities of the country, including Salvador Bahia, Belem, Fortaleza and Rio de

Janeiro. While we may not agree with or relate to some of the rituals of Candomblé (which can involve mediumship, possession, and animal sacrifice), we can benefit from Candomblé teachings that describe the characteristics of these nature spirits and show how to communicate with them.

By coming into deep contact with these forces of nature, Candomblé teaches that we open ourselves consciously to the potent wisdom and healing power which resides in rocks, mountains and lakes. We also learn how to co-operate with these forces in nature to help us reach deeper levels of self-understanding and inner alignment. We discover why we are on this planet, what we need to do, and where we need to go. This leads us to a clear understanding of our task in life, and how we can make our small yet unique contribution to the evolution of the planet in total harmony and cooperation with all kingdoms in nature.

The first qualification for working with nature spirits is that we must feel truly drawn to them. Rather than making a mental decision because working with the forces of nature may be interesting or exciting, we need to feel a deep yearning in our hearts to commune and work with nature.

The second qualification is *goodwill*. Our personal attitude must be one of truly aspiring to resolve any inner issues in our lives that block our heart feelings and prevent us from being in truth. While we may not yet have reached the level of perfection to which we aspire, goodwill, compassion and a sincere desire to serve will all naturally attract the benign energies of nature which protect us and guide us in our explorations. We also need to be humble and pray for guidance and blessing in our search for truth.

Candomblé (as well as many other religions grounded in nature) teaches that working with nature spirits empowers us: it gives us both greater physical energy and better mental focus. We learn how to face doubts, fears and challenges squarely and with courage. We function from the center of our being. As a result, we not only begin to transform our relationships, but we begin to discover the deeper, more spiritual aspects of work, study and community service. We integrate truth, harmony and cooperation into all our activities.

We also become deeply aware of our intimate connection with the earth and the responsibility this knowledge and power entail. By doing so, we become a type of "bridge" between the forces of heaven and earth, blending spiritual vision with practicality and realism. Achieving this state of being does not occur overnight, but is the result of many years of deep personal work. It involves progressively discovering who we really are.

The Devic Hierarchy According to Candomblé

In Candomblé tradition, there is an all-powerful and all-encompassing God, called *Olorun*, who created the heavens and earth. Olorun also created all the myriad forms of life who inhabit both the seen and unseen worlds on this planet. Unlike Christian theology which conceives of a personal God, Candomblé views Olorun as a benign yet impersonal force. For this reason, he created an army of helpers in the unseen worlds who exist not only to assist in the evolution of nature, but also to provide personal assistance and support to the human members of Olorun's vast family. These beings, which never take physical forms, are known both in Africa and Brazil as *orishas* (pronounced oar-ee-shahs).

Like other religious philosophies, Candomblé speaks of the inherent dualism in creation, and that *yin* and *yang* energies are inherent in every life form. For this reason, Candomblé teaches that there are both male and female orishas. According to Candomblé tradition, we receive a "father" and "mother" orisha when we are born. The task of these devic "parents" is to provide us with protection and guidance during our evolutionary journey on earth. They are, in fact, considered our guardian angels by Candomblé priests.

Each orisha is connected with a specific element in nature. In order to discover our father and mother orishas, we need to discover the elements with which we best resonate. The places in nature where these elements predominate (and where we feel the strongest resonance) are called our "personal power spots." For that reason, each of us has a "male" and "female" power spot in nature.

The connection between our orishas and our power spots is obvious: our power spot is the earthly home of our orisha. It is in this home that we can receive the fullest measure of the orisha's benign strength, wisdom and healing. Our power spot is not restricted to one or two locations. If our power spot happens to be the forest, *any* forest is our personal power spot.

We also have the potential to communicate with and receive wisdom and healing from orishas that are not necessarily our "parents." If we want to commune with the angelic energy of a waterfall, for example, it doesn't really matter if the waterfall is not one of our personal power spots. The devic energy enveloping the waterfall can provide us with communion, grace and healing. This is especially true in the case of "planetary power spots": places in nature with extremely high concentrations of energy. They often include places long considered as sacred, like Mt. Fuji (Japan), Iguassu Falls (Brazil and Argentina), the Grand Canyon (U.S.A.) and Ayers Rock (Australia).

Orishas are believed to be related to each other as members of a family. In addition to being the subjects of a multitude of stories and myths, each orisha is said to possess unique psychological characteristics which set it apart from the others. According to African tradition, there are over four hundred different orishas, but we will discuss here only eight of the major orishas and their personal characteristics. Most are connected with actual power spots, while one is related to the wind.

Oshalá (Oxalá)

Oshalá is considered the father of all the orishas and the grandfather of all mortals. As an extremely powerful nature being, he resonates with the energy of mountaintops, along with the vast expanses of sky which surround them. Oshalá is said to be androgynous, symbolizing the male and female qualities in nature as well as both the creative and procreative aspects of the universe. On a psychological level, Oshalá represents justice tempered by love, as well as the purifying aspect of conscious awareness.

In Brazil, Oshalá is compared to Jesus Christ or Nosso Senhor do Bomfin Salvador Bahia. Because his favorite color is white, he is said to resonate well with white metals such as aluminum, silver and white gold. His consecrated day is Friday, although he is also worshipped on Sunday.

Yemanjá (Iemanjá)

Yemanjá is known both in Africa and Brazil as the "mother" of all orishas, and is compared to Our Lady of Conception in the Roman Catholic Church. Her domain includes the oceans and all bodies of salt water, and she is among the most popular and revered of the orishas in Brazil. Yemanjá, who represents the maternal forces of nature, is often characterized as a beautiful and exalted figure of spiritual motherhood, coming forth from the sea dressed in flowing light blue robes. Although she is considered a powerful, serene nature being, Yemanjá can be emotionally unstable, with a strong temper and unforgiving nature. Her colors are white, light blue and silver, and she likes sea stones, shells, white roses and perfume. Yemanjá's day of worship is Saturday, when thousands of Brazilians go to the shore to pay homage.

Nanan *(Nanã)*

Legend has it that Nanan is the oldest of the orishas, and is affectionately called *vovô* or "grandmother" by her devotees. Known variously as the wife or lover of Oshalá and the mother of Omolú (the orisha of healers), she corresponds with the energy of St. Anne in the Catholic religion, who is also the mother of the Virgin Mary.

Nanan is the orisha of still, fresh waters, and her domain includes still lakes, marshes and swamps. Clay and mud are Nanan's elements, and white and dark blue are believed to be her favorite colors.

She is often viewed as a wise old woman who dances with dignity. Nanan is said to be calm, calculating and stubborn, and is deeply connected to domestic life. Her consecrated days are Saturday and Monday.

Shangó *(Xangó)*

Shangó is one of the most popular orishas, and is called "the King of Justice" by his followers. He is the orisha of thunder, and resonates with the energy of storms, caves and large rocks. Often compared to St. Jerome, Shangó is seen as the force that makes for justice and wisdom, prosperity and peace. He is also viewed as "the Master of Fire."

Originally considered to be a hermaphrodite, Shangó's contemporary image is basically masculine. He was once "married" to Yansan, the orisha of winds, and is also considered to be an amorous adventurer and fierce warrior. On a psychological level, Shangó is said to possess an explosive temper, but he can also be very calm and reserved. His devotees wear white and red, and his consecrated day is Wednesday. Copper is Shangó's earth element.

Oshoun (Oxum)

Oshoun is the orisha of flowing fresh waters and can be found primarily by rivers, waterfalls, springs, and streams. She is often viewed as the earthy aspect of motherhood, as opposed to Yemanjá who represents its spiritual aspect. As a wife of Shangó (as well as a former wife of Oxossi, the orisha of forests), Oshoun is connected with romantic love, marriage, and human fertility. She is also the goddess of prosperity, and is believed to bring material wealth to her human children.

Candomblé mythology describes Oshoun as a coquettish and vain orisha who likes jewelery, perfume and elegant clothes. Despite these attitudes, however, Oshoun is identified with St. Catherine and several manifestations of the Virgin Mary in the Roman Catholic tradition. Oshoun's consecrated day is Saturday, and her color is yellow. As can be expected, Oshoun's preferred metals are yellow in color, such as bronze and gold.

Omolú (Omulú)

Omolú is perhaps the most respected of the orishas, for he is believed to have control over the powers of life and death. Originally connected with agriculture, Omolú is presently known as the orisha of contagious diseases, with the ability both to begin and to stop epidemics. Considered "the Doctor of the Poor" along the Brazilian coast, Omolú has been identified with St. Lazarus the healer.

Omolú is found primarily in green meadows and open fields with sparse vegetation. His power is connected with the energy produced when sunlight touches the surface of an open meadow or field. Because he is the orisha of life and death, the beginning of the day (when the sun is rising) is considered the time of ascending life; the middle of the day (when the sun is the strongest) is seen as the transition point between life and death, while the descending sun is connected with death. For this reason, people are cautioned to work with Omolú only in the morning and *never* after the noon hour.

Despite his connection with death, Omolú is viewed as a generous, kind and nurturing orisha. The act of healing invokes the presence of Omolú, and all healers are said to enjoy his protection and guidance. His principal colors are maroon, white and black, and Monday is his day of worship.

Oshossi (Oxossi) (pronounced oh-showss)

Oshossi is the orisha of the woods and the jungle. Candomblé tradition describes him as dwelling in an impenetrable forest surrounded by wild animals. Oshossi is, above all, the "great hunter" (his symbol is the bow and arrow), and he is the protector of hunters. As a husband (or, some say, the former husband) of Oshoun, Oshossi is connected to the healing powers of medicinal plants. In Roman Catholic tradition, he corresponds with the energy of St. Sebastian.

Oshossi has been described as a very active nature being, who never rests. He is seen as clever, quick and always alert, with the tendency to be emotionally unstable. The colors worn by devotees of Oshossi are blue, green or a combination of both. He is said to be very fond of corn and wine, and his favorite metal is bronze. Thursday is the day that is consecrated to Oshossi.

Yansan (Iansã)

Yansan is connected with wind and lightning, and is the goddess of storms. Unlike the other orishas who are found primarily in areas uninhabited by human beings, Yansan can be found wherever there is wind, including the roofs of buildings and the decks of ships.

According to Candomblé tradition, Yansan was the first wife of Shangó, and their marriage was a tempestuous one. In Brazil, Yansan has been compared to both St. Barbara and St. Teresa in the Roman Church, and her favorite colors are dark red and white.

Discovering Our Orishas: Preparation

Many of us have felt intuitively drawn to certain places in nature since childhood. We may have spent many hours playing in a favorite outcropping of rocks; perhaps we often returned to sit on the shore of a quiet lake; or we may have become very unhappy without regular visits to the beach. These indicate that our personal orishas are probably associated with these favorite childhood places. Even as adults, we have places in nature we intuitively seek out when we need peace, healing and reflection or when we simply need to "recharge our batteries." Chances are that these special places are related to our "mother" or "father" orishas.

Ideally, we relate best to our personal orishas. However, all of the orishas we've spoken about in this article can provide protection, healing and guidance to all members of the human family who approach them with respect and love. Like the saints in the Catholic Church, we may be attracted to orishas with whom we feel a certain affinity, or may seek to contact those whose help we may need at the time. For example, many Brazilian women in search of a husband seek to commune with Oshoun, the orisha of romantic love. If a person is ill, he or she would probably seek out the help of Omolú.

Communing with the Orishas

There are rituals and practices based on the Candomblé tradition that can help you get in closer touch with orishas. Below are some general things that help, followed by practices specifically for individual orishas. Before you leave your house to visit the domain of the orishas, take a shower to cleanse both your physical body and energetic field. You may also wish to *smudge* yourself, which is the process of cleansing one's energy field with smoke. Long practiced by the Catholic Church and Native Americans (among others), smudging involves immersing yourself in sacred smoke. Sage (available at grocery and spice stores), in combination with sweetgrass, pine needles and cedar chips, is most often used for smudging. Place some sage in a bowl and light it, soon adding small amounts of the other ingredients of your choice. When the smoke begins to rise, bring it to your head, face, arms, chest, back, legs and feet, using your hands or a feather. If you are with a partner, he or she can smudge you in this manner.

After you are smudged, light a white candle that has never been used before. Make a prayer to the Creator, your spirit guides and guardian spirits for protection and support. Include a special prayer to Oshala, and to your orisha for guidance. Ask that he or she may be revealed to you. Leave the candle burning in a safe place while you are away.

As in other native traditions, offerings have long played a role in Candomblé teachings. They are believed to be an important aspect of making contact and working with the orishas. There are many different types of offerings one can bring an orisha.

Oshalá

The suggested offering for Oshalá includes white flowers (preferably chrysanthemums) and cooked white corn or popcorn.

You will also need a piece of white cloth (the size of a table mat) that has never been used, two small ceramic or glass candle-holders (white or transparent), two white candles, a white porcelain or ceramic bowl (which has never been used before) and, if you wish, a small clear or white vase for the flowers. Because you are outdoors, be especially careful to avoid causing a fire with your candles.

To visit Oshalá, you will be going to a mountaintop. Because Oshalá's favorite color is white, you should wear white clothing, or bring white clothing to change into. You may also want to carry a rock crystal or religious symbols, as well as some drinking water, matches or other incidentals you may require when taking a journey into nature.

Find a place where you are especially comfortable, and place the cloth on the ground. Fill the bowl with the cooked corn to be set in the center of the cloth. Place the flowers in the vase and set it by the bowl, or arrange the flowers around the bowl of corn. Set the candlesticks on either side of the bowl and light them. You may choose to use votive candles that are protected from the wind by a glass holder.

There is no one way to commune with your orisha. However, the first task is to ground yourself. You can either stand up or sit down, getting in touch with the earth. By doing so, we become aligned, aware and inwardly calm. Some people may close their eyes, do deep breathing and sit quietly in a meditative posture, open to any communion that may take place. Others may pray and actively ask for help. In Brazil, devotees sing hymns to the various orishas. The following is a special hymn of affirmation for Oshalá:

> Oxalá meu pai
> Tem pena de nos tem do . . .
> A volta da terra e grande
> E Teu poder ainda e maior . . .

> Oshalá my father
> Have pity and compassion for us . . .
> The way around the world is vast
> And your power is vaster still . . .

It is important to remember that contact with orishas is not made through the rational mind, but through intuition. If you feel like lying down in your power spot, do so. If you want to move about and explore Oshalá's domain, do it. You may wish to chant, sing or pray. You may want to ask specific questions about yourself, about major decisions you have to make, or about the direction you need to take in your life. The main challenge is to follow your instinct and move in whatever direction your intuition leads.

Yemanjá

Yemanjá rules the oceans, and the offerings made to her are considered the most exotic and beautiful of those given to orishas. They include white flowers (especially roses), white candles, and women's perfume. Offerings can be made in several ways.

Dressed in white clothing, go to the beach and dig a hole in the sand where you will place offerings of candles and flowers. The hole should be deep enough to protect the lighted candles from the wind. There is no limit on the number of candles you can use; this should depend on your intuition. Many pilgrims prefer to arrange the candles around the flowers. Open the bottle of perfume and place it near the center of the offering.

You can also make your offering by simply walking into the ocean carrying a bouquet of white flowers. Begin making your prayer to Yemanjá as soon as you enter the water, and count the number of waves that wash by. After you meet the seventh wave, cast your flowers (either all together or one by one) into the surf to be received by Yemanjá.

Nanan

Nanan is the orisha of fresh still waters, and is connected with lakes, ponds and marshy areas. When you wish to commune with Nanan, it is suggested that you wear aquamarine blue or white with an aquamarine accessory such as a scarf, ribbon or necklace. Avoid wearing black or solely dark colors when you visit Nanan or any other orisha.

Cooked popcorn (prepared without additives like salt or butter) is considered the primary offering to Nanan, along with white or aquamarine flowers. The candles may be white, aquamarine blue, or a combination of both. Candleholders and a white or deep blue cloth are optional, although a white bowl (which has never been used before) is needed for the popped corn. Place these offerings as close to the water as possible.

Shangó

Shangó is said to like red flowers, white and red (or striped) candles and reddish fruits like apples, plums and pomegranates. Candomblé priests suggest placing the fruits in a new white clay or porcelain bowl, although you can also lay them directly on a new white cloth. The flowers can be arranged around the bowl of fruit on the cloth, and the candles can be affixed directly to a rock or to the ground. While the candles are considered to be an important offering, the fruits need not be offered every time. Pilgrims who visit Shangó wear white or burgundy clothing or a combination of both colors.

Oshoun

When you go to visit Oshoun, dress in yellow or white with a yellow shirt, scarf or ribbon. Her favorite offerings are yellow flowers and white and yellow candles. You can place the flowers on a new white or yellow cloth the size of a table mat as close to the water as possible, or the flowers and candles can be placed directly on the ground. You can also make your offering of flowers by standing by a stream, river or waterfall. Make your prayers and cast the flowers into the water.

Omolú

Those who seek to visit Omolú do so only in the morning while the sun is rising. As with the offerings described before, you will need a new white bowl, white or clear candleholders and, optionally, a vase for the flowers. Cooked popcorn prepared without salt, butter or other additives should be placed in the bowl. White flowers can either be placed in the vase or arranged around the bowl and laid directly on the cloth. Candles should be white and maroon in color. When you make an offering to Omolú, wear white along with dark red, maroon or brown.

Oshossi

Oshossi is connected with wooded areas, forests and orchards. According to Candomblé tradition, Oshossi responds best to people wearing light blue clothing and to offerings of sliced coconut and green and red "tree" fruits like apples, pears, avocados and papayas. Cooked red corn (if available) is also suggested, in addition to white and light blue flowers and candles.

Place your offering of fruits in a new white bowl, which is to be laid on a white or light blue cloth especially selected for this purpose. Place one white and one blue candle (or two blue-and-white striped candles) in white or transparent candleholders, and arrange them around the offering of fruit. Like the offering to Oshalá, the flowers should be placed in a white or transparent vase, or they may simply be arranged on the cloth around the bowl of fruit.

Yansan

When you commune with Yansan, it is recommended that you wear red (or red and white) clothing. White and red flowers are said to be favored by this orisha, as are red and white candles. Since you will be making your offering in a windy place, it is a good idea to surround your candle with a glass or find a votive-type candle available in religious supply stores and some supermarkets or boutiques. The flowers can be simply laid by the candles to be carried off by Yansan.

Communing with one's orishas can be one of the most fulfilling spiritual experiences. In addition to personal unfoldment and inner healing, communication with the forces of nature can eventually empower us to build a new society that will resonate with both natural and universal law. By returning to our roots and learning how to live in harmony with the earth, we can end a long period of alienation from the land and begin to aid in the healing of this planet, our home.

A Final Word of Caution

The subtle realms of existence are populated with a wide variety of beings at different stages of evolution. When we are working in these realms, certain entities may sometimes be attracted to us. However, we can attract only energies with which we resonate and which have affinites with our own energies. By following the guidelines presented here, chances are slim that you will attract any negative or otherwise disharmonious beings when you are working with your orisha.

However, if you should attract some spirit being, ask yourself, "What is in me that attracts this force?" Whenever you meet such a being in the subtle realms, you need to follow your intuition regarding its intent. If you have any doubts at all, speak from your innermost being, "If you come in the name of God, you are welcome. If not, please go away." This should be followed with a prayer to God for protection and clarity.

These final words of caution are not intended to frighten you, nor to prevent you from making contact with your orisha. However, by choosing to work in the subtle realms of the orishas, you are entering an unfamiliar world with its own inhabitants, forces and terrain. By taking the necessary precautions and entering this world with good will and respect, your journey will unfold naturally and safely through your own inner guidance. You will follow your own itinerary and will create your own unique adventure in the world of the orishas.

Bibliography

Bastide, Roger, ed., *The African Religions of Brazil*. Baltimore: Johns Hopkins University Press, 1978.

Booth, Newell S., ed., *African Religions*. New York: NOK Publishers Ltd., 1977.

González-Wippler, Migene, *Santeria: The Religion*. New York: Harmony Books, 1989.

Goodman, Felicitas D., *Trance, Healing and Hallucination*. New York: John Wiley & Sons, 1974.

Langguth, A. J., *Macumba*. New York: Harper & Row, 1975.

da Matta e Silva, W. W., *Misterios e Práticas da Lei de Umbanda*. Rio de Janeiro: Livraria Freitas Bastos, 1981.

Ogum, Jair de, *Fé* (Rio de Janeiro: Agents Editores, 1984.

Rosa, José with Altman, Nathaniel, *Finding Your Personal Power Spots*. Wellingborough, UK: Aquarian Press, 1986.

Torres de Freitas, B., and Cardoso de Freitas, V., *Os Orixás e o Candomblé*. Rio de Janeiro: Editora Eco, 1967.

Verger, Pierre, *Dieux d'Afrique*. Paris: Paul Hartmann, Editeur, 1954.

ANGEL OF UNITY *Arthur Douët*
"I think that the discovery that we can communicate and work with all life in the universe on an equal basis gives a special completion and a fresh beginning to our humanity."

Dorothy MacLean

20
Humans and
Angels Now

DOROTHY MACLEAN

In the early 1960s at Findhorn, where a small group of people were endeavouring to grow a garden for food, and after ten years of daily attunement to the 'God Within,' in meditation Dorothy Maclean was told that she had a job to sense into and harmonize with nature forces. When she eventually did just that, she found herself communicating with overlighting intelligences of various plant species and translating their meaning into her own words. Questions asked by the gardener, Peter Caddy, were answered and put into action. The garden flourished and became famous. Dorothy's contact with these energies, whose nearest name to her was "angel," broadened as she realized that humans also have an angelic self, that even qualities such as serenity have an intelligent counterpart, that gods and goddesses of various cultures were not based simply on superstition nor on human projection, but on these energies.

Maclean continues to contact this world of energies, at present also exploring the oversouls of human groupings such as different cultures and nations. She believes that until we honor the many species and worlds that play their part on the planet, we separate ourselves from planetary wholeness.

Many great teachers, religious or otherwise, have walked the Earth, and from each one we can learn. Yet the angels, from their vantage point and from their interplay with our consciousness, can see what we truly are, can see the steps in front of us, and continue to help us connect to our divine origin and goal. Now we can consciously seek their cooperation. The creative living styles described in Chapter 10 are both the way leading to the angels and the way they, the angels, are becoming and being. Joy, love, flexibility, freedom, harmony are what we are, the essential nature of all life—but we humans have to know it. We simply have not known what we are; but clearly, beautifully, the devas spelt it out for me, shared with me what I am. They said it in the conscious

communion that I developed with them, until I became aware
that the same message was conveyed in Nature, in every particle
of life.

Every flower is shouting at us of our common divinity, of our
transcendent selves. We know it unconsciously. Our paradises
have been gardens. We 'say it with flowers.' Our symbolic pictures
of the universe, our mandalas, are flower designs. But now flowers
are saying, with a new intensity, 'Look, don't think; look directly
at us and see God.' Our minds may translate the call as 'Look at
our colour, at our design, at our intricate delicate beauty.' Their
fragrance joins in the same message: 'Breathe in my scent; that
too is of God.' The touch of the grass, of a pebble, of wood, of
running water, of sun, also exclaims: 'Touch me, feel me, I am a
wonderful life for you to blend with, to admire or carve or shape,
and I too am divine.' Our very taste buds distinguish delectable
flavours and we savour yet another creation of the whole, another
expression of God. Sound, natural or manmade, can lift us to
harmony, and then leave us in the silence necessary for the
thunder of God.

We have caught up with Blake's vision of wholeness: 'Man
has no Body distinct from his Soul, for that called Body is a portion
of Soul discern'd by the five Senses, the chief inlets of 'Soul in
this age.' Even Karl Marx, in his early speculations, called for the
resurrection of human nature, for the human physical senses to
be emancipated from the sense of possession, and then humanity,
free of the domination of the senses, could enjoy them for the
first time. I believe this is what Krishnamurti says when he urges
us to watch Nature without thought, without judgment, without
wanting to continue the joy, because when thought takes over
the joy, it becomes pleasure, mechanistic, back in the round of
pleasure/pain. It is not by wanting to experience another realm
that we get there, but by being completely aware of every action,
every sound and colour around us, every relationship. Or, as don
Juan said, apprehending the world without interpretation, with
pure wondering perception.

Through the senses and minds of mankind, a clod of earth
talks of the millennia of its history, of the myriad invisible lives
contained within it, of the manifold visible life that grows from
it. The animals speak directly through their incredible grace and
instinct, birds through song or their unerring migrational flights.
Man talks most of all and with greatest complexity! Hidden
behind his speech is a being whose glance can mean heaven or

hell to another, a being who can be judged as ennobling, degrading or anything we like. A strange, powerful creature whose touch of individual spirit is ever beyond knowing. A miracle. 'What is man, that thou are mindful of him. . . . Thou hast crowned him with glory and honour. Thou madest him to have dominion over the works of thy hands. . . . O Lord our God, how excellent is thy name in all the earth!' (Psalm 8)

Although man is a miracle, to many the flower is a more compelling expression of perfection. So perhaps it is easiest, through awareness of flowers in particular, of their radiant beauty and purity, their uncomplicated stillness, their vibrant colour, to come to the excellence of the One and be uplifted beyond thought to our devic selves. We see white spring blossoms bursting from a grey stick, and we know that Nature is the glory of God. 'There is one holy book, the sacred manuscript of nature, the only scripture that can enlighten the reader.' (Inayat Khan) To me, with eyes open or closed, tuning into the essence or beauty of any wild place is heaven. And that glory is infinitely enhanced by knowing that we can relate to it in the realm of consciousness, that we can unite with and translate its intelligence, since we are the same intelligence.

Of course, Nature does not speak in the same language to everyone, and can even bring fear to some. And God cannot be heard by those whose every effort is directed toward finding the next meal. Still, a mathematical equation may awaken the soul of a mathematician. The arts, which are a blend of devic and human energies, may speak most clearly to many of us, through a Gothic cathedral, a painting, a poem, a ballet or, most universally of all, through music. A smile, a sexual experience, or an athletic achievement may give us a transcendent experience. With a sense of wonder, something in our environment uplifts our whole being, and we are more whole than before.

We are all wayfaring to our future. We have in common, as Goethe said, 'the constant striving upwards, wrestling with oneself, the unquenchable desire for greater purity, wisdom, goodness and love.' That means effort, and perhaps heartache. Although our innate desires will bring us to our future, we can save ourselves a lot of grief by relating *now* to our future, to our devic selves, as well as to our transcendent experiences. In fact, we are continually doing that and always have been, but we were not aware of it. Consciousness of this ability not only makes us relate more concretely to the whole of ourselves, but to the whole of our surroundings. In all we do we can recognise that we belong to a great universe of life. We can apply our relatedness to everything, and we, and everything, become more alive.

Take, for instance, our technology: There is nothing wrong with technology, only the way we apply it. Technology is destructive only in the hands of fragmented, over-specialised people who do not realise that they are one and the same process as the universe. However complicated machinery may be, approaching it, or anything, in the spirit of divine wholeness is relevant. For instance, the singing group, the New Troubadours, when trying to record a tape had constant trouble with the various pieces of equipment. Just as everything seemed perfect, one or other of the numerous units would break down. Not until each person concerned had recognised the need to evoke a 'higher' energy was a successful recording achieved.

Of course, this approach could give rise to a cute cult that appeals to the deva of this or the deva of that for everything. That would miss the point, which is that we first recognise and act from our own wholeness, and then from that point of consciousness relate to the similar consciousness in our surroundings. The angels that we encounter in this process are not little kitchen pixies come to clear up our messes. We can only recognise a mess without because it is part of our experience within. Only our whole selves, with the aid of the angels, can untangle our confusions and create a new world. By broadening our view, we change our lives and become more aware of life everywhere, even of the beauty in a rusted tin can. In fact, the power that is increasingly available through science and technology is an agent of change, because of its very vastness. We have to learn the responsible use of technology as an instrument of love. It can begin by caring for and appreciating our tools, our knives, pins or scissors.

In North America we must, in fact, reclaim the heritage of the Continent, a heritage which we have almost destroyed. Whatever our backgrounds, we will not be truly American or Canadian or Mexican until we, like the native peoples, recognise the Earth as our mother, and show respect for every form, function and power of Nature. To the Native Americans, Nature was indeed a holy book of profound value, and though I do not think that we need revive their rituals, the shamanistic veneration for life is essential. Other cultures were similar. As Edward Hymans wrote in *Sources*:

For the ancient farmers, and even for those not so far from us in time, every plant and animal and stone and the very Earth herself was alive and animated by spirit. And since, from self-knowledge, man knew that mind and matter, soul and body must be in harmony, in order that the whole should function, he also knew that in manipulating the body of the living world, he must be at one with the spirit animating it.

No civilisation has manipulated the environment as much as the modern North American; no civilisation needs the Native American heritage more than we do.

This fact was once clearly illustrated for me in the San Francisco Bay area. When attuning to the devas in a wild valley there, I found them in a state of shock. This was incredible! Never before or since have I encountered them in other than a high free state. Evidently, the rapid and continuing encroachment of the white man, whose huge machines brutally and thoughtlessly attacked the landscape, was responsible for their state. In Europe, environmental change has come about more gradually through the generations, with a certain rapport between man and Nature. In parts of Scotland, tenant farmers still contract to put manure back onto the land, and to cultivate it on a four-year crop rotation basis. But in America, where man once had such a close relationship with Nature, the white man has taken over with complete indifference to the value of the environment except as something for his own use. It might even be that much of the violence we experience in America is a karmic result of the violence with which we have treated the land. And perhaps those devas that I had encountered in the lovely unspoilt valley had been upset because they had foreseen the machines that would be at work in the valley a year later.

In most ancient societies trees were not wantonly felled, because each tree was believed to possess a soul, and these beliefs were, in fact, effective soil conservation regulations. We need a modern equivalent; and the devas can provide it.

The devas can also provide conscious cooperation with humans who seek their aid from holistic motives. They will cooperate in annulling the destruction man has inflicted on the planet, as we play our part. They will cooperate in joint creative efforts to improve the plant life that they have already created, with hybrids and new experiments, as we play our part. They will cooperate with scientific ecologists in ways yet to be developed. We can each start to play our part by being more considerate in simple ways. We can plant shrubs that grow to a height of five feet when we wish a five foot hedge, instead of planting trees that have to be clipped each year to prevent them attaining their normal fifty feet. We can stop using poisons and start using natural fertilisers. I think our eating habits will eventually change, as we realise the truth of the devic statements that there is more nutrition in small 'natural' vegetables and fruits than in large, chemically treated produce.

For humans, for angels, for all planetary life, wilderness areas are necessary. Nature forces are at their strongest and purest where thinking man has not interfered. I found, for example, more power in a little wild violet in the sand dunes than in the most cosseted garden flower (see Appendix, p. 209). We humans, creators of comparisons leading to the divisions of good and evil and to the development of wisdom, with minds that have cut us off from our souls, need places free of materialistic concepts, free of comparing thoughts, for the restoration of that soul. In addition, the angels need places free of humans. When I flew over the Arctic, devas told me that even the empty frozen wastelands were necessary for certain planetary work. The tree devas have stressed the important role of the forests in helping men and women to find their balance. Every little garden is better off with an area untouched by humans, where the nature spirits can be uninhibited. And, of course, wild animals need wilderness. To be good stewards of the harmonious allotment of the natural resources of this closed system called Earth, we need to use our angelic intelligence as well as our trained minds.

In regard to animals, here again we can learn from the Native American, to whom each animal reflected a particular aspect of the Great Spirit (man reflected all aspects). The Native American believed that knowledge of his oneness with the universe and all its powers could not be realised unless there were perfect humility, unless man humbled himself before the entire creation, before the smallest ant, realising his own nothingness. Only in being nothing can man become everything, and only then will he realise his own essential brother/sisterhood with all forms of life. His centre, or life, is the same centre of life of all that is. And our brother/sisterhood from such a centre is a vital link between the different forms of life. A case in point is that of the rats who, at my request, did not disturb me for four years. After that experience I felt a loving link with rats, which they seemed to reciprocate; it might have been my imagination, but it was a constructive imagination based on reality. To have that sort of relationship with all life is a wonderful vision, one that I think appeals to all lovers of life, and it is not impossible. We are all ultimately St. Francises, especially now that we realise that men, not animals, are the villainous destroyers of life on Earth. When we communicate with our pets as equals, not talking down to them, we get a deep response. An attitude of respect, of knowing that all life has a place, is imperative. Unless we wish all wild animals to become extinct and tame animals to be further exploited (and ourselves thereby lessened), it is up to us to exercise our dominion, not against but for the animal world.

Instead of forcing the creation of disease resilient insects by our chemical sprays, we can have a cooperative exchange. As a beekeeper, for instance, I enlisted angelic help, tuning into a wonderfully wise Being who, above all, told me to be peaceful in my handling of the bees, to study and harmonise with the bee ways and then follow my own feelings. My subsequent treatment of them resulted in a honey yield greater than that of others in the area—apart from the joys and sharp sorrows of relating to these fascinating insects.

Regarding humanity, we have many great teachers to show us the way to our future. Do the devas add anything new, anything to help us relate to each other? Yes, in their complete freedom to live wholly. In great living teachers we may glimpse feet of clay, but the devas all have winged feet. That is no criticism; to err is human and often that which we find lovable about human beings is precisely their imperfections. Precisely because so many erring humans are now attuning to their own Christhood, it is nice to have an archetype supplied by the angels. Example can still be helpful.

At least I found angelic example helpful. I would ask myself, for instance, if angels were humble. Not a bit of it; they gloried in their power. Then were they egotistical? Never. They gloried in God and each other. I do not see why humans eventually cannot attain the same state, which, idealistic or not, is the avowed purpose of man's highest endeavour, formalised in all religions. In the present state of the world, in this time of pervasive disclosure of human misdeeds and selfish actions, in this time of the very breakdown of society, we are not in danger of becoming idealists or losing the common touch, but we are in danger of completely losing sight of our angelic selves. We need to re-value ourselves, to recognise our feminine 'diffuse awareness' and focus our consciousness according to its holistic views. As various modern thinkers are pointing out, this is already happening in certain areas here in North America, which is still, for better or worse, a world exemplar. To fulfil the American destiny, to make real the statement that 'We hold these truths to be self-evident, that all men are created equal,' we have to look to our angelic selves. (Obviously, we are not all equal on other levels.)

A devic approach new to humanity is that they learn without suffering. Suffering has been our human way. The First Noble Truth of Buddhism is that all life is sorrowful. The Second Noble Truth is that sorrow is caused by attachment, and the Third Noble Truth is that the release from sorrow comes through giving up attachment. This release is called nirvana. Many people believe that nirvana is this world itself, just as it is, when experienced without desire and fear. I believe, also, that we can be as free as the devas in this world if we function with all our capabilities. Looking back on my life, suffering was, admittedly, the spur that drove me to seek within, but I no longer wallow in misery, anguish in indecision, or look for some panacea or drug. Now I attune to myself to discover purposes and actions.

Consciousness is the knowing faculty. When consciousness has no object to be conscious of, it is pure intelligence. If we believe that we have no intelligence or love, we cut them out of our worlds. How can we be loved if we carry the thought that everyone who sees us dislikes us? We are our own worst enemies. I know that I create my own world, and while I can still suffer in it, not being able to blame anything or anyone else does negate emotional and mental stress and turns me to the area where I can make effective change: myself. The very energy of asking for help from Christ, God, Allah, the angels, is a catalyst for change and is as strong as the strength of my belief. This is not new teaching; but what is so marvellous is the refreshing, magnetically joyful and light approach of the devas.

If the angels bring anything new, it is the quality of joy— appropriate now, because humanity is at the stage where we can express joy in ourselves as we make that giant step from intellect to intuition and leave behind the days of martyrdom and suffering. The devas would point out some shortcoming of mine in such a lighthearted way that I could see it impersonally and not be bound by my error.

It has taken years for the belief that I draw to myself all that happens to me to become an integral part of my living. At present we seem to need time and constant realignment to become accustomed to our vastness and to bridge the gaps in ourselves. We continue to make excuses for ourselves, and until we truly see that our own thoughts and memories, both cultural and individual, are behind all our acts, they will continue to fragment us. Our minds will fight to retain their familiar supremacy until we admit that direct perception, higher attunement, transcendence, intuition, or whatever we call it, is valid. Then we can begin to link with all of ourselves and change the way we live.

The devas suggested customary approaches or teachings, which we humans do not yet seem to apply, like being loving, thinking affirmatively, using our energies positively, attuning to inner peace for protection at all times. If we respond to chaos and suffering, we are stuck on that level, stuck to the old, separated, departmentalised world. Let go of the mind and let joy explode! To some people such an approach may appear, not only as an ostrich view of life, but inhumane, narcissistic, unrealistic. They are right, if we cut ourselves off from any part of life. We *are* our society. We have to discover where we fit in, have to be true to ourselves and follow the leads that life gives us. Let others who are much better cooks feed the starving millions; for my part, I am more likely to find, on some level of consciousness, a secret for better food production.

The constant devic reference to life as movement, as energy, as change, is in keeping with our fast modern world. The old static codes and moralities are dead shells. Yet the eternal value of goodness still applies, and those who break it for power or material success find, even in this lifetime, destruction, not fulfilment. Modern titans, such as the corporate oil companies, could follow the same self-destructive path unless, like the power-controlling devas, they serve the whole. We can no longer deny the inter-relatedness of life. But we can, like the devas, blend with the new waves of energy we encounter as we live in harmony with that still small voice within, doing the best that we know in our circumstances. As we attune to our divinity, all creation attunes to us. We find our acts bear fruit, that a book opens at the page containing the answer we seek, or that the very person we need suddenly turns up. We ride the crest of the wave, until the natural rhythm of our life takes us through the hollow to another crest. We start generating more subtle energy. In the whirling devic forces problems vanish, as we see solutions from that level. Our finest thoughts become powerful enough to take form on Earth, in new relationships, in a garden, in the arts.

The first step in cooperation with a new dimension is to choose it, which is another way of saying 'I believe' or 'I know.' We humans are strange mixtures; while we do not believe that we are the gods that the devas say we are, nevertheless we act like gods. We have been true pagan deities on this planet, taking for granted that we have sole control of it, yet not invoking our divinity. While we gaily admit the devil in us, we are ashamed to admit the god in us. The angels say that it is high time that we know what we are, and join our warring parts together. Disillusionment is a good clean starting point. Only in unity can we, and the whole Earth, survive. As we realise our basic oneness with all life, we appreciate our differences more. First we have to attune to our uniqueness, our part of the vastness, our Godhood, before we can know and work with it, and from that growing awareness mingle with others in this diverse world.

The devas have made it easier for me to link up with my fellow man. Having learned that behind the so-called 'stupid' green vegetable is a lively intelligence, I can more readily acknowledge a lively intelligence behind the pitted face of my fellow human or the one I see in the mirror. As the angels awaken joy in me by their joy, some day, maybe even today, I can be joyful enough to awaken joy in others. Or I can call on the 'higher' realms for joy or any other quality, and receive some sort of response to my invocation.

But I think that the discovery that we can communicate and work with all life in the universe on an equal basis gives a special completion and a fresh beginning to our humanity.

My own eternal quest took me as far as I could then go, into the hub of myself and of the universe. From there I was directed to what I thought was a new realm, the angelic world, which in sharing itself kept taking me back to that common hub. From that world I learned more than I could have dreamed about my own pragmatic environment. I learned that we can deal with all levels of our world in a truly creative, reciprocal way and, in joyous company, move to still more creative realms along with the brothers and sisters who make the totality of planetary life.

So far, we have only scratched the surface of the devic world 'within' and 'without' us. We and the universe are full of unknown, changing dimensions, and no space journey could be as interesting or as far-reaching as the journey into our own many mansions. Our angelic brethren, co-builders of our 'inner' and 'outer' universes, show us how to apply our talents in a different way.

Just as in the land of Britain I discovered the art of walking, because there people walk, so in the land of the angels I began to discover the art of creative cooperation with my environment.

There is a long journey ahead but, splendidly endowed as we are, we move. And, as the devas said, what matters is that we, the knowing, growing tip of Earth, consciously act from our divine centres.

Benediction

A flutter of feathers, a song, a
stir of air—"Keep the faith,"
they sing; "human dreams are angel food,
human deeds are angel drink.
When you gather together like this,
imagination deepens across the heavens,
and we see your souls trafficking between the worlds.
Through the crossing point pours a living fountain;
your art will guide you to its waters.
Farewell. We are with you always. Feel
in your inner eye our iris crystal
and under your feet the web of the swan.

M. C. Richards

Index

Muhammad, and Gabriel, 21-22,
205-209
Mullican, Lee, 240
Mystery(ies), Egyptian, 179;
rite, of bridal chamber, 103;
schools, 54, 57, 62, 66;
systems, 57
Mystic, mysticism, 185
Mystic marriage. *See* Marriage
Mystical theology, 64
Myth, myth-making, mythology,
12, 16, 35-36, 68, 99, 137,
151-166 *passim*, 195, 216,
243-253

Nature, 38, 43, 70, 87, 236, 260;
and effects of ritual, 236; as
sacred manuscript, 257; communion with, 56; cooperation
with, 252, 255-265; humans
and, 233, 255-265; Kingdoms
of, 140, 143, 148-149; Laws of,
40, 67, 70, 72, 141-142; planes
of, 140, 143; spirits, 65, 229,
241-242
Near-death experience, 137
Neoplatonism, 59, 63-64, 166,
179, 183
Newman, John Henry Cardinal,
101-102
Noumenon, 56
Numinous, 42-43, 46, 79, 193

Occult philosophy, 226, 228. *See
also* Esoteric philosophy
One, Absolute, 146; and Many,
53, 59, 62, 64, 67, 72, 99, 148-
149, 209, 224; transcendental,
65; Unknowable, 170; Life,
Ain Soph as, 94
Opposites, 76, 146, 153, 190,

193-194; balancing of, 197;
uniting of, 97, 183, 195
Opus Sanctorum Angelorum,
127
Order, Cosmic, 70, 72, 79;
of the Golden Dawn, 145
Origen, 129
Orishas, 244-53
Osiris, as daimon, 180
Oversoul, 56-57, 255. *See also*
Soul, World

Paalen, Wolfgang, 19
Padre Pio, 128, 133
Pagan, paganism, 51-58, 64, 66,
68, 165
Pagels, Heinz, 28
Pantheon, 61, 63, 70-71
Paranormal, 137
Parapsychology, 133-136, 183-
184
Parente, Father Alessio, 133
Personification, 13, 39, 54, 67, 70,
74, 127, 133, 135, 201
Philo, 169
Physics, 25, 28, 109
Pistis Sophia, 102
Plato, Platonism, 30, 55, 102, 166,
177-178, 182-183
Plotinus, 56
Plutarch, 178, 180, 183-184
Polarity. See Opposites
Polytheism, 127-128, 155, 170
Power(s), 107-108, 215, divine,
66, magic of asuras, 78; of
thought, 81; of will, 193;
specialization of, 68; to
restrain evil, 223; godly in
humans, 76; intelligent in
Nature, 142; magical, 193; of
being, 166; psychic, 5; soul,